The Rise and Fall
of
Social Psychology

SOCIAL PROBLEMS AND SOCIAL ISSUES
An Aldine de Gruyter Series of Texts and Monographs
SERIES EDITOR
Joel Best, *University of Delaware*

David L. Altheide, **Creating Fear: News and the Construction of Crisis**

Nancy Berns, **Framing the Victim: Domestic Violence, Media, and Social Problems**

Joel Best (ed.), **Images of Issues: Typifying Contemporary Social Problems** (Second Edition)

Joel Best (ed.), **How Claims Spread: Cross-National Diffusion of Social Problems**

Cynthia J. Bogard, **Seasons Such As These: How Homelessness Took Shape in America**

Augustine Brannigan, **The Rise and Fall of Social Psychology: The Use and Misuse of the Experimental Method**

James J. Chriss (ed.), **Counseling and the Therapeutic State**

Jeff Ferrell and Neil Websdale (eds.), **Making Trouble: Cultural Constructions of Crime**

Anne E. Figert, **Women and the Ownership of PMS: The Structuring of a Psychiatric Disorder**

James A. Holstein, **Court-Ordered Insanity: Interpretive Practice and Involuntary Commitment**

James A. Holstein and Gale Miller (eds.), **Challenges and Choices: Constructionist Perspectives on Social Problems**

Philip Jenkins, **Images of Terror: What We Can and Can't Know about Terrorism**

Philip Jenkins, **Using Murder: The Social Construction of Serial Homicide**

Valerie Jenness and Kendal Broad, **Hate Crimes: New Social Movements and the Politics of Violence**

Stuart A. Kirk and Herb Kutchins, **The Selling of DSM: The Rhetoric of Science in Psychiatry**

Ellie Lee, **Abortion, Motherhood, and Mental Health: Medicalizing Reproduction in the United States and Great Britain**

John Lofland, **Social Movement Organizations: Guide to Research on Insurgent Realities**

Donileen R. Loseke, **Thinking About Social Problems: An Introduction to Constructionist Perspectives** (Second Edition)

Donileen R. Loseke and Joel Best (eds.), **Social Problems: Constructionist Readings**

Gale Miller, **Becoming Miracle Workers: Language and Meaning in Brief Therapy**

Elizabeth Murphy and Robert Dingwall, **Qualitative Methods and Health Policy Research**

James L. Nolan, Jr. (ed.), **Drug Courts: In Theory and In Practice**

Bernard Paillard, **Notes on the Plague Years: AIDS in Marseilles**

Dorothy Pawluch, **The New Pediatrics: A Profession in Transition**

Wilbur J. Scott and Sandra Carson Stanley (eds.), **Gays and Lesbians in the Military: Issues, Concerns, and Contrasts**

Jeffery Sobal and Donna Maurer (eds.), **Weighty Issues: Fatness and Thinness as Social Problems**

Jeffery Sobal and Donna Maurer (eds.), **Interpreting Weight: The Social Management of Fatness and Thinness**

Michael Welch, **Flag Burning: Moral Panic and the Criminalization of Protest**

Carolyn L. Wiener, **The Elusive Quest: Accountability in Hospitals**

Rhys Williams (eds.), **Cultural Wars in American Politics: Critical Reviews of a Popular Myth**

Mark Wolfson, **The Fight Against Big Tobacco: The Movement, the State and the Public's Health**

The Rise and Fall
of
Social Psychology

The Use and Misuse of the Experimental Method

AUGUSTINE BRANNIGAN

ALDINE DE GRUYTER
New York

About the Author

Augustine Brannigan
Professor of Sociology, Department of Sociology, University of Calgary, Canada.

ALDINE DE GRUYTER
A division of Walter de Gruyter, Inc.
200 Saw Mill River Road
Hawthorne, New York 10532

This publication is printed on acid free paper ∞

Library of Congress Cataloging-in-Publication Data
Brannigan, Augustine, 1949–
    The rise and fall of social psychology : the use and misuse of the experimental method / Augustine Brannigan.
        p. cm. — (Social problems and social issues)
    Includes bibliographical references and index.
    ISBN 0-202-30742-5 (cloth : alk. paper) — ISBN 0-202-30743-3 (pbk. : alk. paper)
1. Social psychology—Methodology. 2. Social psychology—History. I. Title. II. Series.
    HM1011.B7 2004
    302'.01—dc22

                                                                                    2003027326

Manufactured in the United States of America

10 9 8 7 6 5 4 3 2 1

This work is dedicated to Terry M. (Wilcox) Brannigan,
my beloved companion, lover & wife.

Contents

Preface

Why Social Psychology Fails

This book is about the attempts over the past half-century to forge a science of social life based on the systematic use of experiments. Experimental social psychology is unique in the social sciences in that it has committed itself almost exclusively to the use of the experimental method to create new knowledge. In my view, this attempt has failed, and the rise of the institutional review boards and human ethics boards promises to bring the discipline as we know it to an end. The conclusion of this book is that experimental social psychology is *at present* an impossible science with little possibility in its current configuration of establishing any credible new knowledge. There are many reasons for this. The subject matter of the field is already part of the competence of people in everyday life. Certainly, scholars in other fields must face this problem, but social psychology occupies an unusual scientific space. Where the historian researches documents that capture, say, acts of genocide, the historian is merely telling a story that links the documents in a coherent way. His or her knowledge may be more "thorough" than what the witnesses to genocide might individually report. By contrast, the experimental social psychologist claims to be exposing processes that explain genocide or other topics in a nonobvious way, typically with reference to processes and mechanisms of which the original actors are unaware. Otherwise, he or she is merely repeating the obvious without the advantage of the historian, whose research of the *primary* documents puts facts before the reader that would not be known otherwise.

Furthermore, the experimentalist has to conjure up a proxy or a shorthand artifice or substitute for the original event. Rather than going to primary sources to study the phenomenon firsthand, the experimentalist has to visualize a way of reducing the process to something that can be studied in a laboratory over a short period of time, whether or not this is the best method of elucidating the phenomenon. The result is not a study of genocide but a metaphor of genocide, a dramatization or allegory that enacts certain key processes that the psychologist feels are critical, though these are frequently researched in a complete empirical vacuum with respect to the original events that characterized the genocide.

In this process the experimentalist is at elevated risks of importing into the study deeper moral and/or philosophical presuppositions. In other words, not being constrained by any set of "hard facts" that arise from studious observations of the phenomenon *in situ,* and not being informed by what is found in the historian's documents, or the clinician's interviews, or the demographer's age-gender tables, the moral substructure of social science inquiry is given free play. The evidence that I will examine in this book suggests that moral issues often make "consumers" of experimental social psychological research, students and the public at large, overlook the obvious empirical deficiencies of experimental designs. This explains the popularity of the field, and its attraction to psychology and sociology majors in spite of its scientific weaknesses. Social psychology is like divinity in the nineteenth-century liberal arts curriculum—interesting, but not really practical, deeply relevant to everyday life without being a source of definitive or scientific understanding of the social world.

THE END OF SOCIAL PSYCHOLOGY

This work explores these ideas in the case of a number of the classical contributions to experimental social psychology, experiments to which every student in the field would be exposed. I refer to the group influence tradition of Muzafer Sherif, Solomon Asch, and Stanley Milgram, all of whom were wedded to the experimental tradition, were seized by the problems of everyday life, and each of whom had a moral interest that animated his research and that explains its enduring appeal. This moral appeal is highly evident in the study of IQ and teacher expectations, and worker productivity and employment conditions in two classical studies of expectation effects: Pygmalion and Hawthorne. Both were methodologically indefensible investigations that nonetheless captured the hearts and minds of millions of students and members of the public. Their attraction was in their moral subtext, not their findings. The practical application of psychology is explored at length in the more recent experimental study of violent media and the allegedly worrisome effects of aggressive fiction on viewers. The rise of pornography in recent decades has fueled enormous public concerns about violence against women, and psychologists have enjoyed tremendous opportunities as expert witnesses in prosecutions trying to control sexually provocative fiction. I review the psychological evidence as well as its impact on the common law of obscenity to determine whether any "hard facts" were identified in this research and whether its adoption by the courts was warranted. I also explore whether there is any such thing as "social learning" and whether it explains the origins of antisocial behavior.

The balance of the book examines the impact of feminist and Darwinian agendas on the study of gender, although in this case, the methodologies are not always experimental. Again I ask whether the social relevance of the research is based on scientific considerations, or moral and philosophical perspectives parading as science, i.e., "living better" through science.

The final chapter explores the idea that the institutional review boards created to safeguard the treatment of human subjects in medical and psychological research may end social psychology as we know it—short-term, low-impact studies, based on laboratory simulations with subjects whose consent has been obtained through deception. The end of social psychology as an experimental undertaking is an outcome the book examines sympathetically. However, rather than leaving off on a negative note, the new ethical environment created by the institutional review boards may help us rethink what the objectives of social psychology should be. The prescriptions that tend to eliminate social psychological studies based on the willful deception of the subjects might lead us to rediscover the sorts of questions that ought to rehabilitate our work, and how we could approach the new questions in methodologically more authentic ways.

Acknowledgments

I want to thank the many friends and colleagues who read the manuscript and offered support and insight: Sharon L. Williams, Mike Lynch, Travis Hirschi, Michael Overington, Gwynne Nettler, Rod Cooper, Tullio Caputo, Rick Linden, Doug Skoog, Hank Stam, John Mueller, John Ellard, Erin Van Brunschot, the late J. Edwin Boyd, Bob Stebbins, Dick Wanner, Sophie Bonneau, Nick Jones and Ron Roisen.

1

The Sunset of A Golden Age

Reflections on the Gap between Promise and Practice

The Classical tradition is now dead and not mourned by those who hastened its demise, a cabal of some cognitive social psychologists, human subjects research committees, Protestants, and female social psychologists.

—Philip Zimbardo, "Experimental Social Psychology: Behaviorism with Minds and Matters"

HUMAN EXPERIMENTATION AND CAUSAL EXPLANATIONS: PROMISE VERSUS PERFORMANCE

Philip Zimbardo was president of the American Psychological Association in 2003. If the classical tradition is dead, surely he would know. Whether its demise was hastened by female scientists and Protestants is another matter. In my view there was a huge gulf between the appropriate use of experiments and what psychologists actually did in their laboratories, and this was the case not at the periphery of social psychology but at its very core. In other words, there was a gap between the promise and the performance after experimentation dominated the arsenal of social psychologists in the 1950s. In this chapter I want to identify the scientific strength of experimentation and contrast this to how experiments actually developed in the golden age of experimental social psychology.

THE PROMISE

In the methodology of the social sciences, it is well accepted that experimentation is the key to objective knowledge, and is superior to rival methodologies, at least in principle.[1] The ideal design in scientific research

1

is the *true* experiment, where subjects are randomly exposed to various treatment conditions and then tested to determine the effects of the different treatments on the outcomes. Since the designs are formal, replication of results is typically quite straightforward. What made the experiment superior to other methods such as cross-sectional surveys, ethnographies, or interviews was, according to its proponents, its ability to combine certain features of inquiry: first, an association between two or more variables (a link between a potential cause and an effect); second, the ability to identify temporal precedence of the cause, i.e., the appearance of the cause *prior* to the identification of the effect because of the time-ordering of the events in the experimental designs; and third, an ability to determine whether the connection between cause and effect is nonspurious. In addition, true experiments have three things associated with them: two comparison groups—minimally, an experimental group and a control group, variations in the independent variable before assessment of change in the dependent variable, and random assignment of subjects to the two (or more) groups.

In theory, this combination of factors is supposed to give some confidence in the validity of the causal connections between the "treatment" and the outcomes. And our confidence is further enhanced by two things: the identification of the causal *mechanisms* that underlie the observed changes and the experimenter's control over the institutional context of the experiment. This said, it must also be acknowledged that not all experiments have a pure "exposure" and control or "no exposure" design. Sometimes a design will have several different *kinds* of exposures. Imagine looking at the effect of exposure to violent films, versus nonviolent films versus no films at all. The "no film" condition would be the true control group and the other types of exposures would be comparison groups across experimental treatments. In addition, true experiments do not actually require *pretests* on the variable or outcome of interest. If one was interested in the effects of certain types of films on attitudes (for example, propaganda and attitudes to certain minorities), it might be possible to get a pretest measure of attitudes *prior* to the treatment. However, the logic of the design is that those in the control group are in effect a pretest group because they have not received the treatment. Because they have been randomly assigned to the control condition, they are logically identical to the "before" group. The random assignment of subjects to various treatment groups avoids the potential artifact that arises from administering the same measures to the same subjects twice.

A related point has to do with randomization. Of course, it would be a mistake to believe that the people who end up in the treatment versus the control group are all exactly alike. They obviously are not. But what the logic of random assignment suggests is that the various salient things that might affect the outcomes have an equal probability of occurring in each group, so that their effect is neutral.

A different issue concerns random *sampling* versus random assignment. In a survey, we engage in a random sampling of a population to ensure that we can generalize from the persons in the sample to the larger population, since each S has the same probability of being selected for inclusion in the survey (Frankford-Nachmias 1999:481). By contrast, in experiments, randomization does not ensure generalizability, nor is it designed to. It is designed to ensure internal validity. Internal validity covers a number of issues, but for our purposes suffice it to say that what it ensures is that the design gives us confidence that the only important difference between the control and the treatment group is the treatment itself. The issue of generalizability is perhaps the main Achilles' heel of experimentation in social psychology. The logic of experimentation is that the sorts of things being investigated are of such generality that they are present in whatever sections of the population from which subjects are drawn. At least in theory, the lack of a careful selection process designed to ensure representativeness is irrelevant. Obviously, with these attributes, the experiment has earned a reputation as a powerful tool in the arsenal of social scientists. How did the experiment work out in practice? A rather different picture emerges.

THE GOLDEN AGE OF EXPERIMENTAL SOCIAL PSYCHOLOGY: REFLECTIONS FROM THE YOSEMITE CONFERENCE

In 1997, a group of senior American social psychologists gathered at Yosemite National Park to take stock of the growth of knowledge in experimental social psychology and to record some of their personal memories and professional reflections. They were the leading lights in psychology, who were active in creating the profession in the period of its heyday following the Second World War and in the decades thereafter.[2] All the participants took their doctoral training in the period 1948–1959, and were major contributors to the field during its impressive growth in the fifties, sixties, seventies, and eighties. Their postmortem deliberations on the achievements of the field provide a rare window on the history of social psychology. They identify a number of ambiguities in the development of the field that appear to be associated with its commitment to the causal explanation of social behavior through the use of experimental methods.

What important conclusions emerged from this celebration of a century of research? There were recurrent observations that the golden age was over, that the field had not accumulated much reliable new knowledge, and that it had not achieved much consensus about important matters. The

sociology of knowledge warns us to treat collective reflections about a
field's origins with a grain of salt since often times these "memories" are
myths about the turning points in history that eventuated in the current configuration of knowledge. Rodrigues and Levine (1999), who edited the proceedings, trace experimental social psychology to the work of Norman
Triplett. In 1897, Triplett had published an experimental study of children's
task performance based on observations of bicycle racers. Triplett knew
that the individual performance levels of racers are influenced by competition. Typically racers "pace" each other before putting on the final sprint at
the end of the race. Triplett measured children's performance on a fishing
reel undertaken alone and in competition. His work introduced the concept
of "social facilitation" into individual productivity as well as the effects of
the related concept of "rivalry." What is ironic is that his research received
rather mixed notice in the years that followed, and, aside from being experimental, created no research legacy.[3] Indeed, in the early decades of the
discipline, G. H. Mead criticized the use of experiments for social psychology since he favored the method of introspection. However, social psychology gradually acquired scientific respectability, not because of its
theoretical progress, but because of the adoption of the methods and logic
of the hard sciences. The break between social psychology as a *sociological*
discipline and social psychology as a *psychological* discipline emerged in the
fifties, when experimental methodology became the orthodox approach in
professional psychology while the sister sciences remained relatively diver-
sified in their approaches. Experimentation established itself as the gold
standard because of its ability to link connections in a nonspurious, tem-
porally informed fashion, and to explore relationships causally.

Several contributors at the Yosemite conference noted that social psychology had become a field in which practitioners appeared to know little
of the history of their own discipline, and had become alienated from
cognate areas on sociology and anthropology. In this celebration of the discipline's achievements, Aronson (1999:108) lamented the fact that contemporary social psychologists were ignorant of research prior to 1975, and
Raven (1999:118) warned that new scholars were in danger of "reinventing
the wheel," or of failing to credit an idea to its originator because of disciplinary amnesia (Berkowitz 1999:161). There was a consensus that the field
had become increasingly abstract, specialized and divorced from issues of
everyday life. There was also a sense that "the golden age" of experimentation had come to an end, a victim of the new institutional review boards
instituted in the 1990s to protect human subjects from unethical conduct
by experimenters. Pepitone said, "The golden age was quintessentially the
age of experimentalism and the passing of metatheories like field theory
or systems like S-R learning theory and psychoanalytic theory" (1999:
180–81).

The review boards were created in the 1990s to ensure protection of human subjects from harm and discomfort. While originally directed at medical research using human subjects, the boards have probably sounded the death-knell of experimental studies of human psychology. In such studies, consent is often obtained from subjects through deception about the purpose of the research, a condition that renders the consent uninformed, and hence invalid. In addition, in the search for realism in the lab, some psychological experiments have entailed very detailed dramaturgical manipulations that have resulted in high levels of trauma among subjects. For example, in the disturbing study of obedience to authority, Milgram (1963) reported that many of his subjects experienced nervous fits, "full-blown, uncontrollable seizures," in some cases so violent that it was necessary to terminate the experiment. Zillmann and Bryant's (1982) nine-week study of pornography reported that changes in callous attitudes among subjects were "nontransitory" (i.e., permanent). In their study of the dynamics of emotions, Schachter and Singer (1962) injected subjects with chlorpromazine (a medication used in the treatment of schizophrenia) or epinephrine (synthetic adrenaline) under the pretext of testing a new vitamin, "suproxin." The passing of high-impact experimentation was noted by Zimbardo in the quote at the head of this chapter. Zimbardo claimed that the ethics review boards "overreacted to the questionable ethics of some of the research by the oldies but goodies in experimental social psychology." By imposing limits on what can now be done and said to research participants, the boards have provided safeguards "to the end of eliminating some of what could be called traditional experimental social psychology" (1999:138).

The dominant understanding about the defensible treatment of human subjects in experimental psychology has been that there has existed a trade-off between short-term deception and edgy manipulation of subjects on the one hand, and long-term benefits to science and society on the other. But there has never been an annual general meeting of the consumers of psychological knowledge to determine whether this investment was justified. In fact, Zimbardo's own work raises some of the deepest questions. In the Stanford "prison study," he reports that some of his mock guards assaulted the mock prisoners, and that many prisoners had to be released prematurely because of intense emotional trauma. In his 1972 account in *Society*, it appears he dragged his heels in terminating the "experiment" until it could be recorded on videotape by a local television station. But what was learned about prisons that we did not know? If the ethics boards overreacted in recent years, this may be due to an absence of effective internal self-regulation in the past. But that was not the only problem associated with experiments in the golden age. Evidence suggests that in many of the key studies, researchers would not take no for an answer, that the experiments simply became devices for demonstrating a relationship arrived at beforehand, and that the field could not grow because falsification of a hypothesis was virtually never recognized.

KURT LEWIN AND FIELD THEORY

In my view, experimental social psychology began, not with Triplett in 1897, but with Kurt Lewin and his students in the mid- to late 1940s. Lewin was a German émigré whose "field theory" (1951) was based on the German gestalt tradition in which individual actions and attitudes were interpenetrated by socially based, cognitively coherent frames of reference. After the war, Lewin established the Research Center for Group Dynamics at the Massachusetts Institute of Technology. The Center moved to the University of Michigan after Lewin's death in 1947, but not before Lewin had assembled an impressive group of graduate students and coinstructors. By all accounts, Lewin was an effective "tribal leader" (according to Deutsch 1999:9). He combined a commitment to the rigors of experimentation with an intellectual agenda that fostered practical engagement with everyday life, including the potential of social psychology for ameliorating social problems. Lewin's own work demonstrated the greater effectiveness of democratic versus autocratic forms of leadership in lab studies. This in itself had a tremendous attraction among the graduate students who enrolled in social psychology after participating in the war against European and Japanese dictators. The field had a further caché since experimentation was the sole methodology in the social sciences expressly capable of suggesting not mere correlations, but causal connections. At the Yosemite meeting, Kelley recorded the attitude at the time: "We were 'real scientists,' using the experimental method, drawing firm conclusions about cause and effect, and not fooling around with mushy correlational data" (1999:41). According to Gerard (1999:49) Cohen and Nagel's *Introduction to Logic and Scientific Method* (1934) was standard reading for these scientific protégés.

The late forties and early fifties were very consequential for the subsequent directions of the discipline. Lewin's gestalt orientation appeared to lead psychologists away from a focus on stimulus-response behaviorism in their theoretical modeling since it expressly celebrated the distinctive role of perception, recollection, and normative action in human social behavior. However, the commitment to the method of experimentation was subsequently to result in a narrow focus on cognitive *mechanisms* that were suitable for laboratory investigation however remote they might be from pressing problems in everyday life. This narrow methodological focus was subsequently to stifle the search for general, integrative theories. By contrast, at the start of their careers Deutsch, Gerard, Berkowitz, and Pepitone (among others) attested to the remarkable breadth of social psychology, and to the common definitions of problems in "sociological" and "psychological" social psychology. There was a tremendous interest in racism and discrimination, the related problems of school desegregation, and concerns over world peace. As the field developed, experimentalists became increasingly preoccupied with, in the words of Berkowitz (1999:162) "within-the-skin" versus "between-skins" phenomena. The "social" in social psychology became more associated with the idea of "information" and "information processing" than with meaning, culture, and context. And the focus on "cognitions" qua cognitions created "a spurious conceptual generality" (Pepitone 1999:191).

One of the casualties in the institutionalization of social psychology was psychoanalysis. Morton Deutsch, one of the earliest proponents of experimental studies of group behavior, was trained in psychoanalysis and enjoyed a long clinical career outside academic psychology. "The practice was personally rewarding. I helped a number of people, it enabled me to stay in touch with my own inner life, and it provided a welcome supplement to my academic salary" (Deutsch 1999:15). Similarly, Harold Gerard turned to "depth psychology" later in his career, entering psychoanalysis at age fifty-nine and becoming a psychoanalyst at age sixty-nine— thereafter switching his experimental work to a focus on "subliminal activation." But these clearly were the exceptions.

As the field became more lab-oriented, such "soft methods" and general theories fell into disfavor. The single leading proponent of experimental social psychology—Leon Festinger—viewed such "applications" with suspicion. According to Aronson, "Leon was not interested in improving the human condition. Not in the least. . . . Trying to understand human nature and doing good research (not doing good) were more than enough to keep him excited" (1999:87). Indeed, Festinger held Aronson's other mentor, Abram Maslow, a leading humanist, in obvious contempt. Festinger once told Aronson, "That guy's ideas are so bad that they aren't even wrong" (ibid.:92). In the end, Festinger's scientific model overshadowed the humanistic methods and theories of Maslow, and Freud's theories became unwelcome in the era of experimentation.

THE IMPACT OF COGNITIVE DISSONANCE

Festinger's attitude to humanism is difficult to fathom. In his own work, he attempted to ground research in provocative issues taken from everyday life. The dynamics of everyday life could be distilled in the formal light of causal ordering in the controlled experiment and applied back to the outside world. His study of group conformity and rejection of deviants arose from a field study of political consciousness among graduate students in college residence (Festinger, Schachter, and Back 1950). The famous field study, *When Prophecy Fails* (Festinger, Riecken, and Schachter 1956), was one of the most important intellectual foundations for his studies of cognitive dissonance. In *When Prophecy Fails* Festinger et al. discovered that a failed prediction of the imminent destruction of the earth led its proponents to become *more* attracted to the prophecy after its failure, not *less* so, as might be predicted by behaviorism. This study had far more potential for understanding irrational behavior than anything subsequently "discovered" empirically in the lab. The passing of such brilliant fieldwork was another casualty of the experimental "turn" in psychological methods. This brings me to what I believe was the pivotal role of the experimental study of cognitive dissonance, a move that appears at several levels to be indicative of the sea change that occurred in social psychology.

Aronson reported at Yosemite that he read Festinger's manuscript, *A Theory of Cognitive Dissonance*, in typescript as a graduate student at Stanford, and that he found it revolutionary:

> [It] revitalized social psychology . . . and offered a serious vehicle for challenging the smug dominance of reinforcement theory. It did this not in a vague, philosophical manner, but in a powerful, concrete, and specific confrontation, exposing reinforcement theory's limiting conditions as well as its inability to predict some of the more subtle and more interesting nuances of human behavior. (1999:86)

This was strong testimony to the impact of Festinger's vision on the field, and the agenda-setting implications for his students in social psychology. When he arrived at Stanford, Aronson (ibid.:85) reported that he eagerly enrolled in Festinger's "seminary" in social psychology (an interesting Freudian slip). What is ironic is that, prior to joining the faculty at the Massachusetts Institute of Technology (and later Stanford), Festinger had not taken a course in social psychology, nor had his leading student, Stan Schachter (see Festinger 1987:2), nor apparently had another leading light in the field, Donald Campbell (see Raven 1999:115). Furthermore, those who had studied psychology at the New York universities as undergraduates experienced little indoctrination in behaviorism (if the work of Solomon Asch or Floyd Allport is any guide). The new generation of social psychologists appeared unacquainted with the leading social psychology texts of the 1930s, which, in any case, were *not* primarily behaviorist. Cognitive dissonance simply opened a new page for social psychology, one that was dogmatically experimental, indifferent to practical applications, and focused on the underlying mechanisms of sense-making.

In debates about psychology's apparent lack of progress, reference is often made to the "infancy" of the field. I believe another hypothesis should be examined: The potential for growth in social psychology perhaps was stifled precisely *because of* the impact of cognitive dissonance and the subsequent "cognitive revolution" in the field, something fostered by the dominance of the experimental method. The concept of cognitive dissonance is based on the idea that the human mind resists the simultaneous appropriation of two cognitions that are inconsistent. If one believed dearly that the world was going to end, and shed all one's worldly goods in anticipation, the realization that the world had *not* ended when expected would create a cognitive disequilibrium that would create a drive designed to restore cognitive consonance. One would have to accept the fact that one's beliefs were mistaken, and that one had foolishly given away one's material resources. In that way, all the facts would cohere consistently. Alternatively, one could reject the failure of the prophecy and revise the date of doomsday. Either way, the mind seeks an equilibrium in "cognitions." This is what Festinger had recognized conceptually before taking the matter to the lab.

In the lab, Festinger and Carlsmith (1959) enlisted naïve subjects in a series of repetitive, ostensibly boring, mechanical exercises. The naïve subjects were told that the experimenter's assistant was unable to instruct new subjects, and that a replacement was required. Subjects were recruited to replace the assistant, and to coach new subjects. Specifically, the recruits were required to tell the new subjects that the experiment was very exciting and interesting when nothing could be further from the truth. After the naïve subjects (turned recruits) had delivered this false information (to a confederate of the experimenter), they were tested to determine what they themselves thought about the experiment. They were asked *how enjoyable* the experiment was, how much they thought they had *learned,* how scientifically *important* it was, and their *desire to participate* in similar experiments. The first critical dimension of the experiment was that the subjects were manipulated into lying to someone they thought was as naïve as they themselves had been. The second critical dimension was the amount of money they were paid as recruits to (mis)inform the new subjects (who, it turns out, were confederates). In the one case, they were paid a large amount of money (twenty dollars), in the other they were paid a small amount of money (one dollar).

What was the effect of the level of compensation on the subjects' personal estimation of the degree to which the experiment was interesting, exciting, etc.? If you were paid a lot of money to lie about such matters (twenty dollars), would this salve your conscience? Would this payment mollify the lie, and leave your estimation of the experiences unaltered? On the contrary, if you lied for peanuts, would you experience an anomaly that would compel your mind to think that the experiment was more exciting in retrospect than it had been originally, and that, as a consequence, you had not really lied at all? In short, did the dissonance (between what you experienced personally and what you told the other) create processes in which your sense-making devices reordered the significance attached to the original events below the threshold of consciousness after you were paid? Or did the compensation (twenty dollars) in effect justify the misinformation given to others, and leave your original memories unaltered? If so, cognitive dissonance would become a paradigm for opinion consolidation and change, and presumably predict some concordance between opinions, values, and behaviors. *When Prophecy Fails* suggested this happened in everyday life. What was revealed when the experimental microscope was focused downwards to look more closely at the phenomenon in the lab?

The original experiment reported four predictions, but only one was corroborated (i.e., estimation of "enjoyment"). Persons paid poorly found the experiment more enjoyable than persons paid well. The cup was three-quarters empty, but rather than reevaluate the theory, the experimentalists returned to the lab. There followed a torrent of tests of cognitive dissonance exploring the dynamics of dissonance in a myriad of innovative, experimental contexts.

In 1964 Chapanis and Chapanis summarized the findings from several dozen tests of the theory of cognitive dissonance. They concluded that there was no evidence that subjects actually experienced the dissonance that the experiments were attempting to induce, that the manipulations were not credible social situations (paying someone a day's salary—twenty dollars—for half an hour's work—16 percent voiced suspicions or refused to be hired in the original Festinger and Carlsmith design), that the designs were confounded by classical reinforcement processes, that there were massive problems in the rejection of cases and arbitrary reallocation across treatment groups, and that some studies used unusually permissive statistical criteria for rejecting the null hypothesis. "Experimental manipulations are usually so complex and the crucial variables so confounded that no valid conclusions could be drawn from the data. . . . A number of fundamental methodological inadequacies in the analysis of results . . . vitiate the results." They reiterated Asch's conclusion in his 1958 review of Festinger's book: the case for cognitive dissonance was "not proven."

THE DISAPPEARANCE OF FALSIFICATION AND THE DECLINE IN CONSENSUS

One would have thought that such damaging criticisms would have given serious pause to the field. But that does not appear to be the case. In *Reflections on 100 Years* (Rodrigues and Levine 1999), there are dozens of references to dissonance theory but not a single reference to Chapanis and Chapanis. Chapanis and Chapanis were not part of Lewin's tribe, and those who were simply ignored the critique! Not surprisingly, the report of negative findings was quite rare in experimental social psychology during this period, as noted by Pepitone: "An overall summary of experimental research would show that findings infrequently lead to an outright rejection of the hypothesis being tested . . . in the vast majority of published research articles findings confirm hypotheses" (1999:193).

The problem with this is that a science that cannot say no to anything does not actually have the capacity to grow. Experiments had taken on a life of their own, and research had lost contact with everyday life. Events researched in one lab were designed to explore effects not found in everyday life, but in other labs. Zajonc (1997:200–1) voiced some difficulties with the consequences in terms of the progress of the field. He noted looking backwards that "social psychology (like psychology itself) is not cumulative." If one were to take any textbook, he says, and randomly reshuffle the chapters, it wouldn't matter since "there is no *compelling* order." So in a century of psychology, nothing accumulates. As we shall see, this observation has been recurrent in the history of the discipline. Zajonc then noted that "the scientists of a given discipline agree about the core subject matter of their inquiry. . . . But psychologists and social psychologists do not. We have no consensus about the core of our field's subject matter." Zajonc attributed this to disagreement about the fundamental characteristics of human nature (whether the mind is rational or irrational), but I would say that this cannot logically be a *cause* of the lack of consensus as much as another manifestation of it. In his reflections, Pepitone similarly noted that despite the volume of brilliant and creative work produced by experimentalists, "the theory-research programs have produced few absolutely general, context free, and universally valid principles or laws" (1999:192). Pepitone further observed that research traditions in social psychology seem to come and go like fashions, without achieving higher-order conceptual integration, or acquiring any enduring set of "hard facts."

In the 1970s, there was widespread discussion about the lack or progress, relevance, and consensus in psychology. This is sometimes referred to as the "crisis literature." At the time, many critics pointed to the liability of the experiment whose scientific allure outstripped its actual potential since the majority of the experiments involved low-impact, short-duration interactions between strangers drawn overwhelmingly from the ranks of college sophomores. High-impact designs such as that employed by Milgram eventually raised ethical questions for members of the ethics review boards. In their textbook, *Experimental Social Psychology,* Murphy, Murphy, and Newcomb had warned of the limitations of the experimental method and its potential misapplication decades before experimentation became the *sine qua non* of social psychology: "It has become very evident in recent years that the social psychologist . . . has succeeded in experimental and quantitative control by leaving out most of the variables about which we really need to know" (1937:10). It is not surprising that Albert Pepitone came to the same conclusion when he suggested that the current lack of progress derives from the "*successful* development of the lab experiment as the principal method of testing hypotheses and the principal source of hypotheses." As for the lack of theoretical progress, "This deficiency is also due to the exclusive use of experiments" (1999:193). Rodrigues and Levine appeared to agree: "Many of the current criticisms of the field today—for example, an overemphasis on experimentation, a lack of humanism, an unwillingness to focus on the applied—are part of Festinger's legacy" (1999:218). Festinger himself appears to have abandoned experimental social psychology in the midsixties after cognitive dissonance encountered heavy weather. But the field persisted, and continued to examine social processes in the lab at an ethereal level, testing for relationships in a pure or context-free fashion, looking for what might be called a geometry of interaction, divorced from the bite of infernal life. Gerard reported that "by the 1970s, social psychology had become dominated by the cognitive revolution that had swept most of psychology. . . . I developed a sinking feeling that we social psychologists were missing the boat. . . . I became dissatisfied with the bland cast that had overtaken social psychology" (1999:67). Pepitone similarly observed that the experiment "systematically constrains the field to leave out of theory and research much of what is observed about the influence of culture and social structure" (1999:193). So the approach that gave the field its scientific credibility constrained how problems were defined and actually smothered its growth.

SITUATIONAL ANALYSIS AND THE EXPERIMENT

Another bias that students of Festinger and Lewin seem to have inherited is a sense of the primacy of "the situation" as a fundamental fact of social life. This is a legacy of the phenomenology that underpins gestalt psychology. Phenomenology emphasizes the role of embodiment, consciousness, and temporality in our immediate experience of reality. But these may not be important from the point of view of causal explanation. Borrowing from another context, this is evident in Jack Katz's criminology, in which he attempted to explain participation in crime by reference to the foreground of experience: the embodied attractions of doing evil. The problem he ran into was that things like robbery, no matter how pleasurable and seductive, had certain recurrent features: robbery is overwhelmingly the pursuit of youth, of males, and of poor blacks, characteristics that point to background structures. Phenomenology can describe processes, but an explanation that equates exogenous causes with an account of the processes that need explaining is circular.

The parallel deficiency in social psychology is the importance that is attached to "the situation." The experiment is premised on the idea that the essential elements in social interaction are situational and can be scripted into short-term experimental dramas. This overlooks compelling evidence from life course studies about the stability of traits like temperament and aggressiveness over the life cycle (Glueck and Glueck 1950; Moffitt 1993).

A good illustration of the frailty of this line of thinking was suggested by Aronson's discussion of anti-Semitism. At the Yosemite conference, Aronson (1999:104) reported that he was forged as a social psychologist at the age of nine following harassment by neighborhood kids who intimidated him en route to Hebrew school. "They were caught up in a powerful situation that produced that prejudice" (ibid.:104). As a social psychologist he said he strives to create interventions that can produce "redemption" through a situational remedy. In other words, both the causes and the remedy to anti-Semitism are "situational." This flies in the face of national and institutional patterns of animosity that have marked centuries of European history from the time of the Romans. This "situationalism" is not the legacy of thinking experimentally, but the legacy of thinking *only* experimentally. What the Yosemite conference suggests is that in the pursuit of a methodology designed to confer confidence in causal connections, social psychology lost some of its purchase on the complexity of everyday life, on depth psychology and emotional attachments, on life-course persistent traits, and on much of what preoccupies us as requiring social reform. The rise of the institutional review boards that censure deceptive cover stories and threatening manipulations—the stuff of classical experimental social psychology—may be a blessing in disguise.

IS SOCIAL PSYCHOLOGY A MORAL SCIENCE?[4]

Social psychology is paradoxical. It is one of the most popular subjects in the undergraduate curriculum but very little of its subject matter is practical, or can be applied in specific settings to overcome problems that would plague society in its absence. It strikes students as highly "relevant" but its theories do not exhibit evidence of accumulation either in empirical findings or in the consolidation of nonobvious theories. The scope of the field is colossal but its achievements are questionable. It does not appear to have generated a set of "hard facts" or "main effects" that ground a consensus of what is truly important. What coherence does exist appears to derive from adoption of the method of Galileo—experimentation—

arguably the most powerful technique for making causal inferences in the relationships between social variables. But even here, many of the key experiments are allegorical, theatrical, or metaphoric since the important questions that arise in the study of everyday life often are rarely amenable to short-term, low-impact situations, nor can the important things that preoccupy us—violence, trauma, misery—actually be examined experimentally with human subjects for obvious ethical reasons. The rise of institutional review boards designed to mitigate the harm to human subjects in medical and social science research, as noted earlier, may spell the end of an approach to social research frequently premised on deception of the subjects. The field shows evidence of painful crises of confidence as investigators confront the disappointments and contradictions of the field. The Yosemite conference provides ample evidence of this crisis but misgivings about social psychology's progress have been common in the field for decades. We turn to some of that literature now.

NOTES

1. For example, Campbell and Stanley, reflecting on McCall's pioneering work on the use of experiments in educational research, hold up the experiment "as the only means for settling disputes regarding educational practice, as the only way of verifying educational improvements, and as the only way of establishing a cumulative tradition in which improvements can be introduced without the danger of a faddish discard of old wisdom in favor of inferior novelties" (1963:2).

2. The participants included Morton Deutsch, Harold H. Kelley, Harold B. Gerard, Elliot Aronson, Bertram H. Raven, Philip G. Zimbardo, Leonard Berkowitz, Albert Pepitone, and Robert Zajonc. Stanley Schachter's terminal illness unfortunately precluded his attendance.

3. Triplett's legacy might have been better served had he played a role in educating graduate students who would continue his legacy. In order to assess the impact of his work, I examined the collection of social psychology texts published prior to 1950. The University of Calgary collection holds twenty-one such volumes. Triplett is cited in five (Allport 1924; Murphy et al. 1937; Murchison 1935; Newcomb and Hartley 1947; LaPiere and Farnsworth 1949). There is no reference in the other sixteen volumes (Ginsberg 1942; Karpf 1932; Robinson 1930; Dewey [1922] 1950; Blum 1949; McDougall 1919; Znaniecki 1925; Lowy 1944; Perry 1935; Dewey 1901; Hopkins 1938; Sherif 1936; Klineberg 1948; Lindesmith and Strauss 1949, Ross 1908; Krech and Crutchfield 1948). While not dismissing his impact, one would have thought that work considered pioneering would have attracted more consistent attention.

4. This is asked in the sense of J. S. Mill in *On the Logic of the Moral Sciences*, not in the sense, "Are psychologists moral?" We do not use Mill's term today. We substitute "social" for "moral," but the question raised here is whether the emphasis should be on the concept of our research as *science* (moral or social) at all—as opposed to morality *presented* as science.

2

Crisis and Controversy in Experimental Social Psychology

Four Hypotheses

What extremely busy and productive field of modern psychology has no clear-cut identity and not even a generally accepted definition? Social Psychology. It is less a field than a no-man's land between psychology and sociology, overlapping each and impinging on several other social sciences.

—Morton Hunt, *The Story of Psychology*

CRISIS AND CONTROVERSY IN EXPERIMENTAL SOCIAL PSYCHOLOGY: SELF-DOUBTS IN A CAUSAL SCIENCE

Is social psychology a "no-man's land" that does not have a commonly accepted definition? How could such an ill-defined field prove so popular as an undergraduate subject? What is its attraction? As we enter the new millennium it is essential to take stock of our scientific progress to determine whether the questions we have raised and the methods we have used to explore them have actually yielded genuinely new knowledge and have perceptibly moved the field forward. As an undergraduate student I subscribed to a wide range of courses in the social sciences, including social psychology. Psychology struck me as extremely relevant to everyday life, and as a profoundly relevant way of understanding human nature and the trials and tribulations that mark our ordinary lives. Like other students of the sixties, I was hungry for an understanding of human life that was based neither on the religious orthodoxy of my forebears nor the materialism of the market. I was also struck by psychology's commitment to a methodology believed to be superior to those found in the other social sciences like sociology and economics. Experimentation epitomized the scientific mentality. It permitted the psychologist to test his or her ideas under controlled settings in which causal inferences were valid, and in which it would be possible to distinguish direct, indirect, and interactional effects. On this basis, a genuine science of human nature would come within our grasp. And with it, people could design social arrangements capable of mitigating harm and injustice and encouraging the open development of self-expression—in other words, Walden Two in postindustrial society, without imperiling freedom and dignity.[1]

However, even as an undergraduate I was impatient with the overreliance on knowledge derived from the study of white lab rats in artificial conditions. The comparability of rats and humans was taken on faith. To be fair, the parallels were drawn between basic learning processes of reinforcement, and not higher cognitive functions. I was also uncomfortable with the confinement of methodology to experimentation and the exclusion of research questions that could not be tackled within that framework. And finally, I looked without consolation for any persuasive perspective that integrated the field theoretically. Except for experimentation (methodology), academic psychology seemed fragmented. And what appeared the most interesting and speculative development in the century—Freud's study of the unconscious—was beyond the pale conceptually, methodologically, and clinically. Rat conditioning attracted more confidence than the interpretation of dreams.

Nonetheless, much of the substance of the field intrigued me, particularly what I have come to view as the classic contributions. Later in life as a professor teaching courses in social psychology, my interest in the questions that motivated these classic studies has continued to grow, but so have my misgivings about their theoretical and methodological premises. This book attempts to lay out my concerns, and to do so in the context of work that will be familiar to most students of psychology.

It is hard to convey to an audience in Europe, Asia, or Africa the importance attached to experimentation in social psychology in North America. That should not be surprising since it is hard to convey it within North America to academics who are not psychologists. It is the dominant methodological approach, and it has become one pursued to the virtual exclusion of every other methodological strategy in the social sciences. As Stam, Radtke, and Lubek argue, "The acceptability of ideas in the field came to depend largely on the ability of authors to couch them in the language of the experiment" (2000:365). Yet, it has been used to tackle some of the trickiest social situations known to humankind. These include the general formation of social norms in Sherif's experiment on the autokinetic effect, the causes of compliance to the European holocaust in Milgram's study of obedience, the nature of workplace determinants of productivity in the Hawthorne studies, the causes of minority school failure in Rosenthal's study of teacher expectations, the contributions of violent and pornographic media to aggression and misogyny in everyday life in the work of Bandura and Donnerstein among others. These studies are just a sampling of the classic contributions.

My interest in the work of social psychologists has been deepened by my own studies of the causes of crime and delinquency and by the evidence amassed in criminology about patterns of crime and its analogs, the characteristics of offenders and their social distribution in society. Is racial-ethnic hate crime explained by obedience to authority? Is street crime explained by youthful exposure to media violence? Both propositions would seem obvious to the student of social psychology but neither would attract much confidence from students of criminology. How could the fields be so mutually insular? When the leading criminology textbooks view the contribution of social learning from mass media models to imitative crime as minimal, are they ignoring sound science? Or do the experimental investigations of media effects so overstate the explained variance of media exposure as to overshadow far more important determinants of violence (gender, class, and individual impulsiveness)? Much hangs in the balance.

For example, a number of national inquiries in Canada, the United States, Australia, and elsewhere have sought input from social sciences in respect of the effects of violent media in order to set guidelines for fictional portrayals of violent and erotic stories. In some jurisdictions, the courts have heard evidence from experimental social psychologists to determine if certain films are so threatening to public security as to put the liberty and capital of individuals who distribute them at risk under criminal obscenity laws. In fact, the introduction of work from experimental social psychology has been important in many areas of litigation, including forced busing in the United States, limits on industrial action at the Chancery Court in the United Kingdom, and the suppression of pedophilia and pornography in the United States and Canada. For many psychologists, acknowledgment of their accomplishments in legal decisions is strong corroboration of their social relevance and a vindication of their methodology. I cannot think of comparable contributions to jurisprudence from sociologists or criminologists, and I believe that the advantage that psychologists claim is their adherence to a superior methodology.

But the relevance of this controversy is not limited to the field of social psychology and public policy. There is a lively debate about the epistemology of social science in what has come to be called the "science wars." What is the evidence for the "existential determination" of the content of science?[2] The Sokal hoax is the most recent installment of this debate. Alan Sokal, a New York physicist who taught mathematics to peasant children during the Sandinista revolution in Nicaragua, duped the editors of *Social Text* with a bogus description of what he labeled a poststructural physics. His "transformative hermeneutics of quantum gravity" was a spoof on the claims about science running through the leading figures of the French intellectual establishment spiked with the usual impenetrable jargon and buzzwords (Sokal 1996a). The parody was published in a special issue of *Social Text* designed by the editors to rebuke the criticisms of their antiscientific agenda by leading scientists. Sokal simultaneously published an exposé in *Lingua Franca* (1996b). The hoax ignited a storm of criticism on both sides. The Sokal affair turned the tables on the sociologists of science and raised questions as to whether their charges of social and cultural reductionism in respect of the natural sciences were not more appropriately applied to the social sciences and humanities. My current inquiry raises the question of the extrascientific determination of conclusions in the area of psychological knowledge, and the autonomy of social scientific knowledge from everyday life. If my suspicions are borne out, much of what passes for science in psychology is morality in an experimental idiom.

The topic of experimentation merits reevaluation on other grounds. There is recent historiography in respect of one classic study—Milgram's study *Obedience to Authority*—which suggests that specification of the causal dynamics was seriously amiss, and that the subsequent results, no matter how internally eloquent, did not actually explain what happened. It "explained" what the perpetrators in retrospect said happened, but the historical evidence suggests that this was not the process that needed explaining. Milgram's work is the single best known contribution within the experimental tradition in social psychology. However, it is an open question as to how much light it shed on what it purported to explain. In retrospect, Milgram's operationalization tended to reify the excuses that the Nazis gave at their trials (i.e., "just following orders") making the murderers the victims of the Holocaust. Here I am referring to the work of Daniel Goldhagen (1997) and Christopher Browning (1998). They reject Milgram's supposition that fear of authority was a prime factor in soldier compliance in the extermination of European Jews.[3] The evidence suggests that the Germans were willing executioners not fearful of authority, and that this is likewise true in recent ethnic conflicts in Africa and the former Yugoslavia.

There has also been a revival of debates about the foundations of intelligence with the publication of the *Bell Curve* (1994). Where Rosenthal's *Pygmalion* (1968) argued that students' IQs responded to teacher expectations, the *Bell Curve* authors, Herrnstein and Murray, argued that the origins of variation were largely hereditary, and implied that such patterns might have a racial basis. One could not imagine approaches more diametrically opposed. Both studies purported to contribute constructively to discussions of public policy and both fueled debates that were at times incendiary. But what light has emerged from all the heat? Has psychology clarified anything in the public mind?

I think this inquiry is timely because it captures the chorus of voices from within the field who have registered a sense of both angst and ennui over its lack of progress. In my view this chorus groans over the methodological focus that makes experimentation the lynchpin of scientific authority. My inquiry might suggest why this frustration is a natural outcome of the development of a psychology artificially confined within this methodological frame of reference. In this book there is an assortment of problems that I am trying to sort out and for which I am going to offer some specific hypotheses.

As Morton Hunt points out, the position of social psychology is puzzling. On the one hand, we must acknowledge the tremendous attraction of psychology to contemporary students. In North America, psychology is arguably the single most popular subject in the undergraduate curriculum, though its practical or career consequences are unclear. Even so, there is the recurrent fear among practitioners, as we saw in Chapter 1, that this subject is not actually going anywhere scientifically—this despite its orthodox devotion to the methods of Galileo and its tremendous attraction to its "end users," i.e., the undergraduate students. This has bred periods of hand-wringing within the discipline that are never formally resolved. The hand-wringing is contradicted repeatedly by psychology's ability to address virtually any current social topic without developing cumulative theories with strong coherence and predictive validity. How can these various facts be reconciled?

FOUR HYPOTHESES ABOUT THE CURRENT STATE OF AFFAIRS

My first hypothesis is that many of the classical experiments on which the credibility of the discipline is based are not experiments in the sense of the natural sciences. They are not tests in the strict sense designed to compare outcomes on human subjects in experimental designs based on random assignment to different treatment groups. They are something else—they are demonstrations or dramatizations, not scientific tests. A demonstration has a lesson that is primarily pedagogical. It oftentimes contains a moral lesson about everyday life. By contrast, a test is empirical and its logic is primarily "falsificationist," i.e., designed to test the validity of a causal relationship against the possibility that no such relationship exists (Popper 1959). It seeks to build up a body of theory based on successive empirical observations, and its outcome is in principle aloof from moral or political preferences. Frequently, we confuse these two processes and treat demonstrations as tests—translating certain moral visions into facts. This problem is intensified because we emphasize the "objective" studies of things of greatest "subjective" relevance to us. This also happens in the natural sciences but the process of replication there seems to put a check on the reproduction of empirically vacuous or ambiguous claims.

In social psychology, it is often possible for a claim to be honored even after its empirical foundations have been invalidated. As we shall see, the Hawthorne effect is a good illustration of this. This suggests that an idea may be more attractive than the evidence that supports it. How can that be so? Although there may be many different reasons, there is strong counsel in the field to ignore negative findings. Festinger advises:

> Negative results from a laboratory experiment can mean very little indeed. If we obtain positive results—that is, demonstrably significant differences among conditions—we can be relatively certain concerning our interpretation and conclusion from the experiment. If, however, no differences emerge, we can generally reach no definitive conclusion. (1954:142)

Why? The failure may simply arise from difficulties of achieving an effective operationalization—a point that, even if granted, seems to dispose a priori of the null hypothesis. Cold fusion was a great idea in physics but no credible source in the natural sciences would acknowledge that it has been established. In my view, social scientists following Festinger's counsel would not have been so skittish about the evidence.

If we allow that many of the classic studies are simply demonstrations, my second hypothesis is that many of the experiments borrow heavily from commonsense knowledge of social structure and simply reiterate the obvious in an abstract methodological form. The experiment gives the sense of terrific scientific precision in the form of knowledge without actually discovering anything substantively new. However, it would be inaccurate to equate experimental knowledge with what is familiar and trivial. On the contrary, I hope to show that many of the great studies have a profound moral appeal that makes them qualitatively different from the experimental tests in the natural sciences. Why is this so?

This leads to my third hypothesis. The natural sciences are governed by a concern for the identification of things whose existence is more or less a question of fact, i.e., oxygen atoms have a weight of eight times that of hydrogen atoms, H_2O freezes and expands at lower temperatures that can be identified and measured. And natural science is concerned with relationships between variables—fluorocarbons either eat up the ozone layer or they do not. Pasteur's vaccinations either protect against smallpox or they do not. Genetically altered potatoes either make rats sick or they do not. We can describe a methodology to determine whether these conclusions are valid and how much confidence can be attached to the evidence. This permits an assessment of the merits of the claim, particularly in the long run. However tricky it may prove to establish a claim in the short term (Latour and Woolgar 1979), it would be irrelevant if it could not be measured empirically and defended conceptually. By contrast, the experiments in social psychology are often motivated to demonstrate a condition that cannot be resolved by reference to facts and whose conceptual appeal is more subjective than objective. Many classic studies raise fundamental questions about human nature that are more the province of philosophy or divinity than empirical science.

My fourth hypothesis is that professional anxiety rises when these conditions appear. On the one hand, the discipline does not always follow the methodology of experimentation from which its call to legitimacy is based. And on the other, the sort of insight that is advanced as empirical knowledge is often not the sort of thing that accumulates like a body of empirical facts. Advances might better be described as contributions to philosophical anthropology or psychological ontology—disciplines intimately engaged in the experience of everyday life, but disciplines in which social judgments about historical experience are far more relevant than warehouses of transient facts or general theories.

SELF-DOUBTS IN THE DISCIPLINE

Few academic disciplines appear to be as subject to self-doubts about their scientific achievements, prospects, and credentials as psychology.

> Anyone familiar with the broad field of psychology knows that it is in theoretical disarray. The different branches . . . proceed in relative isolation from one another, at most occasionally borrowing like a cup of sugar a concept here and a method there from a neighbor. Within each branch, psychologists also fail to reach consensus. (Buss 1994a:1)

This sweeping judgment was David Buss's opening salvo in a symposium devoted to evolutionary psychology, which he identified as a possible science of first principles in an otherwise fragmented discipline. As we shall see, Buss's recent misgivings about the state of psychology were not unprecedented. They are remarkably reminiscent of the earlier thoughts of Kenneth Smoke, who reviewed the contemporary state of social psychology in America. He noted that the textbooks varied enormously in what topics they covered, with the result that a reader conversant in one book could be "painfully ignorant" of the content of all the others:

> It might truthfully be asserted that [social psychology] is largely an amorphous mass, that in so far as it is able to formulate any generalizations, they are to be regarded as hypotheses rather than laws; that the worker in this

field, unlike the physical scientist, is never quite sure whether he is studying stones or stars; . . . [and] that there is much metaphysical speculation in this field which is not ordinarily recognized as such. (Smoke 1935:541)

These two observations are not unprecedented reflections sitting like monstrous gargoyles guarding the beginning and the end of more than a half-century of experimental psychology. The misgivings about the scientific credentials of the field, especially in the case of social psychology, have been a recurrent subtext in methodological writings throughout the history of "scientific psychology" (Koch 1992:7ff.). Indeed, the "crisis in confidence" (Elms 1975) has propagated what many refer to as the "crisis literature." While many of the contributors to this literature have become outcasts from mainstream circles, other voices are at the core of the discipline, for example, Leonard Berkowitz, who stated: "Social psychology is now in a 'crisis stage,' in the sense that Kuhn used this term" (cited in ibid.:967). Elms suggested that

many social psychologists appear to have lost not only their enthusiasm but also their sense of direction and their faith in the discipline's future. Whether they are experiencing an identity crisis, a paradigmatic crisis, or a crisis in confidence, most seem agreed that a crisis is at hand. (ibid.)

Writing in 1980, Festinger commented about the field he left in 1966 in a piece entitled, "Looking Backward." He recalled that "much of the field seemed to me to be fragmented. Unfruitful disagreements and controversies arose all too often. New work that appeared could be quite ignored by others" (1980:247–48).

In the 1950s, when sociologists following Bales began to experiment on small group dynamics, the practice of operationalization that was integral to experimentation was criticized by Pitirim Sorokin in his classic discussion of "the illusion" of operationalism (1954). Sorokin decried what he called the "conversion" of laboratory psychologists to an "orgy of operationalism" in an attempt to mimic the success of the hard sciences. "The operationalists firmly believe in the infallibility of operational incantations [yet their] operational manipulations often resemble the 'scientific methods' of 'the scientists' in *Gulliver's Travels*" (ibid.:33). Sorokin's target was the "sham operationalism" that mimicked natural science methods with abstract jargon that overshadowed questions of context and meaning. For the most part, Sorokin was a voice crying in the wilderness as experimentation increasingly became the single leading methodology of scientific psychology and small groups sociology.

Irwin Silverman (1971, 1977) has chronicled a long list of similar misgivings about the logic of experimentation under the title, "Why Social Psychology Fails." He refers to Brewster Smith's 1972 review of the series

Advances in Experimental Social Psychology: "Social psychology still trades more on promise than performance. . . . We must conclude that the predominant experimental tradition in the field has contributed rather little for serious export in enlarging and refining our views of social man" (Silverman, 1977: 353). The following year Smith wrote: "Our best scientists are floundering in search for a viable paradigm. It is hard to tell the blind alleys from the salients of advance" (1973:464). Rosenwald writes similarly: "Theoretical progress, as envisioned within the discipline of social psychology, is slow to arrive. . . . even our laboratory-derived knowledge exhibits little of the cumulative character we associate with the scientific method" (1986:303).

Daniel Katz, in his closing editorial in *Journal of Personality and Social Psychology*, wrote that "the concern with technology and the marginal interest in theory are related to what seems to be the most critical problem we face today in social psychology—the continuing and growing fragmentation of the discipline" (Katz 1967: 341). Similarly, Moscovici wrote:

> The fact is that social psychology cannot be described as a discipline with a unitary field of interest, a systematic framework of criteria and requirements, a coherent body of knowledge, or even a set of common perspectives shared by those who practice it. . . . From time to time the interests of the researcher are mobilized by themes or areas which appear new and important at the moment; but sooner or later these prove to be sterile or exhausted and they are abandoned (Moscovici 1972:32)

Kenneth Ring (1967) wrote: "Experimental social psychology . . . is in a state of profound intellectual disarray" (cited in Silverman 1977:354).

Even the most enthusiastic proponents of experimental psychology sense that the discipline is in trouble. Raymond Cattell opened the authoritative *Handbook of Multivariate Experimental Psychology* with the following observation: "Psychology is young as a systematic study and still younger as a true science. For many reasons its growing pains have been unusually severe and its progress fitful" (1966:1; unchanged in the second edition, Nesselroade and Cattell 1988). Unusual growing pains? Fitful progress? Allusions to the novelty of the discipline are often cited as the reason for its disappointing progress. Even Smoke permitted that despite its lack of focus, social psychology was "on its way," as though time would put the doubts to rest. However, this has not convinced R. M. Cooper:

> In the past any criticisms that have been voiced against psychology have most often been shrugged off as a reflection of its infancy. After 100 years or so this answer begins to wear thin, particularly given the exponential growth in activity of the past 20 years. One begins to suspect that psychology's failure is to be attributed not to immaturity but to retardation. (1982:265)

Cooper goes on to conclude that "my stance is that psychology is generally a failure. . . . Every year psychologists turn out thousands of books and articles. I find it difficult, however, to see much in the way of fruits from these labors" (ibid.). Cooper, like Schachter (1980), believed that psychology faltered because psychologists failed to appreciate how biology controlled much of the behavior claimed by psychology.

Another gloomy confession was turned in by K. G. Ferguson in a piece entitled "Forty Years of Useless Research?"

> After almost 40 years as a student of clinical and abnormal psychology . . . I don't really know many more facts in the area than I did in the beginning. Watching the facts accumulate in one's field is worse than watching the hour hand on a large clock; you are tempted to wonder often if the clock has stopped. (1983:153)

Silverman writes with similar misgivings: "After more than three decades of progressive expansion, the social psychology establishment finds itself bereft of substance and direction" (1977:353). With respect to the textbooks, he draws conclusions reminiscent of Smoke: "Not only is there great diversity of content, but they are devoid of common definition of the field" (ibid.:354)

George A. Miller characterizes the current intellectual plurality in psychology as an "intellectual zoo" (1992:41). He writes that

> no standard method or technique integrates the field. Nor does there seem to be any fundamental scientific principle comparable to Newton's laws of motion or Darwin's theory of evolution. There is not even any universally accepted criterion for explanation. What is the binding force"? (ibid.:42)

Faith! "When reason fails, one resorts to faith. . . . I believe the common denominator is a faith that somehow, someone, someday will create a science of immediate experience" (ibid.) Note that these conclusions are not drawn by outsiders. They come from psychologists talking about their own discipline.

It is difficult to determine how representative such utterances are. Systematic probing of psychologists that explored their perceptions of crisis would be rife with social approval bias, and might reflect their sense of individual success as opposed to collective progress. The statements quoted here were not solicited by any investigator, and their credibility is enhanced by the fact that they were given at great risk of condemnation by colleagues. Many disciplines, particularly in the social sciences, experience misgivings about their scientific progress. In sociology, there are recurrent debates over positivism and the relative merits of quantitative versus qualitative approaches to methodology (Popper [1961] 1976;

Cicourel 1964). As for economics, while outsiders may question the accuracy and predictive validity of macroeconomic models, this skepticism is not a view shared widely by insiders, with few exceptions (Leamer 1990). The dismal science keeps economists quite buoyant about their intellectual credentials. But in neither sociology nor economics do disciplinary limitations give rise to the sorts of recurrent frustration and soul searching witnessed in psychology. Psychology's plight would appear to be peculiar, and, in my view, its angst is most acute in the field of social psychology. Why should this be the case?

WHY PSYCHOLOGY?

Silverman captures a broad band of opinion when he argues that the adoption of the experimental method at the inception of the field was a Trojan horse destined to undermine the field's potential. "Social psychology became an institution solely on the basis of the vision that complex social phenomena could be fruitfully studied by experimental laboratory methods" (1977:355). The pitch was made effectively by Wundt in his labs at the University of Leipzig beginning in the 1870s to which he attracted many American students who in turn imported his approach to North America, over the vocal objections of William James, the doyen of American psychology, and contrary to the influential work of G. H. Mead (1934). Social psychology developed under the wing of existing departments and, in the absence of any theoretical cohesion that would have dictated specific methodologies, it adopted, by default, the method that had supported Wundt's studies of perception and Pavlov's studies of physiological psychology, studies that went some way toward establishing the discipline's intellectual credibility. In a similar vein, Koch observes regarding the whole field that "psychology was unique in the extent to which its institutionalization preceded its content" (1969:64). Experimentation subsequently became the dominant medium of exploration, and this particular methodological focus inadvertently hindered the progress of its practitioners. Rosenwald, speaking of experimentation, put it in darker terms: "To cut through the Gordian knot, we have set our hopes and tightened our grip on one of the dullest blades available" (1986:328).

EXPERIMENTS AS SHORT-TERM, LOW-IMPACT DESIGNS

Silverman concluded that after decades of experimental orthodoxy, psychologists were beginning to realize that "complex social phenomena cannot be fruitfully studied by experimental laboratory methods" (1977:353).

Social psychological experiments are typically short-term, emotionally innocuous, low-impact designs calculated to have very little lasting effect on the subjects. However, many of the problems that interest psychologists, like the causes of human violence and aggression, are not amenable to direct study in the lab. The social psychologist is forced to examine short-term analogs whose fleeting effects are measured immediately. Silverman concludes that this means that psychologists' generalizations are "never beyond the realm of speculation" in regards to their relevance to everyday life. "The conclusion which I draw is that experimental social psychology can never be serious" (ibid.: 356). There are exceptions. Some cases have resulted in high-impact work that has potentially traumatic and/or long-lasting influence on the subjects. Milgram's work is reported to have produced trauma in numerous subjects and Zimbardo's prison study resulted in worrisome interpersonal aggression among those role-playing as guards. But these studies raise deep ethical questions and tend to be "one shot" affairs, exposing the researcher to professional criticism for risking human subjects and/or exposing them to harm on the one hand, while precluding the prospects of replication on the other.

Gadlin and Ingle similarly argued that the laboratory experiment was not always an appropriate format for the things that interested researchers. "Psychologists have begun to wonder about the external validity of the results of laboratory experimentation. . . . Rather than selecting for research those phenomena suited to our methods, we ought to shape and develop our methods to fit phenomena" (1975:1003, 1007).

DECEPTION AND ETHICS

Related to experimentation are two further issues that have worried social psychologists. The first concerns deception, the second concerns ethics. Because psychologists study actors who have a common stock of knowledge about society, the subjects are not naïve in the sense that animals in medical experiments are naïve about medicine, or electrons in science labs are oblivious to the laws of physics. As Orne (1962) has pointed out in his still classic discussion of "demand characteristics," subjects in experiments are role-playing, are seeking information from the environment, and fashioning their conduct in response to the expectations and information communicated to them, sometimes explicitly and sometimes inadvertently by the setting.[4] This has raised questions about bias arising from "experimenter effects" (Rosenthal 1966). One remedy has been to make the subjects naïve by deliberately misleading them about the objective of the study. Social psychologists often devise elaborate cover stories to camouflage the object of their inquiry to ensure a "natural" response from subjects who, had they been informed directly about the point of the study, might have thought and acted differently. For example, Schachter (1971) led his subjects to believe that he was exploring the effects of a vitamin called "suproxin" on vision, when in fact he was administering doses of epinephrine (adrenaline) and chlorpromazine to alter levels of arousal to test its effects on the drive to affiliate. Milgram told his subjects he was trying to determine whether punishment helped people learn, when in fact he was studying the role of authority figures in the mediation of aggression.

There are two concerns about deception. The first purely pragmatic concern is whether it succeeds. There has been some doubt as to how successful such deceptions actually are in keeping the subjects naïve (Stricker 1967). The issue is exacerbated due to debriefing. Since ethical considerations require the removal of the misapprehension or deception during the debriefing, there is concern that the cover story actually remains intact for future subjects after the initial subjects are debriefed. Although subjects typically are encouraged to keep their experiences to themselves and not to tell other potential subjects about the experiment, some evidence suggests that they do not comply, effectively undermining the cover for potential future subjects. In their replication of Schachter's anxiety and affiliation study, Wuebben, Straits, and Schulman (1974) found that a plurality of their subjects did not in fact respect the experimenter's counsel and conveyed enough about the study to potential new subjects to undermine the design. In addition, in Leon Levy's study where the researcher's hypothesis was *explicitly* leaked to naïve subjects by those supposedly leaving the laboratory after the experiment, during the debriefing the majority of those in receipt of the insider information denied being told despite the obvious impact of the communication on their performance (Levy 1974). The task involved verbal conditioning. Subjects were presented with cards on which verbs were printed and asked to make up a sentence using a pronoun. If the subjects chose "I" or "we," the experimenter reinforced the behavior by saying "good." Subjects in the experimental condition were met with a person who appeared to be leaving the setting having just completed the experiment. This was actually a confederate who said that the researcher was a Ph.D. student worried about getting the right results, and that the subject had done "OK" once he figured out that he was supposed to say "I" or "we." The results showed a steep learning curve for reinforced behavior but the informed subjects started at a significantly higher level of compliance from the very start of the trials. During the debriefing, the vast majority of the subjects denied having been informed of the point of the investigation. These beneficent subjects feared spoiling the results and invalidating the research.

A second major concern with deception concerns ethics. If human subjects are deliberately misled about the nature of the research, in what sense can their decision to participate—which is voluntary—be informed? Consent presupposes what deception precludes. Though some researchers excuse the practice in terms of the benefits to society from the insights that result, others are uncomfortable with this instrumental logic, particularly as the returns to the investment in deception studies have been questioned (Baumrind 1985). Even if we allow a trade-off between short-term temporary deception and long-term scientific advancement, at what point is the profession prepared to present evidence of the long-term gain in knowledge and to justify deception? The claim to social benefits is gainsaid.

Others take a more absolutist view and argue that the systematic reliance on deception is categorically inconsistent with a professional treatment of human subjects irrespective of a general social good. However, without deception, the presupposition of subject naïveté is precarious. How does one strike a balance between full disclosure and informed consent on the one side, and normal (i.e., naïve) subject responsiveness on the other? However one comes to a compromise, this raises an important substantive consideration in social psychology, which pertains to the use of experimentation with naïve subjects: the need for "naïvité" (and hence deception) arises because subjects are not by nature naïve about the motives and signals of others, including social scientists, nor are they disinterested in them.

COMMON SENSE AND SCIENTIFIC KNOWLEDGE

What makes deception seem necessary in some quarters is the fact that people already have concepts and beliefs about the way society works independent of the leverage associated with an experimental method. Cattell attributed the "fitful progress" of the scientific study of human conduct at least in part to our preexisting folk psychology. "Scientific writing has found it almost impossible to disentangle itself from semi-scientific, popular terminology, modes of reasoning, and 'theories,' since 'psychology' is such an enormous daily preoccupation of all mankind" (1966:1). In a rare essay, Harold H. Kelley similarly noted the interplay between commonsense psychology and scientific psychology, and explored it at length. Commonsense psychology is "found under such rubrics as 'common sense,' 'naïve psychology,' 'ethnopsychology,' 'indigenous psychology,' and 'implicit theories'" (1992:1). If science and common sense are interchangeable, scientists have no claim to superior authority, and the utilization of esoteric methods of fact finding (i.e., experimentation) is superfluous. On the other hand, if the two fields of knowledge are more or less distinct, and if professional theories are more penetrating and reliable, resort to specific methods of research is both desirable and necessary.

Part of the crisis in social psychology appears to have arisen from the observation that laypeople are already conversant with a lot of what passes for professional insight. John Houston's study of "lay knowledge of the principles of psychology" suggested that introductory psychology students and subjects contacted in a public park reported correctly on tests of cognitive processes at a rate far higher than what one would have expected by chance. Houston: "A great many of psychology's basic principles are self evident" (1983:207). Manzi and Kelley reported a similar conclusion in a study of unequal dependence in pairs of couples: "The 'principles' we derive from the study of interpersonal relationships are already part of common knowledge" (Kelley 1992:3). However, Kelley was not prepared to conclude that there was no room for a scientific psychology. His essay was an attempt to clarify the mutual relationship between common sense and scientific psychology. What did he conclude?

Kelley observed that the interplay between commonsense psychology and scientific psychology was unavoidable because of the common linguistic and cultural immersion of psychologists prior to their elevation to the scientific frame of mind. Since scientific problems do not arise in a vacuum, common beliefs and terms "inevitably influence the concepts and theories we develop for our scientific purposes" (ibid.:4). Indeed, Kelley pointed out that there was often a strong correspondence between commonsense terms and scientific concepts, on the one hand, and between commonsense beliefs and scientific propositions on the other. Operationalizing commonsense terms like "commitment" or "closeness in a relationship" obviously borrows from everyday usage. However, an analyst may coin usages that are more precise or technical, and that organize observations in nonobvious, theoretically justified ways. The risk here is that this can eventuate in a level of jargon composed simply of pseudoscientific concepts. This was Sorokin's conclusion alluded to earlier.[5]

PROTOTYPE ANALYSIS

Obviously, Sorokin's concerns will temper any attempts to hypostatize commonsense understandings with scientific abstractions. Kelley identified a method for moving from commonsense terms to scientific concepts via what he termed "prototype analysis." Prototype analysis permits the theorist to poll ordinary language users to extract a family of interrelated concepts in both a "horizontal" and a "vertical" way, and hence to become more precise about their meanings. Horizontal variations tap different manifestations of a common idea: for example, *love* versus *caring* versus *protectiveness*. The vertical dimension reveals kinds of attraction (infatuation, liking, respect, etc.). Presumably, the analysis allows the researcher to reduce the ambiguities of a concept before entering it into a theoretical model. Kelley cites by way of illustration Buss and Craik's (1980) concept of "dominance," which was developed by asking subjects to describe behavior that illustrated this concept. Among the many illustrations we find the following:

- He forbade her to leave the room.
- On the auto trip, she decided which direction to take when they got lost.

Kelley argues that the first illustration is marked by an implicit threat ("forbade"). The second by a positive initiative (i.e., "decided"). He calls the first a "promise threat scenario" (where does the promise come in?) and the second an "initiative taking scenario." What is the importance of this? Does this mean that the distinction of dominance-by-threatening versus dominance-by-initiative is unfamiliar to common speakers? I suspect that the only reason any of us can draw the distinction is that it is already self-evident to everybody—including those persons who were asked to contribute to Buss and Craik's list in the first place. In contributing to the list, they were never enjoined to stick to a single narrow sense of "dominance" but to supply a family of illustrations. Prototypical analysis does not seem an exercise in scientific reasoning as much as an exercise in drawing commonsense distinctions—or at least it does not appear that these are qualitatively different activities conceptually, although they might be quite different pragmatically. If that is the case, the transformation of commonsense terms into scientific concepts by prototypical analysis seems quite improbable. Indeed, the whole transformation of Wittgenstein's philosophy of language from the *Tractatus Logico-Philosophicus* (1922) to the *Philosophical Investigations* (1951) questions our capacity to put binding stipulations that can convert natural language concepts into definitive scientific terms.[6] We may limit our scientific analysis to specific nuances of terms although there is no guarantee that our readers and colleagues will similarly confine their readings to such nuances. To be fair, Kelley is skeptical about the project, noting that explorations of the "horizontal" dimension have outpaced the explorations of the "vertical" dimension (1992:11). Since higher order precision is based on vertical layers of meaning, this uneven development leaves open the question of the discipline's claim to a superior source of concept formation compared to commonsense theorizing. Kelley seems to sense this when he writes:

> I am expressing here some uneasiness about undue dependence on common thought for clues about how ψ-PSYCH should slice up its phenomena. There must surely be an important role for ψ-PSYCH analysis that enables our conceptual work to come partially under the guidance of logical and theoretical considerations and to avoid total dependence on common terms. (1992:12)[7]

If one were seeking a clear demarcation of the two realms and a lever to establish scientific concepts independently from common terms, although he surely believes these to be desirable, Kelley fails to identify them. But why should we presume that logic and theory can be found only among professionals, and that, by contrast, other individuals are basically unscientific? Similar problems are raised when one compares the parallels between common beliefs and scientific propositions. The problem that Kelley tackles is the familiar charge that social psychology is the rediscovery of the obvious. "It reveals no new information, only what people already know" (Kelley 1992: 13). Kelley counters that "what is obvious is not always obvious," particularly when viewed prospectively. He adds that commonsense beliefs are frequently "self-contradictory"—suggesting that ψ-PSYCH theories are not. The work of the psychologist then is to disentangle the conditions under which alternative outcomes arrive from similar premises, shifting attention away from large main effects to the more fastidious analysis of smaller interaction effects.

In a section titled "How to Make Science Interesting," Kelley suggests that a focus on the nonobvious should be a priority for psychologists since it generates interest in science. Kelley draws on the rhetorical analysis of Murray Davis (1971), who argues that "all interesting theories" dispute the "taken for granted world of their audience." However, Davis's position is that a lot of humbug passes as knowledge because of the way it is presented, and the powerful rhetorical tools of presentation are independent of the validity of the claims they convey—not that scientific innovations attract our attention because they are interesting. Indeed, from Davis's perspective, the validity of an innovation is of less relevance than the interest it provokes. Hence, pursuit of the nonobvious character of the obvious may make psychology "interesting" in Davis's sense, but this has nothing to say as to the scientific relevance and value of such work. Part of the crisis in social psychology arises from the realization that much work restates the commonplace in scientific jargon. Indeed, Kelley concludes that commonsense psychology is probably most reliable at the molar level—the level of everyday, face-to-face interaction:

> Common beliefs are most likely to be veridical when they concern the mesolevel of behavioral phenomena, the familiar, and those events of which the person has principally been an uninterested observer. . . . Beliefs about that behavior and its occurrence under various conditions should thus be fairly veridical. (ibid.:17)

Kelley is skeptical about commonsense beliefs when they move to the microlevel and the macrolevel—but these are levels of analysis typically outside social psychology, suggesting that the familiar territory of social psychology is situated where commonsense rules of thumb are already typically reliable ways of understanding the world, dispensing with the requirements of the special leverage of a scientific approach, and the specific methodology of deception and experimentation.

Kelley notes that many commonsense terms come with cultural implications that imply behavioral relationships. The psychologist who discovers such relationships empirically is basically only discovering how language works in the construction of reality.

> This suggests that CS-PSYCH can become a foundation for ψ-PSYCH theory. The creative work lies here in analyzing CS-PSYCH and revealing its underlying framework. Once any such theory is completed, we should hardly be surprised that, taken separately and viewed from the CS-PSYCH perspective, most of the specific ψ-PSYCH propositions will appear to be truisms. (ibid.:21)

If that were the case, the interplay between the commonsense and the scientific apprehension of reality would not be particularly fruitful. In fact, many would find it fatal. Kelley's own conclusion is ambivalent: "It is impossible for us to avoid the effects of CS-PSYCH, but easy for us to be unaware of them" (ibid.). The problems arising from the role of common sense in scientific concept formation "deserve more widespread attention than they presently receive. . . . The inevitable effects of CS-PSYCH on ψ-PSYCH are neither all good nor all bad" (ibid.:22).

The main problem for this reader is that the case for the role of commonsense psychology is far more convincingly put than the case for the alternative. Certainly, Kelley remains a proponent of scientific psychology, but his optimism is based, like that of Miller and others, more on faith and future expectations than on actual performance. Kelley's psychologists are relegated to discovering main effects that are truisms or obvious to common sense, or to fossicking for complex interaction effects whose generalizability is so hedged with conditionals as to be of questionable utility outside the lab. One is reminded of Bannister's observation in "Psychology as an Exercise in Paradox," when he writes, "I am intrigued by the notion of discovering new knowledge. I have yet to witness this process. I have seen people inventing notions and then discovering sometimes to their cost where the notions led to, but I have never seen them discovering new knowledge" (1966:25). The paradox is that the scientific analysis never gets far beyond common sense, and the subject matter of the discipline is, in Cattell's words, the "daily preoccupation of all mankind."

A consequence of this observation is that much important work in social psychology will inevitably be the common preoccupations of "lay psychologists" concealed in operational clothing, and dealt with abstractly through analogs. This makes social psychological experimentation a qualitatively different strategy compared with experimentation in chemistry or biology. The social psychologist studies, for example, how social norms form by showing how perceptual illusions are interpreted, or how mass media promote physical violence by studying how aversion to violence is taught in the laboratory. We are asked to treat the one as if it captured the other, but these are "as-if" analogies, not direct tests of social norms or physical violence *in situ*—and for ethical reasons this is unavoidable. As I noted earlier, I think this renders many critical experiments little more than demonstrations of things already taken for granted or believed in commonsense psychology. This interpretation will be explored in some classic studies of group influence to suggest that the penetration of pretheoretical ideas into scientific concepts is more critical than Kelley allows. The cases of Sherif, Asch, and Milgram are good places to start since they are universally discussed in social psychology courses and textbooks. However, despite general familiarity with them among students of psychology they are probably among the least compelling evidence for the successful utilization of experimental methodology. They do show something else, however. They illustrate how the experimental form can be fashioned into an idiom to convey some pressing existential problem, and how this subtext leads audiences to lend a charitable reading to research whose relevance would otherwise foster serious methodological misgivings. The upshot is that the psychologist as a cultural actor can speak to pressing issues of the day and can draw inferences about them as though they were based on the special leverage conveyed by scientific method.

In this view, experimental social psychologists are dealing earnestly with the perplexities of existence at arm's length through the use of experiments, but they are operating schizophrenically, often unaware of how their pretheoretical knowledge guides their investigations. On the formal level, they are conducting tests and observations in the tradition of Galileo's discovering science, searching for new laws. Despite the fact that they never make comparable headway in identifying the *mathesis universalis* for the human sciences, the exploration is therapeutic. Like an analyst with society as a patient, it allows them to confront what troubles people in everyday life. For example, Rosenwald argues that Festinger's forced compliance study of cognitive dissonance

> derives its persistent interest from the fact that it [i.e., dissonance] exhibits the formal characteristics of a perplexity—it illustrates how social cohesion can be obtained at the expense of the individual's rationality and self-transparence.... It deals with the irrational manner in which we often resolve contradictions in our social experience. (1986:309)

Viewed this way, the experiment is more like a therapeutic exercise than a logic of inference and, if Rosenwald is correct, it is more successful as the former than the latter. In this sense, his critique of operationalism in experiments points beyond the usual questions of ecological validity or ethics. The scientific progress of the experiment is illusory as science, but at a deeper level, it contains an important unacknowledged subtext without which the ostensive work of inquiry would hold no attraction. Morton's "no man's land" has its finger on the pulse of society. It is the medium through which the scientist confronts the pretheoretic perplexity of life, not directly, but obliquely through the drama of the experiment. Is the experiment then merely a device or illusion used by the experimenter to illuminate or dramatize everyday life? That is what we examine next.

NOTES

1. *Walden Two* was the name of B. F. Skinner's 1948 utopian novel based on the principles of operant conditioning. Skinner's utopia was labeled after Walden, the 1854 account of Henry David Thoreau's two-year solitary sojourn at Walden Pond, near Concord, Massachusetts. Thoreau's ideas about the ideal life emphasized the need for a close contact with nature and freedom of the individual from unjust state interference. *Walden Two* was Skinner's attempt to sketch how post–World War II American society could optimize the "contingencies of reinforcement" to maximize human self-expression in an egalitarian, noncoercive society.

2. The term "existential determination" of science was coined by Karl Mannheim in *Ideology and Utopia* (1954) to refer to the cultural and other nonscientific influences on the content of scientific ideas. Rosenwald (1986) uses the term "extrascientific incentives" to identify the same process. Others refer to "pretheoretical" knowledge to suggest how common sense influences "theoretical" or scientific knowledge.

3. There is some difference in approach here. Goldhagen (1997) argues that Milgram's experimental study was undertaken in a complete empirical vacuum in the sense that it presupposed that German soldiers were intimidated into complying with murderous orders. The examination of the war records of Police Battalion 101 in Poland suggests otherwise. No one was forced to murder civilians. The policemen complied with orders, were permitted to avoid executions, and in many cases volunteered for "Jew hunts"—the extermination of Jews who had run away from the ghettos to eke out survival in the forests. Milgram's portrayal misscripted the actual situation. People complied because it was ordered, and they acted differently from how they would have acted had the decisions been up to them—something probably true for the entire war effort. Browning (1998) is more sympathetic to Milgram, but not to the influence of authority figures. In fact, he points out that the authority figures in Police Battalion 101 were quite effete. Men complied for other reasons—peer pressure, careerism, loyalty to the unit, the perceived legality of the orders, and the like.

4. Martin Orne (1962) reported that the information-seeking characteristic of students recruited as volunteers in experiments employing deception was often responsible for the main effects reported by the researcher. In his search for a base-

line of normal compliant behavior needed for an understanding of hypnotic compliance, Orne found that subjects undertook the most inane challenges with gusto. He asked subjects to add up blocks of random numbers on numerous sheets of paper—and then to tear them up into pieces, and to repeat the whole process ad nauseam. He terminated the exercise after many hours since the students showed no sign of giving up. During the debriefing they communicated that they had figured out what was "actually" sought from them: perseverance! And once they got that into their heads it didn't matter how apparently boring the job was since it actually amounted to a test of their character, and on that count, they were not going to let the experimenter find them deficient!

Orne generalized this conception of demand characteristics to the phenomenon of sensory deprivation effects. The conventional wisdom in the late fifties was that sensory overload and sensory deprivation could result in a breaking down of ego coherence, i.e., nervous breakdown. Sensory deprivation experiments suggested that subjects lost all sense of time, experienced hallucinations as well as intense bouts of anxiety, confusion, and fear. Because of this, subjects were asked to sign release forms waving their rights to sue researchers and their institutions for emotional damage. Orne replicated many of these diverse effects without actually exposing subjects to sensory deprivation. However, many of the trappings of the previous experiments—the conspicuous placement of a "panic button" for emergency rescue, the intimidating release form suggesting the possibility of hallucinations and emotional trauma, as well as the presence of a medical emergency station with appropriate medical personnel—conveyed the impression of risk so effectively that subjects experienced negative effects merely sitting alone in an office (Orne and Scheibe 1964).

5. For example, human happiness in marriage was studied on the basis of a score assigned by a self-report Likert scale—a measure that had tremendous convenience and quantifiability but that was, in Sorokin's view, so little penetrating as to be meaningless. Another operational error was to substitute untested opinions for measures of combat performance evaluations. "Instead of directly studying the phenomena, and in lieu of making their own analysis and definition of the phenomena, they [the researchers] simply 'pass the buck' of study and definition to somebody else" (Sorokin 1954:39). An error of a different type was to model social processes on "concepts, definitions and formulae transcribed and imported from the natural sciences" as did S. C. Dodd in an analysis of social change. Dodd argued that "in symbolic terms, if I represents the change, P, the population changed, and F, the societal force, $F = T - 2IP$ = societal force." This led Sorokin to comment that "however impressive this simplified transcription of physical concepts . . . these definitions are empty and useless" (1954:41) Sorokin suggested that even when claiming to stick strictly with operationalism, researchers in the psychosocial sciences could not escape reliance on "supralogical and suprasensory intuition," "empathy and co-living the experiences of historical persons and groups," "historical observation," analysis of relevant statistics—all of which would contribute to multidimensional approaches, and which would incorporate knowledge of everyday life into a systematic science without confining research to experimental operationalization.

6. There is a similar discussion by Rudolf Carnap regarding a movement from everyday usage to a more formal transformation via the concept of "explication." See Carl G. Hempel (1952:11ff.)

7. ψ-PSYCH refers to scientific psychology. CS-PSYCH is commonsense psychology.

3

Experiments as Theater
The Art of Scientific Demonstration

From my biased point of view, there was some confusion between "relevant" and "newsworthy." Certainly, if some finding was picked up by the mass media, that was clear evidence that it was relevant. One can improvise a jail and have subjects volunteer. . . . One can then report some interesting reactions of certain individuals. It's an important topic and clearly newsworthy. But it's not research, does not seriously attempt to look at relationships between variables, and yields no new knowledge. It's just staging a "happening."

—"Looking Backward," Leon Festinger

Although experiments in chemistry and physics often involve shiny equipment, flasks and electronic gear, an experiment in social psychology smacks much more of dramaturgy or theater.

—Stanley Milgram quoted in Thomas Blass,
"The Social Psychology of Stanley Milgram,"

INTRODUCTION: EXPERIMENTS AS THEATER

The work Festinger appears to be referring to was undertaken by Philip Zimbardo at Stanford University over three decades ago. Zimbardo screened seventy potential volunteers from the Stanford University student body before selecting "about two dozen young men" (Zimbardo 1972) who were randomly assigned to roles of guards and inmates in a makeshift prison. They were paid fifteen dollars per day although the guards only served an eight-hour shift while the prisoners were detained twenty-four hours a day.

The prisoners were unexpectedly picked up at their homes by a city police-
man in a squad car, searched, handcuffed, fingerprinted, booked at the Palo
Alto station house and taken blindfolded to our jail. There they were
stripped, deloused, put into dress-like uniforms, given a number and put
into a cell with two other prisoners where they expected to live for the next
two weeks. (Zimbardo 1972:4)

By the fourth day, three prisoners were dropped from the experiment
due to "acute situational traumatic reactions such as crying, confusion in
thinking and severe depression" (ibid.). Five out of the eleven prisoners
would eventually leave the study prematurely because of trauma. Many
of the guards began acting with cruelty and brutality toward the mock
inmates. Although he reported that what he saw was "frightening," Zimbardo let this go on for another three days, filming some of the behavior
for television news, before canceling the experiment (Haney, Banks and
Zimbardo 1973; Haney, Craig, and Zimbardo 1977).[1] During this period
where was the American Psychological Association? One wonders
whether the provocative detention of the subjects by the Palo Alto police
raised similar questions among civil libertarians. The study also raises
questions about whether citizens can "voluntarily" agree to suspend their
rights to physical security without knowing that they will be stripped
naked in front of strangers and sprayed with deodorant, and asked to
dress in female frocks without underwear for a week.

Festinger's point is that the prison simulation study was merely staging
a happening, more like guerilla theatre than serious science. There was no
hypothesis identified in advance except the implied idea that people who
were otherwise of average or normal backgrounds will take on situational
roles no matter how much for the worse. "The mere act of assigning labels
to people and putting them into a situation where those labels acquire
validity and meaning is sufficient to elicit pathological behavior" (Zimbardo 1972:6). The research was a fishing expedition, less designed to test
relationships between variables and to advance theory than a device to
dramatize the supposedly well-known proclivity of prison guards to treat
their inmates with inhumanity. It suggested that the deplorable misconduct of some guards in some institutions arises from the situational roles
of dominance and subordination, and not from individual traits. If true,
this would be quite a breathtaking inference, and would assign role theory
pride of place in the theoretical arsenal. Yet Zimbardo reports significant
variation in the posture of the guards and reports that half the prisoners
had to be dropped from the experiment prematurely. Zimbardo's perspective makes a virtue out of the experiment's inability to tap the stability of
traits over the life course and across different contexts by implying that the
frictions of prison life reflect the largely situational conditions that short-
term experiments can turn on and off at will.

I do not quite know what to make of the Zimbardo study. If it was as traumatizing as he alleges, I cannot understand why he was not sued, dismissed, and/or censured for ethical misconduct by the APA. On the other side, if the students were merely pretending to be cruel, i.e., acting, then Zimbardo's conduct is less culpable, but his conclusions are less relevant.[2] Either way, Zimbardo's work illustrates a point from the last chapter— much research is simply ethics in disguise, in this case, a telling criticism of prison life.[3] Festinger's dismissive summary seems to imply that Zimbardo's use of the experiment as a stage is wholly at variance with the field. My view is that this use of the experimental idiom as a stage to dramatize something is actually more common than people allow, however little attention is paid to this practice in methodology courses and textbooks. That is what is candidly suggested in the quotation from Milgram. Indeed, a great deal of the work that appears to devolve from formal theory testing is on the contrary quite serendipitous. This chapter explores these possibilities, not as an exception to what social psychologists normally do (although I think Zimbardo's work was exceptional), but as practices that reflect many studies at the heart of the discipline.

THE AUTOKINETIC EFFECT AND THE
LIABILITIES OF AN ILLUSION

In 1936 Muzafer Sherif published his classic study, *The Psychology of Social Norms*, in which he reported his elegant research on the autokinetic effect. The key experiments appeared initially in his 1935 article in the *Archives of Psychology*. The book was an attempt to publicize the work and spell out its implications in a much broader framework, and was followed by an extension of the paradigm to attitudes in the first volume of *Sociometry* in 1937. A norm is defined as "an authoritative standard" or model; "a principle of right action binding on members of a group, and serving to guide, control and regulate proper and acceptable behavior" (*Webster's* 1977). The basic design was quite simple. Sherif exposed subjects to a stationary pinpoint of light projected toward them in a darkened room. Subjects watched the light for a few seconds and were asked to estimate how much movement they saw, since it appeared to shift around in a ghostlike fashion. When asked to estimate how much the point of light had moved, subjects gave estimates similar to those reported verbally by other naïve subjects like themselves. These estimates converged. In contrast, estimates given by individuals privately without overhearing one another were disparate and independent, and tended to be stable between sessions and even across different days. In other designs, Sherif used confederates of some prestige to influence the estimates of naïve subjects. In addition, the experimenter in some cases directly suggested that the subjects were under- or overestimating the movements. The results showed that the naïve subjects tended to change their own range of estimates to bring them into line with the prestigious subject, and into line with the experimenter's cues. Sherif argued that the results were indicative of the process by which norms emerge naturally in society.

Sherif points out that the perception of movement is an optical illusion. The light appears to wander in the absence of a frame of reference. Consequently, the "group" effectively frames the individual's perception—as does the prestigious person or experimenter-expert. Sherif acknowledges that this was well-known to the Wurzburg psychologists from the previous century: "That aspect of the stimulus field is especially observed which the subject is set to observe" (1937:90). Presumably, external influence from others would set the field for the subjects. So how do norms evolve? Sherif suggests that ego is influenced by others (in dyads, in groups, and by leadership figures) when the natural world is an ambiguous source of information. Individuals rely on one another to define reality when the environment fails to give clear clues. While no one would dispute this, it is doubtful that this is actually discovered empirically in the experiment. This would be more like a general supposition of empiricism as opposed to a hard-won fact established in the lab. We should also ask whether norms only arise under such conditions or whether they evolve in other ways. This would steer us toward a general theory of the evolution of norms—quite a tall order. In such a general theory, it would be natural to ask whether they also arise when the natural world is unambiguous. What does he mean to tell us by saying that this is how norms arise? This is not a historical study of specific norms. It is an investigation of norms at large. Yet it is improbable that one could deduce that the behavior of several strangers watching a point of light, an optical illusion, could be indicative of the formation of norms in the sense defined earlier for a number of reasons.

There is no evidence that any reference group in a sociological sense existed in these experiments, no leader, no common history, no censure of misconduct, nor any of the usual things we ascribe to social groups. This does not dispute that there was *social* behavior. Certainly, strangers who spoke in one another's presence engaged in mutual turn-taking and reported similar estimates. However, the subjects' responses to Sherif's requests for estimates of movement would appear to be demand characteristics—ego hazards a guess since he or she *has been instructed to expect movement* (1936:95), and since it appears as though the others got away with similar utterances beforehand, and this, in a situation where it was really impossible for anyone to say for sure if there really was any movement, and, if there was movement, how much of it occurred. This interpretation—demand characteristics and external compliance—is an obvious consideration for anyone trying to replicate Sherif today. It would also be relevant to ask whether anyone thought the stimulus was an optical illusion and was not moving at all. But the reports of displacement were treated as objective distortions in perception exacted by external influence, while the subjective reports of ambiguity were simply ignored. Sherif recorded some of the impressions of subjects: "Darkness left no guide for distance. It was difficult to estimate the distance. . . . There was no fixed point from which to judge the distance" (1936:97). Significantly, Sherif acknowledges that "the effect takes place even when the person looking at the light *knows perfectly well that the light is not moving*" (ibid.:92, emphasis added). If that were the case, in what sense would this action be *normative* since a verbal estimate measured repeatedly with great precision would correspond rather imperfectly to the subjective uncertainty recorded afterwards, and such exacting estimates could be given even though the subjects knew differently from what they saw. That raises another obvious point—whether the reported convergence was simply a conformity in reporting as opposed to an actual distortion in perception.

Another consideration is whether a series of strangers making the same ambiguous estimates—one hundred times each in a round-robin fashion, and repeating the process four times after short breaks for a total of four hundred trials—constitutes a norm in any important sense of the term. There were no apparent consequences in terms of individual survival or error. Is an inconsequential assent to a number something that norms are made of? Norms are moral. We feel *compelled* to assent to the right answer. Optical illusions are perceptual. Does failure to comply lead to discredit or disorientation? What was the norm Sherif was really studying? Certainly one relevant norm that escaped discussion seems to be that strangers accommodate the sometimes perplexing requests of psychologists even if they fail to make any immediate sense. Also, they seem to rely on one another's utterances where a failure to do so might make them stand out in a crowd. In fairness, Sherif acknowledges that the autokinetic effect "reduc[es] the process to a very simple form" (1936:99). This reduction of the phenomenon to a kind of decontextualized purity is at the heart of Sherif's use of experimental methodology. In my view, this methodological approach ironically undermines its specific empirical relevance while simultaneously giving it an air of complete generalizability. How could that be achieved?

Sherif writes that "our whole point is that the autokinetic effect can be utilized to show a general psychological tendency and *not to reveal the concrete properties of norm-formation in actual life situations*. . . . Our aim is to show a fundamental psychological tendency related to norm-formation" (1937:93–94, emphasis added). In other words, the way that people react to an ambiguous visual stimulus can be utilized analogically "to show" or help understand how social norms are acquired. But this must be done at the highest level of abstraction. Why? In the early chapters of *The Psychology of Social Norms,* Sherif lays the foundation for his approach by stressing that psychological inquiries often are biased by the "community-centrism" of investigators—the taken-for-granted social baggage that often clouds the perceptions of researchers by leading them to treat as normal what are quite idiosyncratic practices of their own cultures. The experiment is a method of putting distance and detachment between the experimenters and the objects of their own environments. The process by which individuals come to report perceptual displacement—something that is completely illusory and ostensibly not a question of moral preference—stands in place of the "concrete properties of norm-formation in actual life situations," which the researchers cannot tackle directly because of their own ethical moorings. For example, if the psychologist were to tackle why conservative males oppose abortion, there would be a temptation to valorize a priori certain "facts of life" that recapitulated elements of the norms and associated beliefs themselves. "This norm evolved because the men had learned to identify with the developing fetus," etc. Sherif advises us to ignore such concrete (i.e., community-centrist) reasoning and turn instead to the social processes of influence by which the norms and beliefs are acquired from others part and parcel with the justifications for holding them.

Sometimes, Sherif appears to presuppose that the processes of perceptual convergence and moral conformity occur in the same way, although the experiment is limited to the perceptual evidence. Other times, he seems to view them as quite distinct. The autokinetic effect is used as a stage to demonstrate or dramatize the larger and more important foundations of social norms that do not lend themselves to such easy exposition because of community-centrism. When he "venture[s] to generalize" from the basic lesson obtained from the experiment to social reality, he contends that "the psychological basis of the established social norms, such as stereotypes, fashions, conventions, customs and values, is the formation of common frames of reference as a product of the contact of individuals" (1936:106). The leap from perceptual convergence (which might be visual agreement, verbal compliance, or some mix thereof) to a wholesale range of normative structures appears like a sweeping revelation in the text, but is a halting *non sequitur* in logic.

For practical purposes, the conclusion that normative structures arise from "common frames of reference" would not shock many social scientists, but whether it would satisfy them theoretically is another matter. Also, few would draw such conclusions from the empirical evidence of the autokinetic effect. There are several specific problems. First, surely we can ask whether it is logical to argue from an optical illusion, an insecurity in visual perception, to social stereotypes, fashions, and customs. Are these not quite different things? Seeing something, agreeing that it has certain material attributes that can be described in common versus determining that it is socially desirable ("normative") are quite different kinds of judgments. Sherif enjoins us to conflate them.

Second, if we accept that "community-centrism" threatens the neutrality of scientific accounts, and agree that we need a general template for normative behavior (achieved via experimentation) in order to capture the common foundations of stereotypes, fashions, and customs, in what sense can the "common frame of reference" explain how norms arise since its existence is already evidence of a normative foundation? In other words, it is tautological to explain the appearance of collective norms by virtue of a prior "common frame of reference" since this amounts to the same thing. The social contact between individuals that results in the common frame of reference constitutes but does not explain the rise of the normative order.

Third, despite the fact that experimentation, at least formally, is a deductive method in which the experimenter makes predictions about various outcomes based on differences in treatment, Sherif explicitly advocates a post hoc form of reasoning that is based on induction. For example: "If the principles established on the basis of laboratory experiments can be profitably extended to the explanation of the everyday operation of norms, then our principles are valid" (ibid.:68). And again: "The test for such an approach lies in the applicability of the principle reached to the description and explanation of norms found in everyday life. . . . Whether or not this is just one more psychological abstraction or laboratory artifact . . . can be decided after it has met facts in the fresh and wholesome air of actualities" (ibid.:88).

It could follow from this that if a researcher can discover an extrapolation to everyday life, that is what the experiment was essentially about in the first place—a position characterized negatively as post hoc reasoning in methodology, but applauded as *serendipity* in theory construction.[4] What makes Sherif's claim less of the latter and more of the former is his suggestion that his experiment was simply "an extension" (ibid.:89) of well-known prior observations in perception, specifically F. H. Allport's earlier work on group mediation of individual perception (1924:260–85). Also, Sherif reviews all the major gestalt psychologists on the ground-figure relationship (Külpe, Köhler, Henri, Wertheimer, and Koffka, among others). One could conclude that its relevance to the all-embracing conception of norms was arrived at in advance. This experiment was a demonstration or allegory designed to explain the general processes of interpersonal influence in everyday life, even if the explanation was more allegory than proof. As Sherif admitted, the autokinetic effect was only "the rudiments of the formation of a norm by a group. . . . We have used laboratory material of a sort which is not found commonly in actual social life, but which, nevertheless, demonstrated the psychological processes in such cases" (1935:17, 47). It was certainly *interesting* in Murray Davis's (1971) sense, but it was hardly a model of scientific methodology in terms of how norms actually evolve, even if we accept that Sherif's insights were extremely valuable, a point to which we shall return momentarily.

WHAT WAS THE EXISTENTIAL PROBLEM FOR SHERIF?

It is difficult to recover exactly what initiated Sherif's inquiries in the midthirties. He reports a concern for the dramatic changes in social life associated with the thirties in America, the rise of totalitarian governments in Europe, widespread hunger and starvation, oppression of the power-less, and the mobilization of mobs through political sloganeering. He sug-gested that "the study of such unstable situations of oppression, hunger, and insecurity and their psychological consequences demand careful attention from social psychologists . . . especially in our time of transition" (1936:193). Again, "When social life becomes difficult . . . the equilibrium of life ceases to be stable and the air is pregnant with possibilities. . . . Such a delicate, unstable situation is the fertile soil for the rise of doubts con-cerning the existing norms, and a challenge to their authority" (ibid.:85).

Sherif was preoccupied with the important tensions in Europe and America that arose during the Great Depression, as were many of his gen-eration. But rather than tackle specific questions such as the popular appeal of the Fascists in Italy and the National Socialists in Germany, he began by thinking about normative behavior in general, and dealing with the breaches in normative behavior in the thirties at arm's length, as though he were examining a geometry of social relations in pure form, with idealized representations of people-in-general falling prey to unidentified sloga-neering and irrational sentiments. Fear of bias from community-centrism made Sherif abandon the specifics of social reality, and the peculiarities of historical situations, in favor of treating everything as an expression of an underlying condition. The former would invite anthropological descrip-tion while the latter could be analyzed in terms of abstractions.

To study the social circumstances created when the equilibrium of social life ceased to be stable, Sherif turned to normatively neutral condi-tions easily operationalized in the lab: the autokinetic effect. To capture the origins of totalitarian norms, Sherif contrives a setting where subjects are scripted into roles that dramatize what the society has experienced at large. He suggests that subjects in a darkened room watching a phantom light actually perceive the movement that they report. And in the responses of these subjects to this illusion, Sherif himself sees the complexity of the society compressed to its essentials. He speculates on the evolution of normative behavior from watching people trying to figure out if a stationary light is perceived as moving a discernible distance as his subjects convey their impressions. Plato's allegory of the cave returns as the autokinetic effect. Berkowitz and Donnerstein (1982:249) have argued that an experimental setting does not have to have surface realism or demographic representativeness to be valid, a point that might recommend the value of Sherif's approach. However, as Baumrind notes, manipulations within specific experiments are so consequential for outcomes that "results do not survive even minor changes in the experimental conditions. . . . When the task, variables, and setting can have no real-world counterparts, the processes dissected in the laboratory also cannot operate in the real world" (1985:171).

Sherif deceived his subjects by leading them to treat an illusion as though it were real. Is it possible that they duped him by telling him what he wanted to hear, making him the object of his own illusion? Sitting in the darkness together, and having been instructed that the light will move and that they will have to figure out exactly how much, the subjects hazard their estimates. Consequently, we find reported not only that a stationary point is moving, but that as far as the subjects are concerned, because no one wants to stand out in a crowd where there would be no point to it since the phenomenon is apparently ambiguous, it is moving three inches for one group, although four or five inches might do as well. The tables are turned on the experimenter. Subjects tacitly conspire to allow Sherif's illusion that they are being deluded in what they see, and consequently that what he sees in them reflects the social order. That at least is what Asch (1955:32) implies in a later article reflecting back on the history of group influence studies:

> There is some reason to wonder whether it was not the investigators who, in their enthusiasm for a theory, were suggestible, and whether the ostensibly gullible subjects were not providing answers which they thought good subjects were expected to give.

In this light, the entire experiment is a kind of optical illusion, both for the experimenter who discovers in it what he finds so pressing in the society, and for his audience whose attention he commands since, like Pasteur and cow pox (Latour 1983), he has captured the phenomenon in his laboratory, and demonstrated its truth. The lab gives the experimenter power over the effect by showing how to unlock it from nature and reproduce it at will, as did Pasteur in his field labs. But in retrospect, the experiment does not survive operational scrutiny. In the context of Sherif's larger vision, the autokinetic experiment appears to be an allegory used to illustrate how individual perceptions are mediated by others and how this can be used as a paradigm to understand the whole nature of social behavior.

Having registered some skepticism about Sherif's work from a purely methodological perspective, I also need to say that the story does not end there. As I hypothesized in the preceding chapter, psychologists often have a prophetic vision concealed in their science. Sherif does not disappoint us on this count. *The Psychology of Social Norms* is not a specialized treatment of group influence on visual perception. It is a brilliant and at times radical treatise on the very nature of social interaction, values, identity, and social change. Like other classical statements in the social sciences, it often blurs the line between ontology—the limitations and tragedies of human experience—and empirical inquiry. Among Sherif's suggestions, we find a call to end friction arising from class conflict—"the classes themselves must be eliminated"—and a call for the removal of "the belief in the divine origin of individual species" (1936:201)—both of which are "survivals" that create palpable harm to individuals. Viewed in this way, the autokinetic effect is what he calls a "prototype" of norms in this more expansive conception, and becomes a vehicle for reflecting on the larger issues of human nature suggested by the social mediation of all our experiences, including sensory perception, by culture. Gardner Murphy suggests in the 1965 reprint that "the laboratory investigation presented to our faculty here is embedded in a matrix of social science considerations, nearly to the point of being completely lost. . . . The details of the laboratory test have now become incidental" (Sherif [1936] 1965:x)—a point with which I agree. The empirical particulars were insinuated into larger considerations—both in the original endeavor reflecting Sherif's global interests in norms and attitudes, and in the subsequent focus on his methodology by proponents of experimentation.

Sherif's work became a classic study but the whole post hoc nature of his reasoning is never openly discussed, and the theatrical or dramatic structure of the experiment was similarly relegated to history. From this perspective, the suspicion that the subjects experienced no genuine shifts in perception resulting from group influence would be immaterial since the process was already a matter of earlier scientific recognition. Some introspective accounts from the 1937 report suggest that certain individuals knew they were being influenced by others, although others apparently were influenced and either did not realize it or would not acknowledge it. Later generations would read Sherif in authoritative collections that suggested that Sherif's approach was methodologically exemplary and his conclusions grounded in experimental empiricism—making them the latest victims of the illusion. The experimental study of social influence did not end there.

ASCH AND THE RESISTANCE TO SOCIAL PRESSURE

Although Muzafer Sherif (b. 1905) and Solomon Asch (b. 1907) were contemporaries, Asch's work appeared a decade and a half after that of Sherif, but is in large measure a response to it. In my view, his work is the second classical contribution to social influence research in American psychology in this period. It appeared just after the Second World War. Where Sherif stressed how subjects were influenced by the group outlook, Asch was interested in the grounds of *resistance* to group pressure. He developed his ideas over the course of several publications (1951, 1952, 1955, 1956) that examined social pressure on individuals working in groups. Where Sherif had studied social influence where the stimulus was inherently ambiguous and where individuals seemed to drift unconsciously into a consensus by exchanging opinions, Asch pointed to the social and individual conditions that compelled individuals to accept or reject opinions that they perceived to be *contrary to fact*. Sherif appeared to attribute the subject's knowledge to "the operation of suggestion and prestige" (Asch 1951:178). Asch stressed the predicament of the individual who can see differently from others but who experiences pressures to mimic them, and whose individual freedom is jeopardized as a result by a majority rule.

WHAT WAS THE EXISTENTIAL PROBLEM FOR ASCH?

As with Sherif, it is not clear what concrete issue initially motivated Asch's experimentation. On the one side, he appears to be making an intellectual response to Sherif. To be sure, he appears to have been involved in Sperling's (1946) M.A. thesis at the New School for Social Research that replicated Sherif's work (in large part), and devotes a significant portion of space in *Social Psychology* to a critical engagement with Sherif.[5] On the other hand, in all his publications, he stresses the context of propaganda and the manipulation of public opinion in the mass media. He proposes a basic study of interpersonal behaviors in order "to make fundamental advances in the understanding of the formation and reorganization of attitudes, of the functioning of public opinion, and of the operation of propaganda" (1951:177). He worries that the technical extensions of mass communications have created "the deliberate manipulation of opinion and the 'engineering of consent'" (1955:31). The final chapter of *Social Psychology* is devoted to the analysis of propaganda.

Social scientists were certainly aware of the enormously important role of propaganda, which had been so influential in mobilizing the German and Italian populations in the 1930s to support the war effort, and which, in the German case, promoted racial hatred resulting in genocide. Asch contested the Sherif-paradigm that suggested that people tend to absorb

their morality (i.e., norms and attitudes) from their social context. In Sperling's replication of the autokinetic effect study, subjects who were told
that the stimulus was an optical illusion did not experience a drift of their
estimates to a common range. And when they were exposed to a confederate whose estimates were wildly off, they did not feel compelled to
absorb them in their own schemes because the other subjects appeared
to be clearly mistaken in their views. For Asch, the individual's experience
is a primary and independent source of information. His experimental
designs focused on the dilemmas created when individuals had to confront vivid discontinuities between their views, and those of their neighbors. Sherif's subjects believed they were sharing the world known to
them in common. Asch's subjects had to tackle the problem of defending
what they knew to be true on the basis of their own senses, a situation that
exposed them to potential ridicule and marginalization—or capitulating
to the group and suffering a loss of self-respect and self-confidence.

In my view, Asch's experiment proceeds at two separate levels—the
concrete manipulation of conditions and the development of the ontolog-
ical condition of the pursuit of truth at personal expense. How could an
individual stand up against misperception and false propaganda? Most
readers will already be familiar with this telling study. What I would like
to remind them of is that this work did not begin with a specific theory or
hypothesis that the experiment was designed to test. It was another fishing expedition designed to explore Sherif's model based on an ambiguous
stimulus with an alternative social pressure that was downright provocative. Asch's device for exploring this interest in the lab was to ask subjects
to match the length of a stimulus line that was drawn on a cardboard sheet
with one of three other lines represented on another sheet. Although the
correct match appeared highly self-evident, the unsuspecting subject
found himself sitting at the end of a round-robin of guesses from seven to
nine others and at odds with them in a third of all the guesses. Unknown
to the real subject, the confederates were instructed to chose incorrectly.
Many subjects were completely floored by the situation and removed their
glasses to "double-check" the stimulus board. In about one-third of all the
critical trials, subjects mimicked the majority. Three-quarters of subjects
were swayed at least once by the erroneous majority. A third of the subjects
caved into pressure at least half the time. Nearly all were emotionally provoked by the inconsistency.

Of what social situation is this an operationalization? Propaganda?
Public opinion? Advertising? It is hard to say. It is presented as a generalized investigation of social influence. The most intriguing findings are that
subjects show tremendous variation in their responses, some acting independently throughout, and others caving into group pressure at every
turn. Asch devotes a considerable discussion to variations in how subjects
reacted to the confrontation that the design produced.

Asch introduced several variations to the basic design to determine the effects that these had on the levels of influence: the presence and absence of an ally, effects of changes in the size of the majority group, and effects of variations in the degree of the group error. What was discovered? Under what conditions do people resist propaganda or other social influence? Asch discovered that errors made by real subjects following group pressure to err declined when *one other subject* chose correctly. Ergo, external pressure is resisted when ego has an ally! But the ally must be constant, for if the ally bails out midway through the trials or arrives late, ego's vigilance for truth declines accordingly. As for the size of the group, a maximum influence occurs with a majority of three. Larger groups exert no higher levels of conformity. And finally (contrary to Sperling), there was little evidence that subjects ignored majorities that reported large errors as opposed to moderate errors.

Just as Sherif tackles social influence allegorically, Asch's entire orientation appears to have little relevance to everyday life. I would again hazard an opinion that this experiment tells us nothing informative about the process of propaganda during World War II. It says nothing about genocide and the political use of scapegoats to misattribute the real misery of German society during the thirties. It says nothing about national animosities, nor the state's legitimation of violence to deal with opponents. Like the Sherif experiment, it borrows from the pretheoretic understanding of the phenomenon of propaganda in order to context the experimental task of line discrimination. In fact, our collective immersion in the moral issues of the day probably leads us to miss the impertinence of the autokinetic effect and the line discrimination task to social instability during the thirties and the later wartime propaganda because our minds have been misdirected from the props of the experiment to the history that researchers were trying to dramatize through them.

It is ironic that though the experiments arise from pressing issues in the life world, protocol dictates that this social relevance be studiously misrepresented in the experiments themselves through a deceptive cover story to prevent the subjects from learning the point of the study—in this case, to study the effects of propaganda—and to prevent them from acting on this definition of the situation—presumably to consciously resist it. Where the consumers of the experiment orient to history for its relevance, the actors or subjects must operate in the dark so as to recapitulate history from the stance of naïveté—again demonstrating that the experimenter can release or bottle up the phenomenon as required. As in a box camera, things are turned upside down as our grasp of the world is used to explain and make sense of the experiment in the lab, and as the same life-world relevance is hidden from the subjects to ensure they do not invoke their own common stock of knowledge of the world to exhibit how propaganda ought to be dealt with.

ASCH'S MORAL AGENDA: RESISTANCE AND CONFORMITY
AS ONTOLOGICAL DILEMMAS

Students of experimental social psychology seem to ignore the fact that the particulars of some of the classic studies are empirically vacuous. Does anyone really believe that Asch discovered a critical number (i.e., 3) that results in maximum social influence in group situations? To which settings could such a discovery be generalized? Or that the role of an ally or friend in opposing false knowledge is any more than what one would guess from common sense and no more or less reliable? Would anyone build an organization based on these specific findings? I believe that would be foolish. Indeed, from an empirical perspective the research is quite casual. There is no pretense that the subjects are representative since they are acquired through snowball contacts. There is no control for gender. The reports also differ significantly in their particulars. The 1951 chapter reports that there were 18 trials with 12 critical tests involving a total of 87 subjects. In 1952, Asch reports 56 subjects involved in 12 trials of which 7 are critical. And in 1955 the number of subjects jumps to 123 in 18 trials. What gives? One is reminded of Harold Garfinkel's experiments in *Studies in Ethnomethodology* (1967) in which he tells readers that his experiments are "aids to the sluggish imagination," i.e., demonstrations, and not to be taken too literally, advice that seems equally appropriate here.

I think readers of Asch overlook such details because the description of the predicament of the subjects is so engaging, and the analysis of their situation makes a point that transcends the original study, although the point is more philosophical than empirical. Some subjects acted with courage and confidence in confronting their situation but most were deeply threatened and disturbed, oftentimes experiencing a "double-take" to confirm that their neighbors were so clearly wrong, sometimes laughing nervously and sometimes withdrawing. Most subjects erred to some extent during the critical trials. Among the yielders, only one subject said his perception of the lines changed after he heard the majority opinion, although, as Asch notes, "we cannot be fully certain of what took place" (1952:469), and certainly he does not think any of Sherif's subjects actually experienced distortions in perception. More likely was the situation where subjects caved in for "the fear of exposing themselves to ridicule" (ibid.:470). Even if they enjoyed a short-term relief from embarrassment, they subsequently experienced a feeling of personal defeat and were racked with feelings of self-doubt and helplessness.

Of what relevance are these issues? Asch frames the problem as an inevitable condition of the social order. Social order requires a degree of consensus for the operation of group life. People enter into social relationships with a certain amount of trust in the value of those relationships but independence is also necessary both at the individual level and at the collective level. At the individual level,

> to be independent is to assert the authentic value of one's own experience; to yield is to deny the existence of one's senses, to permit oneself to become confused . . . to renounce a condition upon which one's capacity to function depends in an essential way. (ibid.:497)

At the social level, the act of independence is essential to prevent the spread of errors and confusion. "The meaning of consensus collapses when individuals act like mirrors that reflect each other" (ibid.:495). Asch says that he "cannot rigorously justify the relevance of the present observations" to the general social conditions that people face, but there is good reason to believe that this juxtaposition between independence and yielding is a central dilemma in social life.

> There are times when one must choose between stark alternatives that have very much to do with the question of independence. Germans who lived near concentration camps could not escape the choice of breaking with their social order or of forcibly suppressing a range of facts and refusing to bring them into relation with their daily experiences. (ibid.:496)

So Asch does tackle propaganda—but at arm's length, by classifying people as independents or yielders. Yet this only idealizes social processes and does not throw much light on actual, historical experience.

Final point. Asch's work has some of the trappings of experimental manipulation of the conditions of influence (role of ally, group size, etc.) but generalizations from these would be trivial if not reckless, especially as the evidence is inconsistent (i.e., of the magnitude of group error). The most interesting part of the study is inductive—the identification of ideal types of reactions among "yielders" and "independents." Now we ask, how does Asch explain this polarity in social life and which trait comes to dominate in an individual? One of the less well-known positions that Asch advanced was that such traits tended to be relatively stable across situations. Such traits were marks of "character" for Asch and were not readily amenable to investigation through experimentation. He rejected the idea that the differences in question were "constitutional" (i.e., innate) and suggested instead that "the present discussion converges on a difficult and intriguing problem: the relation between character and social action" (ibid.:499). He seems to imply that certain social conditions will better foster independent action and build community consensus by drawing on the mutual dependence of personal and social qualities. It is interesting that when Asch's 1951 paper was revised for inclusion in Proshansky and Seidenberg's (1965) edited collection, *Basic Studies in Social Psychology* the

final sentence on "the relatively enduring character differences" he identified was deleted by the editors. This forced greater attention on the experimental variations of the work, but highlighted findings with the least
scientific relevance. The most important element that is stressed in all the
reports of the line discrimination task is edited out, presumably because it
did not lend itself easily to experimental investigation.

THE HOLOCAUST AND OBEDIENCE TO AUTHORITY

The Milgram experiments are the single best-known contribution of social
psychology to contemporary culture (Miller 1986; Miller et al. 1995). They
are also among the most controversial for both empirical and ethical reasons (Orne and Holland 1968; Mixon 1971, 1989; Baumrind 1964; Patten
1977a, 1977b) although textbook writers act as though the story is such
good copy that scholarly dissent cannot be allowed to spoil the effect. Milgram, like Sherif, was a student of Gordon Allport at Harvard, but "the
psychologist who had most to do with his intellectual development was
Solomon Asch" (Sabini 1986). Milgram spent 1959–60 at the Institute for
Advanced Study in Princeton when Asch was also a fellow.

Adolph Eichmann was captured in Argentina on 11 May 1960 and
returned secretly to Jerusalem by the Israeli secret police for trial as a war
criminal several days later. Although Milgram's study was derived conceptually from the work of Asch, the trial of Adolph Eichmann sharpened
the issues for him. Eichmann was the allegedly plodding Nazi bureaucrat
who assisted in the mass murder of European Jewry by masterminding
the concentration of the victims in Poland after the Nazi occupation of
France and most of western Europe. Subsequently, the Nazis developed
factories for the extermination of Jewish victims at Treblinka, Sorbibor,
Auschwitz, and other death camps. Several million innocent people, men,
women, and children, were murdered at these death camps by ordinary
German administrators, policemen, soldiers, and camp guards. In Milgram's experiment, ordinary subjects were cast in the parts of executioners. In the "received view" of this work (Stam, Radtke, and Lubek 1998),
Milgram took people from all walks of life and turned them into the experimental analogs of Eichmann, suggesting that the capacity for evil was fostered in virtuous individuals by monstrous bureaucrats. The existential
problem could not have been more clear-cut. Indeed, all of Milgram's
work has the bite of immediate relevance that is rare in this field.

The study was advertised as an experiment designed to test the effects
of punishment on human learning. Subjects ("teachers") were paid to
teach the "learners" to memorize a long series of paired associations. The

pretext for the study was to advance knowledge about the effectiveness of negative reinforcements on learning. Errors were to result in a shock, but the level of the shock escalated at every mistake in 15-point gradations from 15 volts right up to and beyond 450 volts. The experiment was run with individual teachers and learners, but the role assignment was rigged so that the real subject was always assigned the role of the teacher who administered shocks, while an affable middle-aged man, a confederate, acted as the learner. The teachers were given a sample shock to demonstrate the actual discomfort that resulted from their control of the shock machine. The machine was an impressive electrical appliance with switches, lights, and verbal designations describing the severity of the shock (mild, moderate, high, extremely high, XXX). The subjects were drawn from a wide range of occupations and professions, unlike the usual captive population of undergraduate students. Unlike other psychologists at the time, Milgram *was* concerned about the sampling frame. And the experiment was run under so many conditions that Milgram processed over seven hundred subjects before the research was completed.

The single feature of the research that advanced the influence studies was the utilization of an authority figure who appeared to be the scientist directing the experiment. His job was to pressure the teachers to comply with demands to administer increasingly severe levels of shock (which Milgram equated with aggression), since the learning task was rigged so that the learner's performance attracted increasingly lethal (but illusory) levels of punishment. The experiment produced tremendous anxiety in many of the subjects.[6]

Like the previous studies in this tradition, there was no a priori identification of hypotheses, nor specific examination of alternative theories. More fishing. Ties to Sherif and Asch were absent. Milgram cast his work as though it were generated *de novo* without influence from the earlier tradition. Milgram approached many groups to determine what they thought would be the normal responses to his experimental manipulations, and especially, what people would estimate the refusal rates would look like. Psychiatrists, college students, and middle-class adults predicted that 100 percent of the subjects would defy the authority figure and refuse to administer the lethal levels of shock. People were not asked how many soldiers during war would defy an order to murder noncombatants.

In the *Blackwell Reader in Social Psychology*, Hewstone, Manstead, and Stroebe summarized the study: "There is no experimental design as such; no factors are manipulated. No statistics are reported on the data nor are they needed since no experimental variations were compared" (1997:54). This characterization is not entirely fair. Milgram studied a number of different conditions of aggression, the most famous of which was proximity. He argued that the closer the victim to the context of aggression, the lower the levels of compliance. He also tested the effects of group mediation of compliance. Indeed, he reports eighteen different conditions of obedience, suggesting again that the research was inherently inductive. Milgram found that the majority of subjects *did* administer the maximum level of shock but that this declined the more proximal the victim was to the teacher. He concluded that compliance of individuals in bureaucratic condition results from the force of authority figures on their obedience. His experiment extracted this general human tendency from the reports of the Holocaust killers who reported that their role in genocide was a result of "just following orders." This has been the dominant view of the obedience studies over the last four decades.

Criticisms were raised both in terms of internal and external validity. As for internal validity, contrary to the received view, Orne and Holland (1968), Mixon (1971), and other critics argued that, in psychology experiments, subjects presume that "nothing can go wrong" and that bad things may not be as bad as they seem. Even though subjects are told that the shocking device delivered some 450 volts and are demonstrated through a sample that the volts are, well, electrifying, most presuppose that "this must be OK—no one can really get hurt." Universities cannot permit that to happen.

In the pretests of the study, Milgram reported that "in the absence of protests from the learner, every subject in the pilot study went blithely to the end of the board" (1974:22). Meaning what? Every subject in the pretest administered the maximum shock level without pressure from anyone! No one stuttered, sweated, or shook with anxiety. It was only at this point that Milgram introduced the various feedback conditions—initially a knock on the wall to indicate that the learner receiving the shocks was actually experiencing discomfort. In the *Obedience* film, it is evident to me that when the fake learner exhibits pain by actually shrieking—along prerecorded lines—the real subjects *initially* laugh out loud. They are *startled* that anyone is actually being hurt. In the later designs, when the subjects hear similar complaints from the learner testifying to the painfulness of the shocks, they also have in their presence the "authority/scientist figure"—the actor-experimenter who contradicts their perceptions that something is going wrong, and who reacts passively as people appear to be dying nearby. The subject is drawn between what is heard—a suffering victim—and what is seen—a nonplused authority figure subject to the same information but not alarmed by it. This causes enormous conflict for the subjects. They frequently sweat, stutter, and tremble. They are mortified by evidence that the learner is suffering. This is a rather different scenario from the Eichmann episode where the stench of death in the camps was unmistakable. Nor does this dispose of the Orne and Holland critique.

People may have started with an assumption that nothing can go wrong only to have this contradicted by what they could hear from the learner, but not by what they could see from the authority/scientist. As Orne and Holland (1968:287) note:

> The most incongruent aspect of the experiment . . . is the behavior of the Experimenter. . . . Incongruously, the Experimenter sits by while the victim suffers, demanding that the experiment continue despite the victim's demands to be released and the possibility that his health may be endangered. This behavior of the Experimenter, which Milgram interprets as the demands of legitimate authority, can with equal plausibility be interpreted as a significant cue to the true state of affairs—namely that no one is actually being hurt.

The credibility of the experiment is not furthered by the fact that the role of the teacher is actually superfluous in the experiment since the teaching could obviously be carried out without volunteer teachers. In the same vein, it could not have escaped notice by all the subjects that the learning task was simply impossible, and the demands quite incredible. This was Mantel's observation (1971:110–11)[7]:

> Every experiment was basically preposterous. . . . The entire experimental procedure from beginning to end could make no sense at all, even to the laymen. A person is strapped to a chair and immobilized and is explicitly told he is going to be exposed to extremely painful electric shocks. . . . The task the student is to learn is evidently impossible. He can't learn it in such a short space of time. . . . No one could learn it. . . . This experiment becomes more incredulous and senseless the further it is carried.

In a similar vein, Baumrind noted that

> far from illuminating real life, as he claimed, Milgram in fact appeared to have constructed a set of conditions so internally inconsistent that they could not occur in real life. His application of his results to destructive obedience in military settings or Nazi Germany . . . is metaphoric rather than scientific. (1985:171)

Don Mixon suggests that every experimental manipulation that Milgram developed that introduced less ambiguous evidence that a subject was being hurt reduced the aggression of the teacher. When the learner's pain was signaled through pounding on the wall, compliance dropped from 100 to 65 percent. This was the single, most significant variation tested. It is also another fact lost on the textbook writers. All the elaborate verbal feedback of learner's suffering that was used as the baseline treatment reduced the compliance by only a further 2.5 percent over the knock on the wall—meaning that only one less person in forty resisted going to the highest shock level. Even though the authority figure is central to the received view of the study, his inclusion was actually a later addition to the design. Milgram thought that the verbal designations on the shock levels written across the electrical device would impede obedience on its own. That it did not suggests that people did not expect suffering to come to citizen volunteers. The classic study only emerged when he introduced feedback of harm and equated compliance with a specific agent—the lab-coated scientific "boss." But surely this was illogical since the "harm" occurred at highest levels without the expert authority. The introduction of the latter contributed not power over the subjects as much as ambiguity over the harm.

From this perspective, the study is an inductive exploration, not a deductive test of theory. When the victim's suffering was brought into the room and portrayed dramatically by an actor in the real subject's presence, although the authority figure's comportment suggested no harm, the aggression declined. And when the authority figure was totally removed from the lab, the pain feedback information reduced the shocks to extremely low levels. In other words, the more evident the painfulness of the procedure to the innocent teacher and the more the background expectation that nothing can go wrong was contradicted by experience, the lower the levels of compliance to the authority's demands. In a post hoc questionnaire completed by 658 former subjects, only 56 percent suggested that they fully believed the learner was receiving painful shocks. This involved less than half of the obedient subjects (48 percent) and most of the defiant subjects (62.5 percent). Over 40 percent were unclear as to what they perceived. So it is not clear that the manipulation was nearly as successful as the "received view" suggests, and when subjects *did* perceive harm, they tended to be defiant. On this reading, the experiment should have been grounds for optimism about humankind. However, in the early sixties, this interpretation was not explored as attention was devoted to Holocaust analogies—analogies that appear founded on the excuse of the perpetrators as opposed to an analysis of their original behaviors. The authoritative view was based on the supposition that everything of interest was merely situational—making it ideal for short-term experimental observation. Although, like Asch, Milgram noted dramatic individual differences in responses to group pressure, he declined to administer any personality measures to explore this (Blass 1992:285).

Milgram did not throw any more light on the subject matter than what was already evident from history. The final frames of the *Obedience* film depicting the pulsating force field of the authority figure—crudely tying his work to Lewin's (1951) field theory—end with a warning more appropriate to vintage science fiction movies. "In comparison to the effects tested in our New Haven Labs, one can only wonder at the altogether more powerful influences wielded by governments and bureaucracies on individuals."

This would *already* have been self-evident to any student of the war. It was, for example, laid out in Shirer's brilliant report furnished so quickly after the end of the war based on his diplomatic and journalistic coverage of the events. Compliance in war crimes by whole police and army regiments was documented at the Nuremberg trials. As for Milgram's contributing anything of theoretical significance, the experiment was a theoretical cul-de-sac despite the massive public attention devoted to it. The "agentic state" is as tautological today as it was when invented. Indeed, Milgram only speculated about the state years after the experiments were finished (Blass 1992:279). It is alarming to think that the study that attracted more attention than any other in its generation did not result in any novel, theoretical insight. The experiment's extrascientific attraction was simply this: it allowed the psychologist to dramatize the story of humankind's capacity for ruthless violence in an experimental idiom. By replaying Eichmann in the lab, it did not substantially advance knowledge, nor did it discover anything essential or new about the death camps. Furthermore, it obfuscated the deep anti-Semitism that fueled the destruction of European Jewry by the Nazis, and substituted generic obedience.

In contrast to the view suggested by Milgram, the recent revelations of historians Daniel Goldhagen (1997) and Christopher Browning (1998) suggest that ordinary Germans were overwhelmingly complicit and willing participants in the slaughter of the Jews. Members of the police battalions who carried out many of the initial mass shootings who asked to be relieved from the killing were reposted without recriminations. Furthermore, many executioners inflicted suffering and humiliation on their victims far beyond what was ordered by the state. Goldhagen overplays his hand by suggesting that the genocidal anti-Semitism was the *cause* of the Holocaust, but no one can be left unmoved by his evidence of wholesale compliance. By contrast, Milgram's depiction of the Holocaust transfers our focus away from the real victims by dwelling on the murderers as though they were the victims of *their* bureaucracies and reifying their alibi of "just following orders." Even on this count, his version of events is misleading.

Hannah Arendt (1964) stresses points in the evidence that Milgram seems to miss. The first was that the policy of genocide was the rule of law in Germany during the Nazi period. In other words, like the Allied carpet-bombing of German and Japanese civilians, killing of noncombatants was based on the rule of law at the time, however repulsive it was in its consequences. Milgram's conceptualization seems to depict the Germans as unwillingly executioners, contrary to the historical accounts of Goldhagen

(1997) and Browning (1998). In transporting these issues to the laboratory, Milgram's design is based on the supposition that the teacher's aggression is not only illegitimate but is seen to be illegitimate by the subjects (by implication suggesting that ordinary Germans did not participate in genocide except against their wills). But this conflates two rather different contexts. Subjects have learned from childhood that it is a fundamental breach of moral conduct to hurt another person (1974). But during war do not most people believe that it is morally appropriate to kill to ensure collective survival in self-defense? While people may not like it, failure to do otherwise could be fatal. Also, Milgram's stipulation about what people have learned from childhood seems oblivious to the realities of intergroup hatreds that systematically reduce altruism and escalate intergroup conflict.

There is further moral jury-rigging in Milgram's account identified by Patten (1977a). If Milgram knew during the course of his experiment that subjects were being hurt (i.e., emotionally traumatized), why did he not terminate the experiments immediately? Answer: he thought science might benefit in the long run. However, in characterizing the conduct of his teachers as acting in a "shockingly immoral way," Milgram overlooks the fact that the subjects might be entitled to the same excuse since, during the cover story, they were encouraged to administer electric shocks to advance human knowledge about the effectiveness of punishment. If acting to advance science, would the subjects characterize their conduct as "immoral aggression" (bad) or "reinforcement" (good)? Milgram has it both ways. He describes the task to subjects as a legitimate exercise, then characterizes it as immoral—oblivious to the parallels of his own callousness toward the subjects. Abse suggests that if one wants to view the subjects as so many Eichmanns, then "the experimenter had to act the part, to some extent, of a Himmler" (1973:29). Even if we disagree, we must acknowledge the double standard.

Arendt's second major point was that during the Nazi regime the policy of "resettlement" and genocide would have been impossible without the cooperation of the Jewish leadership, something Eichmann identified as a "cornerstone" of Nazi efficiency. However, the role of the victims and the capitulation of leaders who betrayed them are simply omitted from the experiment. While recognizing that these considerations might present formidable design questions for the experimenter, a failure to tackle them meaningfully has the result that in exploring one of the darkest pages in Western history—and attracting our interest for this very reason—Milgram's experiment boils it down to Punch and Judy simplicity: bureaucracy made good people behave badly. Unfortunately, when we come to other cases of genocide such as the mass shooting of Vietnamese villagers at My Lai, Milgram enjoins us to read it as just another case of the crime of authority. In comparing more recent atrocities with the Nazi massacres, Goldhagen offers an alternative view:

> Who doubts that the Argentine or Chilean murderers of people who opposed the recent authoritarian regimes thought that their victims deserved to die? Who doubts that the Hutus who slaughtered Tutsis in Rwanda, that one Lebanese militia that slaughtered the civilian supporters of another, that the Serbs who killed Croats or Bosnian Muslims, did so out of conviction of the justice in their action? Why do we not believe the same for the German perpetrators? (1997:14)

MILGRAM'S MORAL VISION: ON HUMAN NATURE, FATE, AND VIOLENCE

One of the great attractions of Milgram's work is the latent moral agenda that surfaces in the final pages of his 1974 book. Milgram suggests that the inability of individuals to resist the pressure from authority figures is inherent in our makeup as a species, and as such, represents a design flaw that could jeopardize our survival. The subjects in the obedience experiments acted with violence against an innocent person, but not out of anger or provocation. "Something far more dangerous is revealed: the capacity for man to abandon his humanity, indeed the inevitability that he does so, as he merges his unique personality into larger institutional structures" (1974:188). This "fatal flaw" gives our species "only a modest chance of survival." Human nature "cannot be counted on to insulate" people from "brutality and inhumane treatment at the hands of malevolent authority" (ibid.:189). A substantial number of people will follow genocidal orders "without limitations of conscience, so long as they perceive that the command comes from legitimate authority." Ignoring, for the moment, Milgram's conflation of *malevolent* and *legitimate* authority, this vision of individuals fated inevitably to absorption by institutions, unprotected by a transcendental conscience, and, by nature, prone to violence and mutual destruction is Promethean in its scope. The psychologist as prophet reads the Holocaust only as an instance of this more pervasive condition of humanity that stems from the very core of our being, and that bodes ill for the future of the species.

As with Asch and Sherif, the moral tone is miles from the evidence, and ignores the methodological limitations that exercised the critics. But the ethical appeal is undeniable. It recapitulates the story of genocide stripped of its historical particulars and depicts it as an expression of a side of human nature that cannot be redeemed by conscience. Surely there's a lesson there. Just like there was a lesson in the much more modest experiment of Zimbardo. Festinger seemed to imply that the latter was somehow exceptional. My thesis is that such problems as illustrated here are far more common in experimental social psychology than is usually acknowledged and that this contributes to the lack of growth in the field, and the sense that social psychology fails to get much beyond the common stock of knowledge about war and human nature. Despite the official orthodoxy, experiments serve as platforms for the dramatization of ideas, not for the testing of hypotheses and the building of theories. And that seems unlikely to change given the centrality of the experiment in the arsenal of social psychologists. But the moral tone also explains the enormous appeal of the field to undergraduate students who get an "ethical fix" packaged as science, and who enter the moral high ground under the guise of scientific training.

NOTES

1. Zimbardo's justification for ending the experiment was not as altruistic as one would have imagined but rather self-centered: "in the end, I called off the experiment not because of what I saw out there in the prison yard, but because of the horror of realizing that *I* could have easily traded places with the most brutal guard or become the weakest prisoner" (Zimbardo 1972). Having let this brutality go on so long—if that in fact is what was happening—one wonders how much lower Zimbardo could have fallen from grace. His later charge that the Institutional Review Boards "overreacted" to this sort of abuse of subjects is stunningly hypocritical.

2. The other possibility is that subjects were invited to role-play in a situation where the "play" was *not* simulated. The prisoners did not *pretend* to strip naked, and wear "dresses" and ankle shackles 24 hours a day or dress without undergarments. This actually happened. Zimbardo designed a situation that was intended to humiliate the subjects—and fully half departed the study within days. Likewise the prisoners did not carry toys, but real wooden nightsticks. So the subjects were put in a highly ambiguous field of play where action drifted back and forth across an experiential border demarcating heartfelt impulses and mere acting. Consider the account from a guard-subject: "During the inspection I went to cell 2 to mess up a bed which the prisoner had made and he grabbed me, screaming that he had just made it, and he was not going to let me mess it up. He grabbed my throat, and although he was laughing I was pretty scared. I lashed out with my stick and hit him in the chin (although not very hard) and when I freed myself, I became angry" (Haney et al. 1973:88). Does this mean that the guard and prisoner lost control, began to act "in earnest," and that the subject was consequently assaulted? Another ambiguity in the situation may have arisen from the fact that the experimenters themselves appear to have been swept up in the play and lost their scientific detachment. "Over time, the experimenters became more personally involved in the transaction and were not as distant and objective as they should have been" (ibid.:78) In fact, Zimbardo played the role of superintendent. Did the superintendent carefully censor every outburst of his guards and act as a model of virtue?

No. Yet he would later characterize *their* behavior as "aberrant, anti-social behavior" (ibid.:90) without consideration of whether the subjects took his complicity as approval for their actions. The more one reflects on the shift back and forth between simulation and "spontaneous" aggression, the more apparent it is that the mock prison was not so much an innocent analog of real prisons as much as a species of the very reality it was meant to mimic. In that case, the "revelation" that persons who play certain roles actually come to exhibit traits of the persons who perform them for a living is rather shallow since the "play" here included conditions of degradation that were not mere play, i.e., actually stripping in front of strangers, dressing in demeaning clothes, sleeping in ankle shackles, being wakened from (real) sleep in the middle of the night on the pretext of a count, etc. None of this was simulated. In this reading, subjects were not just tested; they were humiliated. And the experimenter fired off an article to a journal (*Society*) to condemn the sort of behavior in prison officials that he had himself created during his not-so-mock exploration of the same subject.

3. Another vintage demonstration "experiment" was undertaken by Rosenhan (1973), "Being Sane in Insane Places." In that study eight healthy volunteers faked symptoms of mental illness and were incarcerated in various mental hospitals. This study was cited as evidence for the environmental theory of mental illness by suggesting that maladaptive social conduct is a function of oppressive and dehumanizing medical institutions. And certainly the exploratory reports of the new inmates supported the view of callous conditions of treatment. However, this was already well-known to Goffman (1961). What its supporters failed to acknowledge sufficiently was that the normal volunteers acted insane to gain admission. The study was a landmark "demonstration" of the oftentimes inhuman effects of total institutions, but it was not a deductive experiment however much attention it attracted, nor did it advance our theories of institutions in any significant way. It did not explain what type of facilities were more likely to be dehumanizing nor did it throw any light on the factors that lead to dehumanization (cultural beliefs, individual differences, hospital policies, etc.). But it enjoyed enormous appeal because of the moral subtext—people already suffering from a mental handicap were brutalized, if the reports were accurate and representative, by the agents created to ameliorate their discomfort. Unlike Zimbardo's demonstration, this had the bite of reality arising from primary data collection as opposed to simulation, i.e., role-playing (Banuazizi and Movahedi 1975).

4. Zimbardo's prison study helped "explain" friction in jails without bothering to actually advance and test specific hypotheses. While pointing to the primacy of situational factors, his understanding of prisons seems oblivious to the fact that inmate populations have epidemic levels of sociopaths and other personality-disordered inmates who often experience very high levels of recidivism, which reflect a life course stability in aggressive and/or deceitful dispositions.

5. H. G. Sperling's unpublished M.A. thesis was titled, "An Experimental Study of Some Psychological Factors in Judgment," and was presented at the New School for Social Research in 1946. It was reviewed by Asch at length (1952:487–90, 501) to challenge the validity of Sherif's paradigm.

6. Stanley Milgram wrote: "Many subjects showed signs of nervousness in the experimental situation, and especially upon administering the more powerful shocks. In a large number of cases the degree of tension reached extremes that are

rarely seen in sociopsychological laboratory studies. Subjects were observed to sweat, tremble, stutter, bite their lips, groan and dig their fingernails into their flesh. These were characteristic rather than exceptional responses to the experiment . . .

. . . One observer related: 'I observed a mature and initially poised businessman enter the laboratory smiling and confidant. Within 20 minutes he was reduced to a twitching, stuttering wreck, who was rapidly approaching a point of nervous collapse'" (1963:375).

7. Mantel is often cited as someone who "replicated" the experiment but his own views about its ecological validity, i.e., its relevance to everyday life, are often overlooked.

4

Social Psychology Engineers Wealth and Intelligence

The Hawthorne and Pygmalion Effects

How is it that nearly all authors of textbooks who have drawn material from the Hawthorne studies have failed to recognize the vast discrepancy between evidence and conclusions in these studies, [and] have frequently misdescribed the actual observations in a way that brings the evidence into line with the conclusions?

—Alex Carey, "The Hawthorne Studies"

Does research count in the lives of behavioral scientists, teachers and children? If not, we might as well close up shop and refer all correspondence to Family Circle.

—Samuel S. Wineburg, "The Self-Fulfillment of a Self-Fulfilling Prophecy"

INTRODUCTION: WORKER PRODUCTIVITY AND CHILDHOOD IQ AS EXPECTATION EFFECTS

In this chapter we examine the controversies associated with two well-known investigations: the Hawthorne study and the Pygmalion, or the IQ expectation, study. Both were field experiments, one in industry, the other in education. Both purported to discover new, nontrivial information about human nature of tremendous relevance to society. Both had high impacts and apparently long-lasting implications for those who participated. The studies collected vital information over a long period of time, contrary to the usual short-term lab studies such as those examined in the previous chapter, and were heralded as landmark accomplishments and advances in knowledge. Both ultimately attracted close scrutiny, which suggested that the main effects were based on very small numbers of subjects, that both were open to sound, contrary interpretations, and that both enjoyed an appeal, like the studies in the previous chapter, which suggested that they conveyed powerful moral sentiments of more gravity than the evidence on which they were based. In addition, both were in the genre of expectation effects. The Hawthorne study suggested that worker output was limited less by such material factors as fatigue and remuneration than by the social relationships created by a progressive work environment. Pygmalion argued that the intellectual development of children was limited less by their innate biology than by the social expectations of their teachers. Many people continue to subscribe to such beliefs today because they contain a kernel of truth, but the idea advanced here is that the foundations for such beliefs appear to rest on something other than the science on which they were originally based. If these ideas were sound, then human beings could design societies in which industrial productivity and human intelligence would be boundless—and who would want to hope otherwise? That line of thinking makes the discipline of social psychology unresponsive to negative findings while fixating on ideas with tremendous moral appeal that are more responsive to "common sense psychology" than the scientific psychology referred to earlier.

THE HAWTHORNE EFFECT

The Hawthorne studies were the single most important exploration of the human dimensions of industrial relations in the early twentieth century. They were undertaken at Bell Telephone's Western Electric manufacturing plant in Chicago beginning in 1924 and continued through the early years of the depression until 1933. The Hawthorne plant manufactured a variety of electrical equipment and its growth reflected the burgeoning home telephone market that developed in the 1920s. It employed twenty-two thousand workers in 1927 but this number grew to forty thousand by 1930 (down to seven thousand by 1932), reflecting the huge expansion (and contraction) of telephone services during the Roaring Twenties and the depression of the thirties.

Personnel managers with the company undertook a series of experiments to explore the effects of various conditions of work on worker morale and productivity including changes in illumination, humidity, and work rests. In 1928, the company sought the input of several external experts, including Elton Mayo of the Harvard Business School, and Clair Turner, a professor of biology and public health at MIT, to help them interpret the results of their studies. One of the peculiarities of this investigation is that it is not clear who advanced the initial hypotheses in these studies, and what predictions were attached to the various changes in the conditions of work. Like some of the early classic studies in interpersonal influence reviewed in the last chapter, much here appears to have been exploratory. The Hawthorne plant had created an Industrial Research Division. The research was certainly initiated internally at Hawthorne by management personnel including Bill Dickson, Harold Wright, George Pennock, and Mark Putnam, but the subsequent findings are published in reports by people drawn into the project after its initiation, people whose intellectual stature dates to their interpretations of the Hawthorne studies. The classic sources are Elton Mayo's *The Human Problems of an Industrial Civilisation* (1933) and F. J. Roethlisberger and William J. Dickson's *Management and the Worker* (1939). Roethlisberger was a student of Mayo's at Harvard, and the Roethlisberger-Dickson account of the research is usually held as the authoritative one. It appeared a decade and a half after the start of the studies, and it was almost spiked by senior management at Hawthorne who were alarmed by the claims that the management team in the bank-wiring shop was virtually incapable of affecting worker output let alone determining what would be reasonable levels of productivity. The studies at Western Electric are memorable because of the discovery of the "Hawthorne effect." What that effect was, how it occurred, and how it came to embed itself so effectively in the consciousness of social psychologists are not well understood. The term Hawthorne effect appears to have been first coined by Paul Lazersfeld in 1941, two years after the appearance of *Management and the Worker*.[1]

THE ILLUSION OF FAMILIARITY

It is noteworthy that in Mayo's preface to *Management and the Worker*, he alludes to the fact that there was some misunderstanding associated with the findings at Hawthorne. He says that his own Lowell lectures, North Whitehead's *The Industrial Worker* (1938), and Roethlisberger and Dickson's earlier business school account created "an illusion of familiarity when the Hawthorne experiment is mentioned. . . . But this is illusion: many of us have long been aware that there is no sufficiently general understanding of the course that the inquiry ran, of the many difficulties it encountered, and of the constant need to revise and renew the attack on the diverse problems presented" (Mayo 1939:xi). *Management and the Worker* was going to set forth the full record and reverse the illusion by providing a full account of the development of the experiments. Whether it succeeded in removing that illusion is another matter.

There is little doubt that *Management and the Worker* struck a nerve among professional psychologists and personnel directors. Writing in the

Personnel Journal, Charles Slocombe, director of the Personnel Research Foundation, called it "the most outstanding study of industrial relations that has been published anywhere, anytime." Stuart Chase, writing to a general audience in *Reader's Digest,* declared it: "the most exciting and important study of factory workers ever made. . . . There is an idea here so big it leaves one gasping." However, what that idea was and why it left people gasping was not actually clear. The illusion of Hawthorne had staying power.

Today, we refer to the "Hawthorne effect" to denote a situation in which the introduction of experimental conditions designed to identify key aspects of behavior has the inadvertent consequence of changing the very behavior it is designed to identify. When persons realize that their behavior is being examined, this changes how they act, often resulting in their exhibiting socially desirable traits. Obviously, such changes are of interest to psychologists who are trying to understand the rationale of behavior as it transpires in context, and who need to separate aspects of behavior that are natural or spontaneous from behavior that results from the conditions of experimentation.

The original Hawthorne effect referred to the *claim*—for, as we'll see, much here remains illusory—that the productivity of the workers increased over time with whatever variation in the work conditions was introduced by the experimenters. Where Heisenberg had noted in physics that the act of observation changed the field of observation, the Hawthorne effect suggested that this change was motivated by social considerations that led those exposed under the experimental microscope to put their best foot forward—to excel, to show themselves in the most positive light, to produce more and weather the tribulations of industrial work with personal grace and dignity. The changes in productivity or output were a function of tacit expectation effects. The evidence for this was suggested in the preliminary illumination experiments and in the relay assembly test room.

THE ILLUMINATION AND FIRST RELAY ASSEMBLY TESTS

The illumination experiments were initially designed to determine whether increases in artificial lighting on the factory floor could result in fewer accidents, less eyestrain, and higher productivity. The electrical industry had a considerable investment in establishing the returns to enhanced lighting, and the National Research Council became involved with a blue ribbon panel of experts headed by Thomas Edison to explore the effects of changes in illumination. The experiments were conducted at the Hawthorne plant over a three-year period (1924–1927) and involved workers manually winding induction coils for telephone systems. It was clear to the engineers that identification of the contribution of illumination to productivity net of the effects of other changes created by the experimental conditions would be difficult. Baselines of productivity were taken, the women recruited were interviewed about the experiment, changes were made in illumination, and measurements in output during the day were taken by foremen to identify levels of productivity, along with measures of temperature and humidity. A control group of workers not subject to the same enhanced conditions of supervision experienced increases in output because of the development of informal competition between the workers. Roethlisberger and Dickson provided a summary report of the study in the Introduction to *Management and the Worker*. They noted that even when light values were decreased, output increased. In fact, in one variation, even when the light was cut down to 0.06 of a foot-candle, "an amount of light approximately equal to that of an ordinary moonlight night [*sic*] . . . the girls maintained their efficiency" (1939:17). It appeared as though the physical conditions of illumination were less consequential than the psychological conditions. In the eleven periods of the third round of experiments, the control group as well as the experimental group showed an improvement from a prior baseline—whether the illumination was increased, decreased, or remained constant. In the end, "the results of these experiments on illumination fell short of the expectations of the company in the sense that they failed to answer the specific question of the relation between illumination and efficiency" (ibid.:18). But they did motivate the next phase of inquiry: the Relay Assembly Room tests.

The Relay Assembly Room tests started in April 1927 and continued until June 1932, when the demand for relays was so low due to the depression that the study was terminated. The Roethlisberger-Dickson report covers the first thirteen periods, ending coverage in June 1929. This was the most famous part of the Hawthorne study, and the one that has received the greatest empirical scrutiny. It reflects the theoretical ideas derived from Elton Mayo, who suggested that in industrial conditions, people are not motivated by either simple physical conditions such as exhaustion or fatigue nor is their productivity determined primarily by their economic self-interest and material aspirations. Although fatigue and exhaustion were a concern in nineteenth-century conditions of production, heavy labor was increasingly replaced by machines and fatigue in modern workers was viewed as an expression of morale and workplace adjustment. As for income, Mayo suggested that beyond a certain level of material comfort, workers put more stock in the social dimensions of work. They valued the relationships between each other and their supervisors. Paramount was the importance of developing a humane set of relationships that recognized the total situation of the worker and her sentiments. Mayo drew heavily from Pareto and Freud, authorities who held that most behavior was not rational as classical economics had held.

This point is important since most of the postwar criticisms of the Hawthorne study stress the role of self-interest in the level of productivity and in the restriction of productivity by pieceworkers out of self-interest.

The design of the relay assembly test room was more of a "test–change–retest" design based on the performance of a fixed number of workers whose output was examined under successively altered conditions of work. The Relay Assembly Test room included a change of work location in which five operators and one layout worker assembled complicated relay switches consisting of thirty to forty parts in a separate test room. Other changes included a collective form of remuneration calculated on the combined productivity of the test room workers (piecework), introduction of break periods of various lengths at various times during the day, provision of lunch and beverages by the company, and alterations in the weekly work schedule (shortened days, shorter week). The group was monitored by an observer who came to act in a cooperative supervisory capacity with the workers. The output was calculated mechanically with a ticker tape machine, and by manual summaries. The observer made notes about the small talk and social interaction of the workers. To induce them to attend hospital for regular medical assessments, the workers were bribed with ice cream. The workers brought their own cake—and as the experiment developed, the workers, all young women in their late teens and early twenties (with one exception), began to socialize outside the workplace.

The analysis of the changes in productivity is quite detailed but the conclusions were quite simple. If one examines the average hourly output per week during the first thirteen periods of the study, including a reversion to the standard regime during period 12 (in which pauses were cancelled and the work week lengthened), the level of output drifts haltingly upward period after period. "Examination of this chart reveals at once no simple correlations between the experimentally exposed changes in working conditions and rate of work" (ibid.:75). From a baseline of around fifty relays an hour in the first weeks, the women increased their output to sixty or seventy relays per hour two years later. The experimenters noted that the workers appeared to have become a spot "healthier" as gauged by a gain in weight over the period. They also took pains to rule out a decline in fatigue as the cause.

THE SECOND RELAY ASSEMBLY AND THE MICA-SPLITTING TESTS

To tackle the potential contribution of changes in the wage incentive, they created a second relay assembly test group and a mica-splitting test group.

The former worked together in the normal shop floor with the normal form of supervision. For a period of nine weeks they received the small-group piece rate, then reverted to the shopwide form of remuneration. Two operators continued to report inflated productivity after a return to the old method of payment and two did not—from which Roethlisberger and Dickson inferred that "it was difficult to conclude whether the increase in output was an immediate response to the change in wage incentive" (1939:132–33). However, they also reported that because of friction on the shop floor between the special group and the rest of the workers, the foreman demanded that the former method of payment be reinstituted. So this manipulation was inconclusive.

The mica-splitting test group was similar to the original relay assembly group—except for the change in method of remuneration—in other words, they were isolated in a test room—but earned the general piece rate of the other workers. This test began in 1928 and terminated in mid-1930 when the demand plummeted and with it productivity declined for want of work. For this reason Roethlisberger and Dickson employed only the first fourteen months of the two-year series (ibid.:153). Even with this truncation of the series, the gains in productivity were modest and were inconsistent across the different workers. "In both test rooms, output tended to increase in the first year. Also, in both cases the increases followed experimentally induced changes in work conditions. With these two exceptions, however, no parallel developments in the two rooms could be detected" (ibid.:149). And again these changes were estimated on the bases of a handful of workers—five in the case of the relay assembly and five in the mica-splitting test room.

SEARCH FOR THE REAL HAWTHORNE EFFECT

With these inconclusive observations, Roethlisberger and Dickson went into completely different methodological directions, which led to a deeper understanding of the Hawthorne effect than that with which they started. They focused on the qualitative data from the second relay and mica test groups, data that pointed to the dramatic difference in the social situation between the initial relay assembly test group and the subsequent two groups. The original relay assembly group had developed a rare industrial tone in which workers did not feel goaded by their bosses. Indeed, they did not view the observer as a boss at all. The atmosphere was one of a new employee-supervisory relationship marked by a spirit of cooperation, in which "there were no longer any bosses." Absenteeism declined. Group morale improved. Everyone was more likely to assist the others. By contrast, in the later studies with their more modest improvements, there was an "apprehension of management," and a fear of unemployment as the "dreaded depression" (ibid.:153) began to make the future uncertain. That magic first glimpsed in the illumination studies and corroborated in the relay assembly vanished. Having established to their own satisfaction that productivity was not powerfully linked to wages, Roethlisberger and Dickson began to outline the real Hawthorne effect.

The real Hawthorne effect was the potential change in industrial relationships made possible by the insights of scientific management of the sort proposed by Elton Mayo. The bulk of the six hundred pages in this classic book is not devoted to the relay assembly test and its seemingly irrepressible increases in productivity. Instead, we find a program based on widespread interviewing, understanding the nature of industrial conflict based on a novel theory of human nature, and devising a profession capable of achieving industrial harmony through reliance on a scientific management approach that bordered on psychiatric therapy. The interview phase involved some twenty-one thousand employees.[2] It followed an incredible logic of expansion as the short two to three pages of notes gathered in twenty-five-minute interviews exploded into dozens of pages of transcripts. Interviews increasingly came to resemble therapeutic sessions lasting for hours, as the interviewers were alerted to the latent content of worker cognitions in search for the "total situation" of the workers.

TESTS IN THE BANK-WIRING ROOM

The bank-wiring room was devoted to the creation of large electrical switching appliances. The labor force was male, and worker output consisted of two units per day. This was referred to as "the bogey," an informal level of productivity enforced by the workers through informal social control, verbal taunts, and playful shoulder punches. There was no new management intervention and nothing of the magical change in productivity associated with the relay assembly test room. The inclusion of this analysis in *Management and the Worker* is difficult to understand since the conclusions here have none of the implications of the relay assembly room study.

CRITICISMS OF HAWTHORNE

The conflict over what I would call the small h Hawthorne effect arises in a number of works. One of the most provocative is owed to Alex Carey:

A detailed comparison between the Hawthorne conclusions and the Hawthorne evidence shows these conclusions to be almost wholly unsupported. The evidence reported by the Hawthorne investigators is found to be consistent with the view that the material, and especially financial, reward is the principal influence on work morale and behavior. Questions are raised about how it was possible for studies so nearly devoid of scientific merit, and conclusions so little supported by the evidence, to gain so influential and respected a place within scientific disciplines and to hold this place for so long. (1967:103)

Carey's point was that the small-group wage system was the primary cause of worker output among the five subjects in the relay assembly room. The more units they assembled, the higher their pay. Humanitarian management was beside the point, and the so-called Hawthorne effect was a myth.

Carey and other critics pointed to the replacement of two operators in the relay assembly test room who were repeatedly criticized for "excessive" talking and who seemed to be consciously limiting their output in contrast to their peers. Despite the fact that they had been led to believe that enhanced productivity was not an objective of the experiment, they were returned to the shop floor for a lack of cooperation on the issue of output. They were replaced by two new operators whose productivity immediately led the pack—one worker, a fifteen-year-old Italian girl, was particularly productive, and apparently cajoled the others to monitor and elevate their output. As Carey and others have pointed out, her mother had died, and her brother and father were facing unemployment. The observer's record provides fairly convincing evidence that she was instrumental in trying to elevate levels of collective output—a fact from which everyone in the test room benefited materially. The importance of this instrumental action was neutralized by the move to recover the whole technical and human situation associated with the interview phase.

Over two and a half decades after Carey's critique, Stephen Jones again examined the evidence for a Hawthorne effect, i.e., a change in productivity unrelated to economic factors, in an article entitled "Was There a Hawthorne Effect?" Jones modeled week-to-week output by regressing the average hourly rate of productivity on both formal changes introduced by management (form of remuneration, rest breaks, etc.) and inadvertent changes brought about by circumstances (loss of productivity due to repair time, unemployment, radical changes in temperature, etc.). He tested for immediate effects and potential effects up to four weeks later. Again examining the relay assembly room test data, he concluded that

contrary to the conventional wisdom in much research and teaching, I have found essentially no evidence of Hawthorne effects, either unconditionally or with allowances for direct effects of the experimental variables themselves. My results appear to be robust across a wide variety of specifications, alternative samples, and two definitions of experimental change. (1992:457)

H. M. Parsons (1974), writing in *Science,* had attributed the changes in output to operant conditioning—the fact that the workers could constantly monitor their output and benefit from changes in collective productivity, resulting in a long-term increase in skill levels.[3] Parsons and Jones differ in emphasis because the model Jones tests incorporates a simple stepwise change in the method of payment (the mean for change was .97, i.e., unity or no variability).[4]

Jones ends his observations with the following: "A fruitful line of sociological inquiry . . . would explore the social and historical context whereby the Hawthorne effect has become enshrined as received wisdom in the social sciences" (1992:457). In fact that is what Richard Gillespie tackled in his book, *Manufacturing Knowledge: A History of the Hawthorne Experiments* (1991). He takes the position that a conspiracy of Harvard management professors and industry managers emerged to marginalize the relevance of the economic aspirations of workers and their grasp of their working environment. Citing Bruno Latour, he holds further that this type of machination is the normal process by which knowledge is acquired in science generally—a conclusion quite impossible to draw given the repeated empirical dismissal of the conclusions at every turn. The only way I can make sense of this is that the criticisms are noted as though they were *in addition* to the main findings, that the main idea is not undermined by these empirical shortcomings—as though the Hawthorne effect and the Hawthorne evidence were independent, and as though these were different kinds of knowledge.

If my hypothesis is correct, the reason that Hawthorne persists in the imagination is because it paints a picture of workers and industrial production of heroic proportions. The workers are cast as subjects prone to morbid fantasies that they are little capable of understanding. Their complaints to management have to be interpreted in terms of the total situation both on and off the job, in terms of both manifest and latent content. Complaints against management that were discovered in the interview phase often reflected the obsessive thinking of workers—and the analyst risked superficial reduction of feelings of personal insecurity and morbidity to elements of the workplace thought by Mayo to be incapable of explaining them. The scientific manager has to coordinate the technical and the human facts of production to maintain both a personal and social equilibrium. So the task for the industrial psychologists was not simply about improving the manufacture of widgets, that is, production and efficiency (i.e., the empirical illusion of Hawthorne), but maintaining social integrity in an industrial system prone to destroying it, or prone to undermining productivity by failing to account for the human factor (as in the bank-wiring study). Understood in this way, the Hawthorne effect was not a methodological artifact as we have come to view it consequently. It was the clue to social transformation through expert psychological knowledge glimpsed by a mentally healthy work force operating at optimum levels of achievement in the illumination and relay assembly room study. It was about changing civilization by integrating the technical engineering in the manufacturing process (efficiency, productivity, workmanship) while steering workers wide of their obsessions and morbid thinking. That is what made the idea so big it left people gasping. However, at the same time, the dismissal of the economic consequences of the small-group wage system by the authors left the critics shaking their heads. Here may be the key to the persistence of Hawthorne. The moral attraction of the idea finds its continuing relevance as a vision of the humanization of industrial civilization—the quest for paradise in the age of fragmentation—while the empirical evidence points perennially to its negation. (Paradise lost?) Professors of management and industrial psychologists appear fixated on the cultural ideal of Hawthorne's industrial magic and return to the oracle of the relay assembly room test with fascination—only to find the divinations ambiguous. As a result, students of Hawthorne have accorded it a place of pride in the arsenal of industrial psychology, not because of its accomplishment, but because of its promise. Mayo's observations in the preface to *Management* support this line of inference:

> The art of human collaboration seems to have disappeared during two centuries of quite remarkable human progress. The various nations seem to have lost all capacity for international cooperation in the necessary tasks of civilization. The internal condition of each nation is not materially better. . . . In this general situation it would seem that inquiries such as those undertaken by officers of the Western Electric Company have an urgent practical importance that is second to no other human undertaking. How can humanity's capacity for spontaneous cooperation be restored. (Mayo 1939:xiv)

Here was work that was practical, timely, and inspired. And little supported by the evidence. In retrospect, it appears that industrial studies were incapable of dispersing the dark clouds of history settling over Europe when *Management* was published. But it might have represented *an analogy* to Mayo as to how the conflicts in what would become the most fearsome war in living memory might be defused. A relevant lesson could be drawn, however remote from the primary study. The study promised a brighter future. The heroic achievements of five young women in the relay assembly room provided a template for prosperity (as well as peace). In today's schools of business, the myth of Hawthorne survives the deficiencies of evidence noted by Carey, Parsons, Jones, and others.

In my view, there are strong parallels for the improvement of society with the later investigations of intelligence in the Pygmalion research.

Where Hawthorne might unleash unprecedented levels of industrial productivity by creating an optimal working environment and a harmonious industrial community, IQ could be cultivated in an educational environment designed to make it grow unencumbered by extraneous obstacles and prejudices. In this way, racial and ethnic minorities could move forward. This was the kernel of thought behind Rosenthal's famous study, *Pygmalion in the Classroom* (Rosenthal and Jacobsen 1968). Where Mayo alluded to a solution to international conflict based on a template of industrial ideals, Pygmalion promised an end to racial and ethnic inequalities by addressing the impediments to social advancement created in educational institutions.

THE PYGMALION EFFECT

In the Greek myth, Pygmalion was the king of Cyprus who, it was said, created a beautiful female figure in ivory—Galatea—after whom he pined until the figure was brought to life for him by the goddess Aphrodite. This story supports the notion of wish fulfillment that human desire can make the improbable happen. George Bernard Shaw's *Pygmalion* is the story of East Londoner Eliza Doolittle, whose cockney accent marks her lower-class origins, resigning her to a fate of poverty, until her fortune is reversed by language training under the tutelage of Shaw's eccentric Dr. Higgins.

En route to teacher expectancies and IQ studies, Robert Rosenthal examined a family of behavioral studies that pointed in a similar self-fulfilling direction where social expectations brought about the situation they initially only imagined. In the case of Clever Hans, the horse owned by Von Osten, a German mathematics teacher, Pfungst ([1911] 1965) traced the animal's remarkable abilities to the tacit communication of expectations by those who put various questions to the animal. Visitors asked the horse questions of addition, subtraction, multiplication, and division (the answers to which they knew) and the horse answered by tapping his foot to the appropriate number. The tracking of the animal's movements by the audience gave the horse clues about when to start and stop the exercise, creating the impression of great ability. Hans followed the questioners' expectations, although the latter were unaware of their own tacit signals to the animal.

In the "person perception studies," Rosenthal reports that student experimenters were recruited to test subjects for their abilities to perceive failure or success in a set of standardized test pictures. "Half the Experimenters were told that the 'well-established' finding was such that their subjects should rate the photos as of successful people . . . and half the experimenters were told that their subjects should rate the photos as of

unsuccessful people" (1985:441). Those expecting successful ratings report-
edly obtained such results from the subjects. Those expecting failure likewise got what was expected. However, the experimenter used the same
package of photographs in both groups. Likewise, Rosenthal reports that
students given what they believed were "maze bright rats" were able to
teach the animals maze discrimination tasks quicker than students given
what they believed were "dull" rats. But the rats were not in any way different. This led Rosenthal to suggest the foundation for the subsequent
experiment with children: "If rats become brighter when expected to then
it should not be farfetched to think that children could become brighter
when expected to by their teachers" (ibid.:44). *Pygmalion in the Classroom*
provided evidence that this occurred although, like Hawthorne, such a
strong claim attracted close scrutiny and a growing body of skepticism.

But surely Rosenthal's line of thinking was illogical from the start. Did
Clever Hans become literate because people treated him so? Certainly not.
Did rats get smarter? In the case of the person perception studies, is there
any reason for believing that subjects actually found the failure or success
that they were being tacitly coached to find? Just as subtle clues in the case
of Clever Hans suggested to the animal how to behave, why should we not
permit the same explanation in the case of the perception study? The photos used in both the success and failure treatments were chosen because
they were rated as "neither successful nor unsuccessful" as judged by
independent evaluators. No wonder the subjects asked "Did I do
right? . . . I was wondering whether I was doing the experiment the way it
should be done" (Rosenthal 1966:180). Rosenthal presumes that the subjects actually adopted a view internally that most people would not have
thought appropriate given the neutrality of the pictures. It is more likely
that they were simply being polite and were giving the experimenter what
was being suggested by him or her irrespective of what they actually
"saw" in the photos. There is a similar problem with the rats. Students
with so-called "dull" rats could simply have taken more time to permit
them to do their maze runs. They may have handled them more defen-
sively, and indeed, they must have treated them differently because smart
and dull rats were all actually interchangeable, according to Rosenthal. In
addition, their conduct may have actually been observed and scored differently during their performance because of the different expectations.
But none of this means they were actually "smarter" rats after five days in
the maze in the hands of these inexperienced students.

How can we infer that differences in performance mean real differences
in learning when differential expectations are confounded by different
handling? And even if one were prepared to go out on that particular limb,
why should we equate differences in learning under these circumstances
with differences in "brightness"? The entire foundation for the research is

erected on sand. As with Hawthorne, the underlying theory is murky. It conflates changes in the experimenter's cues with changes in the subject's capacity even though the prior case studies—except at the level of myth or analogy—fall decidedly short of that.

Evidence of the impact of teacher expectations on pupil IQs was first announced at the end of Rosenthal's book on *Experimenter Effects* (1966).[5] It was reported more fully in *Pygmalion in the Classroom* by Robert Rosenthal and Lenore Jacobsen (1968). However, Rosenthal was also involved in four other tests of the hypothesis published between 1968 and 1974. Like Hawthorne, this work was extremely relevant to everyday life. It provided a novel explanation of differential patterns of school success by questioning the role of teachers in cultivating the basic raw talent of students under their charge. It was a long-term field experiment covering a period of about two years with superior promises of ecological validity. Because of the nature of the dependent variable and the length of the study, it promised to be a high-impact study with significant consequences for the subjects. And the specific hypothesis about how teacher expectations might influence student IQ certainly was not a commonsensical hypothesis in search of anecdotal support.

The Pygmalion study appeared in a highly charged ideological context in which sizable investments of public money were being poured into "headstart" and remedial education programs to alleviate the dramatic levels of school failure among poor people, particularly poor black and Hispanic communities, and to reverse the cycle of poverty and racial alienation in America. Rosenthal's perspective put a new interpretation on the relationship between poverty and school failure. Rather than arising from a lack of home resources, a lack of parental support, or a lack of home schooling prior to public schooling, the theory of expectation effects shifted the blame for school failure to teachers. Poverty might be related to school failure because middle-class teachers (both black and white) tacitly prepared poor students (usually minority group members) for failure because they *expected* them to fail. The expectation might work as a self-fulfilling prophecy. The political implications of the research were entirely unanticipated by the previous line of inquiry and attracted uncommon levels of public attention.

THE STUDY: MANIPULATING POSITIVE EXPECTATIONS

To explore the self-fulfilling prophecy, Rosenthal and Jacobsen manipulated teacher expectations in the Spruce School of South San Francisco. The school covered kindergarten to grade six. Each class level was divided into a, b, and c levels, reflecting above average, average, and below average performance levels. Students completed a little-used IQ test—Flanagan's Test of General Ability. This examined both verbal and reasoning abilities and was differentiated for various age groups (K–1, 2–3, 4–6). Its introduction into the schools was disguised as a "Test of Inflected Acquisition." Supposedly based on a joint Harvard–National Science Foundation study, the teachers were told the following:

> As a part of our study we are further validating a test which predicts the likelihood that a child will show an inflection point or "spurt" within the near future. This test which will be administered in your school will allow us to predict which youngsters are most likely to show an academic spurt. The top 20 percent (approximately) of the scorers on this test will probably be found at various levels of academic functioning. (Rosental and Jacobsen 1968:66)

The test scores purportedly permitted the examiners to predict spurts in IQ gains in certain students. Approximately 20 percent of the students were identified to teachers in the start of the fall term several months after the initial test. Rosenthal and Jabobsen report that the "bloomers" were chosen at random, although Elashoff and Snow (1971:158) discovered that there were already significant IQ differences between the control and experimental subjects from the start (4.9 IQ points higher for verbal and 13.2 points higher for reasoning IQ). For ethical reasons, only positive expectations were created. The test was administered repeatedly to measure changes in IQ. In fact the test was administered four separate times: (1) in May 1964 to establish a baseline, (2) at the end of the fall term to establish any immediate effects, (3) at the end of a first year to establish the basic posttest results, and (4) at the end of the second year to establish the long-term posttest results.

The results fall into three areas: aggregate changes in the IQ of pupils reported for the experimental and control pupils by class, changes in the school grades by subject, and changes in teacher attitudes to the students. In terms of IQ changes, the following was reported. First, after one school term there was some evidence that the experimental group as a whole showed an IQ increase of 2.29 points, but this was not statistically significant ($a = .08$).[6] Second, after a full year, there was an overall IQ gain of 12.22 points. However, the effects were based on the performance of seven grade one and twelve grade two students (formerly K and 1 in the pretest).[7] Examining these nineteen students, 79 percent experienced at least a 10-point gain, 47 percent experienced a 20-point gain, and 21 percent experienced a 30-point gain.[8] None of the other grades showed any significant differences, i.e., the null hypothesis could not be rejected in two-thirds of the classes tested. Third, as for the long-term effect, after two years, the expectancy advantage was nonsignificant for the younger students but the students in grade five showed evidence of dramatic gains—11.1 points.[9]

In terms of academic subjects, there was evidence of an expectation gain for the experimental subjects in the first three grades after one year. However, it was found for only a single subject—reading—and the scale used to present the differences was calculated in tenths of a letter grade, effectively magnifying small differences.[10]

The final area of measurement concerned attitudes. Rosenthal and Jacobsen compared teacher attitudes toward their experimental and control subjects.[11] The experimental subjects were thought to be more curious, more interesting, more likely to succeed, more appealing, better adjusted, happier, etc. In fact, Rosenthal and Jacobsen reported that where control subjects experienced significant IQ gains, there was some evidence of an attitudinal backlash from the teachers—students were given lower evaluations on these dimensions where IQ was not expected to improve. It is difficult to gauge the theoretical relevance of this part of the work. Certainly, Rosenthal had earlier asked the student experimenters in the rat study about their attitudes toward rats—presumably to establish that at some level the expectation effect (dull versus bright) had resulted in differences in orientation toward the rats. What is so difficult to gauge here is why evidence that appears so strongly to suggest differential attitudes would be found among teachers who after a year could hardly remember which pupils were supposed to be the "bloomers." And if the attitudinal shift was so vivid, it is surprising that it impacted only a single academic subject, and only when the grade range was stretched beyond credulity.

THE EXPLANATION

There were no actual observations made of how teachers treated the subjects. Rosenthal and Jacobsen had to speculate about the mechanism by which the expectations were actually transmitted. Was it the case that the teachers spent more time with each of the students whose IQs were expected to spurt? Probably not—since where the experimental subjects' IQs jumped, so did that of the class as a whole—suggesting that the teachers were not investing time exclusively with the "bloomers." Were the teachers *talking* more to "bloomers"? And was this the way the expectations were transmitted? When we look at the evidence, we see that the greater IQ gains were made in reasoning IQ for both groups.[12] In one year, the experimental group jumped 22.86 points compared to the 15.73 points for the controls. So this line of thinking, according to Rosenthal and Jacobsen, seemed improbable. (Parenthetically, would teachers be so indifferent to student performance that they failed to notice a 23-point increase in IQ? That classes of Don Juans would suddenly became Einsteins?)

According to Rosenthal and Jacobsen, higher expectations must have been transmitted by tone of voice, facial expression, touch, and posture. How this worked is a matter of speculation. These tacit expectations may have impacted the self-concept of the subjects, yielding better performance outputs, higher practice and exercise of abilities, and, ultimately, better performance on the IQ test. There remained two further problems for Rosenthal and Jacobsen. First, why was the basic effect found only for the *youngest* pupils and, two, why was the long-term effect found only for the *older* students? Rosenthal and Jacobsen argued that the young students were more plastic, more malleable, and easier to influence, but also required ongoing reinforcement to sustain the change. As for the older students, if the message did get through, and somehow escaped measure initially, it might survive longer since the older students, because they were more set in their tendencies, would not require ongoing reinforcement. All this was possible, even if it was ad hoc.

IMPACT OF PYGMALION IN THE CLASSROOM

The Pygmalion study received first prize for the Cattell Fund Award for experimental design given by Division 13 of the American Psychological Association in 1969 and the book was reviewed nearly universally in the contemporary press. Rosenthal and Jacobsen (1969: 23) summarized their findings in *Scientific American* and pointed to the need to focus attention on the way teachers structure the performance of students:

> Perhaps then more attention in education should be focused on the teacher. If it could be learned how she is able to bring about dramatic improvement in the performance of her pupils without formal changes in her methods of teaching, other teachers could be taught to do the same. If further research showed that it is possible to find teachers whose untrained educational style does for their pupils what our teachers did for the special children, the prospect would arise that a combination of sophisticated selections of teachers and suitable training of teachers would give all children a boost toward getting as much as they possibly can out of their schooling.

The study was discussed in the *New York Times, New York Review of Books, Times Literary Supplement, Saturday Review, New Yorker,* and many other popular periodicals. Rosenthal was interviewed by Barbara Walters on NBC and the book quickly became standard reading at colleges of education throughout North America. At the time, millions of dollars of federal money were being poured into ghetto education for headstart programs, remedial programs, and cultural enrichment. At the time there was evidence that such spending did boost IQ performance of disadvantaged kids—one study cited a 10-point gain for 38 percent of students, and a 20-point gain for 12 percent of students—but this was over three years. Compare this to the 10-point gain by 79 percent, 20-point gain by 47 percent and 30-point gain by 21 percent in one year in the Pygmalion study! These were spectacular increases and they lent credibility to the notion that racial and class differences in educational accomplishment could be explained in large part by how teachers treated their students. This was the heyday of labeling theory. Given all the attention that it received in the popular culture and in the academy, it was not long before critics ground down their microscopes to examine Pygmalion more closely.

THE CRITICAL RESPONSES

Rosenthal mentions casually that "the bulk of the negative reactions [to Pygmalion] came from workers in the field of educational psychology. Perhaps it is only they who would have been interested enough to respond. But that seems unlikely. . . . . We leave the observation as just a curiosity" (1985:49) to be clarified by historians, sociologists, and psychologists of science. In other words, opposition appeared for apparently extrascientific reasons. Readers can judge for themselves whether science was not better served by these skeptics than by all the yea-sayers who did not want to look too critically at the evidence. The comments reviewed here derive from several now-classic critiques of Pygmalion, including Thorndike (1968), Elashoff and Snow (1971), and Cronbach (1975). In his review of the book in 1968, Robert Thorndike wrote:

> In spite of anything I can say, I am sure [Pygmalion] will become a classic— widely referred to and rarely examined critically. Alas, it is so defective technically that one can only regret that it ever got beyond the eyes of the original researchers. Though the volume may be an effective addition to educational propagandizing, it does nothing to raise the standards of educational research. (reprinted in 1971:65)

Elashoff and Snow reported in a similar vein that despite the attention the book received in official circles, "We retain our view that *Pygmalion* was inadequately and prematurely reported to the general public" (1971:161). Wineburg recorded that "even before the book hit the streets, headlines about it splashed over the front page of the August 14, 1967, *New York Times*. . . . Details of the experiment's failure to replicate, however, received a scant column inch in the continuation of the story on page 20" (1987:31).

Recall why the study was attractive to begin with. Producing changes in performance of a short-term nature, as in hypnosis, or compliance to bizarre short-term demands in an artificial laboratory setting are one thing. But IQ is not plastic and it is not voluntaristic behavior. It appears to be more or less fixed. Control of something like IQ by the act of volition would be impressive if, in fact, that is what occurred.

THE PROBLEMS

There were major problems having to do with the way in which the Test of General Ability was administered. Recall that Flanagan's TOGA, disguised as the test of "Inflected Acquisition," was used partly because teachers might have been more familiar with the Stanford-Binet IQ test—which was the sort of instrument in use in professional educational circles to diagnose learning problems. The test was created for three grade levels: k–1, 2–3 and 4–6. This means that over the course of the experiment, the same base intelligence would be estimated by three different instruments as the children got older. Imagine the tests administered in spring term over three years. In reporting this, I borrow from Thorndike's review. Note that as the children are tested at different dates, they are examined with different versions of TOGA:

- K - - - - - - same-test - - - - - - - - - - →1 - - - - - - - different-test - - - - - -→2
- 1 - - - - - - different-test - - - - - - -→2 - - - - - - - same-test - - - - - - - - -→3
- 2 - - - - - - same-test - - - - - - - - - - →3 - - - - - - - different-test - - - - - -→4
- 3 - - - - - - different-test - - - - - - -→4 - - - - - - - same-test - - - - - - - - -→5
- 4 - - - - - - same-test - - - - - - - - - - →5 - - - - - - - same-test - - - - - - - - -→6
- 5 - - - - - - same-test - - - - - - - - - - →6 - - - - - - - into junior high school
  and out of study

Because there are different versions of the test, different outcomes may be a result of different test measures, not changes in IQ. This is a problem of "reliability." Usually, when tests are administered to large numbers of people, it is possible to identify the degree to which various versions of the test measure the same ability. The "concordance" between different versions of TOGA were not known because the test was not in wide use (and was attractive for that reason in the experiment). Thus, the "consistency" in what was measured was open to question. In addition, if one looks at the older groups, they tended to take the same test repeatedly. This suggests an effect arising from practice. One group would have taken the identical test four times (if we count the pretest, the short-term posttest after six months, the test at the end of year one and again at the end of year two) and this group would show the greatest long-term gains in IQ. Obviously, this is alarming. However, Rosenthal replied that while these deficiencies may have been real, the important thing to look at is the *differences* measured between control and experimental groups—and these were significant even if allowing for practice and inconsistency in the measures.

Thorndike points out that none of the published reports of the study contained the original TOGA scores. The appendices to the report contained the average pretest scores by class for reasoning and verbal IQs. The text reports the "difference scores" calculated by subtracting the posttest means from the pretest means. The case for prophecy effects is based on the performance of the first two grades—specifically, the performance of seven experimental subjects in grade one and twelve experimental subjects in grade two. In Rosenthal's appendix tables, one finds classes with average reasoning IQs of 31, 47, 53, and 54. Thorndike notes that they just barely appear to make the grade as imbeciles! And yet these defective pretest data were used by the authors without caution as to their validity. Thorndike recalculated the average verbal and reasoning IQs combining all three levels (a, b, c) for the first and second grade. They are as follows:

	First Grade	Second Grade
Verbal IQ	105.7	99.4
Reasoning IQ	58	89.1

What kind of test is it that gives a mean reasoning "IQ" of 58 for the total entering a first-grade class in an ordinary school? The pretest data are probably worthless. Thorndike goes further. If IQ = mental age/physical age and if IQ = .58, then it is possible to estimate the mental age of the children. If we assume that on the pretest physical age = 6, then mental age = $x/6$ = .58. Solving for x, we deduce a mental age of 3.5. What score on the original TOGA was required to achieve a MA of 3.5? The tables do not report for such low ages. Estimating a mental age of 5.3, one would need to score 8 out of 28 items. Again, extrapolating downward "we come out with a raw score of approximately 2! Random marking would give 5 or 6 right!" (ibid.: 67).

It is reckless to base any inferences on a test that is clearly so suspect in the identification of its baseline. That is something that most readers would never recognize because the report describes "difference" scores. The raw scores are nowhere produced and initial and posttest scores were put in appendices. Rosenthal (1969) explained that the low pretest scores were not inaccurate. "These low IQs were earned because very few items were attempted by many of the children" (ibid.:690). When one examines the items in question, it is hardly surprising. The reasoning IQ questions displayed abstract geometrical forms with the instruction: "find the exception." Given that the children would hardly be able to read, let alone distinguish asymmetrical line puzzles, the pretest takes on a different significance. Basically, the children were barely literate on the pretest reasoning questions and did much better a year later when the test made more sense to them. On this Wineburg notes:

> A change on the pretest may be interpreted as "intellectual growth," but given what we know about the pretest, we could just as easily attribute it to other factors—misunderstood test instructions, uncontrolled test adminis-tration, selective teacher coaching, teacher encouragement for guessing, or even chance. (1987:43)

Pesky educational psychologists indeed![13]

Many of these problems apparently escaped the readers of the original work. First, the report is based on difference scores, not the initial raw scores. Second, the figures that showed the dramatic spurts in IQ (79, 47, and 21 percent) did not always indicate the small sample sizes on which they were based. And finally, shifts in academic performance, namely reading, were represented as microscopic differences that reported one-tenth grade scales that overemphasized minute differences.

ROSENTHAL'S RESPONSE

Rosenthal replied to Thorndike's criticisms (and others) by arguing that if the pretest scores were unreliable, this made the measurement of differ-ences between control and experiment groups harder to obtain, but the tests find such differences to be (sometimes) significant, and in the direc-tions predicted. In other words, even if one allows that there are issues of validity, this does not entitle one to dismiss the differences that were accu-rately predicted between the groups. However, this is misleading. The major gains come from the first two classes and are based overwhelmingly on the reasoning component. These are conditions that contributed uniquely to the measured gains (i.e., they were not found in these classes in the reading IQ dimension, nor anywhere else in either dimension). Aside from differences between the groups arising from the unobserved expectation effect, we know that a large component of the change arises from a comparison of performance before and after the children learned how to read, fill in the blanks, take tests, and meet other academic expec-tations. We also know that in all the other classes where the pretest means were normal, there was no expectation effect. This puts us in the position of attributing all the difference in reasoning IQ in the first posttest to the expectation effect—which assumes we can sensibly subtract a valid score from the posttest measures from the completely meaningless pretest score. In my view, that logic is foolhardy.

Rosenthal's advice is also perverse in view of his own failures to replicate the same test. We are asked to take the evidence from one study in five
where the gains are discovered for a minority of classes and identified
inconsistently over two periods of measure. Evans and Rosenthal (1969)
reported no main expectancy effect in a middle-class elementary school in
the Midwest. Girl bloomers gained less than controls while boy bloomers
gained more. Conn, Edwards, Rosenthal, and Crowne (1968) studied 258
children in a grammar school (grades 1–6). IQ was the main dependent
variable. "There were no clear expectancy effects" (Baker and Crist 1971:50)
but there were differences in sensitivity to emotional communication, especially among boys. Anderson and Rosenthal (1968) studied twenty-eight
retarded boys. There was no significant IQ gain as a result of expectancy.
There was no evidence of main effects in Rosenthal, Baratz, and Hall (1974).

In addition to Rosenthal's own work, there are several meta-analyses
that summarize the work of other researchers on teacher expectations.
Rosenthal cites these to his advantage. The hundreds of studies that
Rosenthal refers to as supportive of the "Pygmalion effect" are not replications of the IQ study but studies of how expectation effects color the
atmosphere, feedback, input practices, and output opportunities in settings where people have been led to believe that they will interact with
others who are more compatible, smarter, more interesting, and so on.
These studies record *experimenter effects*, not IQ shifts. Two meta-analyses
however do review the latter sort of studies. A short report by Smith in
1980 suggested that the correlation between teacher expectancy and pupil
IQ was $r = .08$. Although Smith's study is cited favorably by Rosenthal
(1987), in point of fact Smith (1980:54) concluded that pupils' intellectual
ability was "minimally affected" by manipulated expectations. Raudenbush's 1984 meta-analysis had a more sensitive focus: examining the magnitude of the IQ affect while controlling for *prior* acquaintance of teachers
with pupils. Raudenbush discovered that the magnitude of the effect was
greatest where prior contact was smallest. Based on the meta-analyses,
Rosenthal suggested that "the educational self-fulfilling prophecy (Merton 1948) has now been well established." He based this conclusion on
eighteen studies and claimed "the effect of teacher expectations were significant for his full set of 18 studies" (1987:39). But Raudenbush deduced
that the correlation was small ($r = .15$) on the basis of the seven studies that
most credibly met the criterion of little prior acquaintance (i.e., less than a
week). With respect to the eighteen studies, in fact four tests of association
were explored. The only one that proved nonsignificant was the one in
which a control was employed for sample sizes. "Larger sample sizes tend
to produce smaller effects" (Raudenbush 1984, cited in Wineburg 1987:43).

A final point from Wineburg: Raudenbush's mean effect size for the
expectancy-IQ link is .11 (standard deviation = .20),

but as any introductory student knows, the mean is notoriously sensitive to extreme values when a distribution is skewed. The median effect size of Raudenbush's 18 studies is but .035; ten studies yielded positive difference and eight yielded negative differences. . . . What kind of phenomenon is it when nearly half the attempts to produce it yield results in the wrong direction?" (1987:43)

So even examining the most relevant cases, the Pygmalion effect is precariously close to zero.

In addition to the points raised effectively by Wineburg, there is another that merits consideration. In recent years, in the face of the paring-down of the expectation effect from a front-page event in every liberal periodical to an R^2 approaching zero, Rosenthal has been promoting the notion that while small, the effect is still precious. His reply to Wineburg in 1987 was motivated to identify "the social importance of these effects" (ibid.:37). This was suggested through what he called the *binomial effect size display* (BESD) and has been seized upon as a canard to keep the Pygmalion myth alive. In the Raudenbush cases in which teachers were unacquainted with pupils for two weeks or less prior to the expectancy manipulation, the correlations between expectancy and IQ was a modest level of association: $r = .14$.[14] In the cases of prior acquaintance, $r = .04$. The BESD is calculated by dividing the effect size (r) by 2 and adding it to .5 (the equal probability of either outcome). The display examines a 2×2 table of outcomes (survival versus death) by intervention (experiment versus control). For $r = .14$, where there are 200 cases otherwise thought to be distributed equally over the 4 cells ($n = 50$ per cell), the distribution actually records 57 survivals versus 43 deaths for the treatment group (divide r by 2 and add the fraction to .5 in the case of the positive outcome or subtract it from .5 for a negative outcome). The values for $r = .04$ are 52 survivals versus 48 deaths—suggesting a net benefit of 4 survivors in a case where R^2 is effectively zero. So here is the small but precious effect. What is wrong with this picture?

For any r that is larger than nil, no matter how infinitesimal, the equation for the BESD will report a nonzero effect, however tiny. If $r = .01$, the survival advantage will be 50.5 versus 49.5—or one person. If $r = .02$, the survival advantage will be two (i.e., $51 - 49$), etc. The problem is that the distribution across the 4 cells is a matter of statistical variation. The BESD will suggest a difference wherever r is not absolute zero. If one accepts that statistical tests are designed to determine the link between populations and samples, then the issue is whether the normal observed variability is more or less what one would expect by chance. In the case of $r = .04$, R^2 is not only small, but nonsignificant especially given the sample sizes typically associated with experimental work in psychology. The BESD is profoundly misleading.

THE LEGACY OF PYGMALION: THE UNDERGRADUATE TEXTBOOK IMPACT

Textbook writers appear to attach a great deal of importance to Rosenthal's conclusions, and seldom is a disparaging word said about the problems associated with the study, as though the methodological issues were something to examine apart from the conclusions themselves. Here are some illustrations.

Louis Penner, *Social Psychology*:

Experimenter effects, like demand characteristics, have implications beyond the social psychological experiment. For example, it has been demonstrated that a teacher's expectancies about a student's ability may influence how the student actually does in school (Rosenthal and Jacobsen 1968). Seaver (1973) was interested in how a teacher's experiences with a student might impact the performance of the student's younger brother or sister. ([1978] 1987: 23–24)

James Vander Zandem, *Social Psychology*:

Rats performed better in carefully controlled tests if their handlers were told, falsely, that the animals had been especially bred for intelligence. Likewise, rats consistently turned in poor performances when their handlers had been falsely told that the animals were dull. And when teachers were falsely told that certain children's IQ tests showed that they were about to "spurt ahead" academically, those children often surpassed their classmates on IQ tests given a year later. (1987:440)

Tedeschi, Lindskold, and Rosenfeld, *Introduction to Social Psychology*:

The experimenter effect has been shown to occur outside the laboratory. Rosenthal and Jacobsen (1968) found that if teachers were led to believe that some of their students had higher IQs than others, these students actually scored higher on standardized IQ tests several months later. Apparently, the teachers' belief that some students were more intelligent than their peers led to preferential treatment, which in turn produced a difference that initially did not exist. Social psychologists have taken the lesson to heart. By using many experimenters in any particular study and by keeping them "blind" or ignorant of the hypothesis, psychologists can reduce and control experimenter expectancy effects. (1985:23)

Charles G. Lord, *Social Psychology*:

When teachers inaccurately expect low ability, as they might if they believe in stereotypes, the teachers inadvertently keep low expectation children from reaching their full academic potential. When teachers inaccurately expect high ability, children can achieve far beyond what they or their parents might have dreamed possible. Expectations work both ways—negative and positive. (1997:438)

Worchel, Cooper, Goethals and Olson, *Social Psychology*:

> Like Henry Higgins in George Bernard Shaw's play *Pygmalion*, the teachers apparently created the person they expected to find . . . Rosenthal and Jacobsen's study drew considerable criticism because, as one might expect, there were deficiencies in this pioneering study. Within fifteen years hundreds of studies had examined the effects of teacher expectations . . . Among the early studies, systematic expectancy effects, or self-fulfilling prophecies, were found in middle-class schools in the East and West (Conn, Edwards, Rosenthal and Crowne 1968; Rosenthal and Evans, 1968) (2000:58). Also, Anderson and Rosenthal (1968) observed the expectancy effect in a class of mentally retarded boys. (2000:58)

What the textbook authors failed to point out here was that the changes in IQ reported in the first reference, the East, were nonsignificant after 4 months, fading further after three terms to nonsignificant mean differences that actually favored the control group. The second source referred to unpublished data. As for the study of mentally retarded boys, IQ *decreased* for boys expected to bloom. Anyone basing their views of *Pygmalion* on these textbook summaries would be materially misled.[15]

Lesson: people who read textbooks are being indoctrinated in Kuhn's sense of the term (1970). The textbook coalesces opinion by subtracting the intellectual debate from the delivery of "the facts."

THE LEGAL LEGACY

Even lousy social science can have powerful political and legal consequences.[16] Pygmalion has been cited in support of actions to force busing in two American jurisdictions. Busing was justified on the need to counter racist attitudes that damage minority students. Pygmalion was used to further social objectives and progressive public policies in spite of its academic shortcomings. From the judgment of Judge Wright in *Hobsen v. Hansen* 269 F. Supp. 401 (1967), a case that supported forced busing to integrate multiracial mixing in the U.S. schools we read:

> Studies have found that a teacher will commonly tend to underestimate the abilities of disadvantaged children and will treat them accordingly—in the daily classroom routine, in grading, and in evaluating these students' likeli-

hood of achieving in the future. The horrible consequence of a teacher's low expectation is that it tends to be a self-fulfilling prophecy. The unfortunate students, treated as if they are subnormal, come to accept as a fact that they ARE subnormal. (*Hobson v. Hansen*, p. 484)

Wineburg commented in the *Educational Researcher*:

To substantiate these claims, Judge Wright cited two studies: one by Clark (1963), which presented no data directly bearing on the self-fulfilling prophecy, and an edited chapter on the Pygmalion study. But unbeknownst to him, Pygmalion dealt with the overestimation, not underestimation, of children's abilities. Moreover, it presented no observational data of teachers and students, so there was no information on how teacher's "treated" students. Further, no interviews were conducted with students to see whether they accepted their "subnormal" status. Although all the points raised by Judge Wright may in fact be true, Pygmalion did not provide the evidence. (1987:33)

CONCLUSION: SOCIAL PSYCHOLOGY AND SOCIAL ENGINEERING

It is not an exaggeration to say that millions of students in North America and Europe have been exposed to the conventional views of Pygmalion and the Hawthorne effect. Many consumers of this information would have been heartened by the potential for improving society through following the "lessons" supposedly learned at General Electric's Hawthorne manufacturing plant in Cicero, Illinois, and in the Spruce School in Los Angeles. They have been seduced by what turn out to be scientific myths. Few would reflect on the fact that the case for the Hawthorne effect was based on a mere five workers (seven if we count the replacements), and, in the teacher expectation study, on just nineteen students. Their methodological flaws should have condemned these studies to the dustbin of scientific history. But the potential for improving society by the social engineering ideas of psychology overshadowed the evidence on which they were based. These apparent miracles of science enchanted generations of students, professors, as well as the general public. Unfortunately, the scientific progress attributed to these studies was an illusion. The lesson suggested by these cases is that their moral appeal has more than compensated for their total empirical bankruptcy. This conclusion is consistent with our earlier findings in the classic group influence studies.

One of the areas to receive detailed attention in social psychology since the 1960s has been the supposedly deleterious influence of violent mass media on human behavior. This has become an area rife with implications based on morality with implications for public policy—in other words, more opportunities for social engineering based on the application of psychological "science" to the critique and control of popular culture.

NOTES

1. Marion Gross Sobol says: "The effect has been referred to as the 'Hawthorne effect' by Lazersfeld in his article 'Repeated Interviews as a tool for studying changes in opinion and their causes,'" (1959:footnote 1) in the *American Statistical Association Bulletin* 2:3–7 (1941). That issue contained a *summary* of Lasersfeld's lecture, which appears to have omitted the Hawthorne reference.

2. If true, this would have been the largest interview study conducted up to that point in social science history. The first mass testing of the IQ, a similarly unprecedented large-scale data collection, was conducted by the U.S. Army in World War I, not by a team of professors from Harvard University. If the average interview took one hour, this would have required twenty-one thousand hours. This represents 525 forty-hour weeks, or just over ten personnel-years. With a team of ten interviewers, this could be done in a single year provided that research staff did nothing but interview—no time for content analysis, interpretation, or the like. It would also have taken an army of secretaries to record and transcribe the interviews. I am unaware of any student of the Hawthorne studies questioning the feasibility of such a colossal interview strategy or the extent to which it was actually carried out as reported. If a researcher could store one hundred interviews in a single archival box, there would appear to be 2,100 boxes containing such materials in a basement library at Harvard University. I am unaware if they were actually archived.

3. Even when the workers reverted to a general method of compensation, their output declined only partially. While the workers' control over take-home pay may have abated in some measure, they had become more skilled because of the reinforcement regime created in the test room.

4. Parsons does not provide a test of significance in output, preferring to report instead graphs that capture evidence of increases in "total output" for 1927–1929, followed by a decline in hours worked and total output from 1930 to 1932 (Parsons 1974:926). In comparing Parsons and Jones we find Parsons noting the increase in output while Jones's test of the effects of remuneration is nonsignificant because there is virtually no variability in the method of payment over his time series. However, everyone agrees that there was some increase, especially in the first thirteen periods of the study. Carey (1968:405–8) puts the increase at about 15 percent.

5. By this time the Pygmalion study had already been under way for two years.

6. See Rosenthal and Jacobsen (1968) Figure and Table 9.1. The references in subsequent notes refer to figures and tables in the original 1968 book.

7. See Figure and Table 7.1

8. See Figure 7.2

9. See Figure/Table 9.2

10. See Figure/Table 8.1

11. See Table 8.5.

12. See Tables 7.3 and 7.4

13. Thorndike tackles similar anomalies in the posttest scores. Table A-6 reports that for one classroom, there are six pupils with an average IQ of 150 points and a standard deviation of 40 points. Again we can estimate the mental age. At the end of grade one, if we assume that the children are 7.5 years old and if IQ = mental age/physical age, then the mental age of students with an IQ of 150 is 11.25. Again, we ask what do the scores of students with a mental age of 11.25 look like? The tables only go to a mental age of 10—and at that level the students would score 26 out of 28. Students with a mental age of 11.25 have to score even higher—but they are already approaching perfection (more than 26 out of 28). With such scores what is the meaning of a standard deviation of 40 points? The data are so untrustworthy as to make inferences based on them reckless. As Thorndike advised, when the clock strikes 13, pitch it!

14. If the $r = .14$ in a bivariate relationship (for example, IQ and teacher expectation), the calculation of the effect of variables that predict IQ in a multivariate regression model that identifies all the important determinants of IQ (for example, gender, class, family size, birth order) is expressed as the square of r. The R^2 of .14 is .0196—a correlation that is precariously close to zero when examined in the context of an appropriately specified statistical analysis. The R^2 of a bivariate .04 correlation is .0016. Such effects are tiny.

15. Contrast Worchel et al (2000: 58) with Wineburg (1987:34): "Years of replications and follow- up studies have shown that strong claims about the relationship between expectations and intelligence are unwarranted. For example, Rosenthal and his associates tried several times to replicate the expectation-IQ relationship they reported in *Pygmalion*. Evans and Rosenthal (1969) found no significant differences in IQ after a year between the treatment and control groups. A study by Conn, Edwards, Rosenthal and Crowne (1968) yielded no statistically significant differences between the treatment and control groups in total IQ after 4 months.... In another study, Anderson and Rosenthal (1968) manipulated the expectations of counselors at a day camp for retarded boys and administered an IQ test at the beginning and end of the eight-week experimental period. The only significant IQ change was a *decrease* on the reasoning subscale for the boys who were expected to bloom, a finding that clearly ran contrary to predicted results."

16. We might also distinguish the ethical legacy from the legal legacy since a number of ethical and professional considerations arise in the Pygmalion study. First, there were no permissions from the parents for the study to be undertaken using their children, no consent from the students themselves, and no informed consent regarding the other teachers who were given the bogus results of the test allegedly used to predict late bloomers. The students were frozen in the initial performance tracks for two years in spite of allegedly massive IQ changes, and no qualification of the research conclusions in the light of mixed results discovered by Rosenthal and colleagues in other field studies.

5

A Guide to the Myth of Media Effects

We do not maintain that comic books automatically cause delinquency in every child reader. . . . But we found that comic-book reading was a distinct influencing factor in the case of every single delinquent or disturbed child we studied.

—Psychiatrist Frederic Wertham, cited in Judith Crist,
"Horror in the Nursery"

In the 20 years since the publication of the Surgeon General's report, research into the TV violence issue has burgeoned. Laboratory experiments continue to provide evidence of a causal relationship between violence viewing and aggression. The results of nonexperimental field studies support the same conclusion. . . . The majority of new investigations suggest that viewing violent entertainment can increase aggression and cultivate the perception that the world is a mean and scary place.

—R. M. Liebert and J. Sprafkin, *The Early Window:
Effects of Television on Children and Youth*

INTRODUCTION

It is difficult to determine when fears about the adverse affects of mass media became a preoccupation of the respectable classes, and motivated attempts to bring the worrisome elements of popular fiction under the control of the state and the courts. In his history of pornography, Walter Kendrick (1988), records how the eighteenth-century excavation of the ruins of Pompeii, buried in 79 A.D. by the eruption of Mount Vesuvius, brought to light household statues and paintings from ancient Roman culture that revealed an extraordinary sexual frankness.[1] Such vivid sexual representation was found so offensive in Enlightenment Europe that the

91

materials were housed in a secret museum in Naples that restricted public access. The very catalog was considered x-rated and access was confined to the male ranks of the privileged classes. What Kendrick calls the "pre-pornographic" culture began to unwind in the nineteenth century. Puritanical sexual inhibitions came under pressure with the spread of literacy in the nineteenth century. Popular fiction exposed readers to the negative influence of permissive writing. "Genteel society" objected to the publication of Mark Twain's *Adventures of Huckleberry Finn* in 1885, and the book was banned from the Concord Library in Massachusetts as "trash suitable only for the ghetto." There are many tokens of this change. In the late 1930s, the appearance of comic books was greeted by alarm, and many U.S. states (as well as Canada, Britain, and several European countries) attempted to ban the comics under obscenity laws. According to Frederic Wertham, a New York psychiatrist, the provocative "comic" covers, the adult crime themes, and the celebration of violence were believed to promote juvenile delinquency, racism, and homosexuality. His book, *Seduction of the Innocents* (1954), and his coverage in popular magazines struck a chord with the public. Here was a psychiatric authority who shared the public's misgivings about the influence of perverse literature.

A public inquiry into the causes of delinquency in the early 1950s chaired by Senator Estes Kefauver raised questions about the influence of mass media on youthful misconduct. Questions of imitation of criminal behavior had been raised earlier in some of the Payne Foundation studies of motion pictures in the thirties and forties. Paul Lazersfeld had studied the influence of radio on political opinions in the forties and fifties, although he found little evidence for significant shifts in political opinion related to campaign speeches (see Hovland 1959). However, U.S. academic funding of mass media effects, especially television, was in its infancy until the early 1960s. The work of Bandura, Ross, and Ross (1963) raised questions about the vulnerability of youth to messages of violence in children's programming, including the popular Saturday morning cartoons. Bandura (1973) advanced a model of influence known as "social learning theory" in which people could acquire new behaviors through vicarious experience, i.e., seeing other people benefiting from a specific behavior and mimicking it with expectations of gaining a similar benefit. The sixties saw the emergence of lab studies of imitative violence, as well as long-term field studies of the correlation between violent media exposure and aggressive behavior. Interest in the question of media effects in America grew as crime rates exploded throughout the fifties, sixties, and seventies.

In 1972 the U.S. Surgeon General issued a report on the effects of television violence that cautiously expressed some concerns about the inadvertent effect of violent entertainment on viewers. Its conclusions were couched in highly conditional language, i.e., television "can" induce short-term mimicry in children, it "can" instigate an increase in aggressive acts, however, the evidence "does not warrant the conclusion that television violence has a uniformly adverse effect nor the conclusion that it has an adverse effect on the majority of children" (National Institute of Mental Health 1982, cited in Liebert and Sprafkin 1988:113). This cautious publication appeared in the golden age of media effects research. At the instigation of mass media researchers, a new report was prepared a decade later under the auspices of the National Institute of Mental Health: *Television and Behavior: Ten Years of Scientific Progress and Implications for the Eighties*. The 1982 report updated the empirical findings, and concluded that the evidence supported inferences of a *causal* link between exposure to violent TV and aggressive behavior among viewers, suggesting that there was a wide consensus among social scientists about this fact, and that the conclusions were based on the "convergence" of different kinds of evidence, none decisive on its own, but convincing when taken together.

The NIMH report created a lot of public and academic debate. Studies of the effects of TV violence on children gave way to investigations of the impact of pornography on male readers and viewers, using many of the same experimental protocols employed in the TV research. Theories of media effects appeared in the court system, sometimes as evidence in support of defenses of temporary media-induced insanity, sometimes in cases where victims of violence sought compensation from broadcasters for attacks resulting from media imitation.[2] In the case of pornography, evidence from experimental social psychologists was influential in revising the common law of obscenity.

After all this time and effort, one would think that psychology had come to some firm conclusions about the way violent media influence human behavior, and that regulatory action could be developed on evidence-based policies. But that is not what occurred. In what follows, I examine the preoccupation of media studies with violence. I then examine whether the social learning theory is a truly distinct form of learning. We shall explore some peculiarities of the logic of experimental social psychology, the difference between statistical significance and effect sizes, and the policy significance of decontextualized effect studies. Finally, I want to explore the extrascientific incentives that underlie the media effects academy. We begin with the preoccupation with media violence.

SOCIAL LEARNING THEORY, TV, AND THE SPECTER OF VIOLENCE

Psychologists are proud to point out that the field is based on three great models of learning. First, there is the classical conditioning model based on experiments with Pavlov's dogs, where he produced salivation by pairing an unconditioned stimulus (a bell) with a conditioned stimulus (food), showing that the animals learned to salivate at the sound of the bell. Second, there is operant conditioning, or trial and error learning, based on (among other things) Skinner's studies of rats and T-mazes, and the differential rewards attached to choosing correct pathways, rewards that accelerated animal responses. In the late fifties, experimental social psychologists sought out a third explanation of learned behavior peculiar to humans, and reflective of their sophisticated cognitive abilities. Bandura's *social* learning theory was the chief theoretical basis for lab studies of the behavioral and attitudinal changes attributed to the new electronic media. However, it had a number of peculiarities that ultimately would impede its success. In retrospect, the first was the remarkable narrowness in what it examined. It was preoccupied with aggression, and it selected stimulus programs from *Batman* to the *Road Runner* cartoons as though aggression was the main "lesson" of such programs and as though this was the only effect worth noting. TV violence was the theory, aggression was the practice. Aggression became a proxy for all that was problematic with youthful behavior. Nobody seemed to wonder whether movies that portrayed theft, prostitution, or narcotics encouraged viewers to steal, prostitute, or get stoned. Did comedies make viewers inclined to tell funny stories and act like comedians? Did *Raiders of the Lost Ark* and *The Temple of Doom* encourage viewers to study archaeology? Did *Caddy Shack* encourage viewers to take up golf?

The virtually exclusive focus on aggression has been remarkably one-dimensional. This has gone hand in hand with a presupposition about the peculiar vulnerability of children. The implication is that social learning occurs primarily in childhood. The famous longitudinal studies of the lagged effect of early childhood TV viewing habits on aggression (Huesmann, Eron, Lefkowitz, and Walden 1973, 1984) ten and twenty years later assume an age-graded developmental model in which violent media exposure creates persistent antisocial behaviors, and that these are determined by media exposure in "the early window."

Of course, this model is contradicted when the same media effects paradigm is applied to pornography. There are reports that suggest that even extremely short exposures to sexually violent, highly arousing pictures can foster rape fantasies and calloused attitudes in otherwise normal men (Malamuth and Check 1981). Men, like children, appear to be extremely vulnerable to the media, especially sexually violent media exposure. But there is no supposition here of an age-contingent impact since the studies of pornography effects deal exclusively with adults, i.e., persons whose dispositions one would have thought were already stable, having been laid down in childhood. When one sees the research agenda of the media effects experts in the sixties, seventies, eighties, it is hard to escape the proposition that the effects of greatest interest were decided a priori in the world of respectable fears about the vulnerability of children and women, and the apparent invasiveness of the new technologies. For every one study on the positive effects of children's programming on literacy, there were twenty-five studies on the consequences of sex and violence. However, even the evidence for the positive effects of *Sesame Street* were probably mediated by child-parent interaction in the context of viewing (Wurtzel and Lometti 1984:36).

In 1971 Leonard Berkowitz wrote an influential comment in *Psychology Today* in which he contrasted the 1970 Presidential Commission on Obscenity and Pornography and the Presidential Commission on the Causes and Prevention of Violence. "Sex and Violence: We can't have it both ways." The former concluded that exposure to sexually explicit fiction was unassociated with harmful behavioral consequences, while the latter found that violence on television promoted violence in everyday life and reinforced attitudes conducive to violence. The former report called for a liberal policy towards sexual fiction, the latter called for elimination of violence in children's cartoons and a reduction in violent programming more generally. While on the surface these looked like radically inconsistent understandings of media effects, we should not overlook the fact that the violence commission was looking at the vulnerability of children and youth, while the pornography commission was looking at adults.

SOCIAL LEARNING AND COMMON SENSE

A second point is that the social learning model appears to be quite a modest intellectual perspective, when we move away from specific technologies (TV) and specific prohibited behaviors (aggression) and when we conceive of it in more general terms. Indeed, it's very commonsensical. Note that there is nothing in the theory that would establish that persons are *peculiarly* vulnerable to TV, as opposed to other sources of information—parents, siblings, peers, school teachers, newspapers, books, neighbors, moral teaching, etc. But social learning theory cut its teeth on television and the subsequent video technology without reference to how social learning worked in all human history prior to the intrusion of the national networks into family life in the fifties, and how it continued to work in everyday life outside television. In other words, the very idea of social learning only emerged with the rise of television. Furthermore, the intellectual study of social learning coappeared with a specific social agenda, i.e., its long-standing interests in censoring children's programming, a position that amounts to promoting certain social values in the name of science and "public health." The social agenda of regulating television was premised on the understanding that it had become one of the most important sources of learning, that it was the source of *decisive* social models and hence one of the most important determinants of behavior, including deviant behavior. This was a *premise* from the very start, and one that the experiments were designed to demonstrate. The early Bobo doll studies were designed to showcase how children learned bad habits from watching cartoons. The fact that the Bobo doll was *designed* to be punched, and that some forms of punching and roughhousing in the context of male play can be wholesome behavior were overlooked. Like other studies in the golden age of experimentation, the lesson was allegorical. Subtract the element of play from the subjects' response, equate the Bobo doll to another innocent child, and, voilà, our worst fears were realized.

There is a definite moral cast in the attitudes of psychologists to popular television dramas and cartoons in the sixties. They assume that the violence in *Batman*, *Superman*, and cowboy fiction is rewarded, and that the viewers are converted to the dark side as a consequence. But the vast majority of so-called violent fiction results in the punishment of the wicked and the reward of the virtuous (Fowles 1999). This is the cathartic attraction of all popular fiction, a point consistently missed by those who believe that catharsis in fiction is only interesting if it alters behavior afterwards and somehow lets the viewer "blow off steam." The catharsis I refer to is the identification with the hero, the suspense experienced as the hero faces danger, our fear and contempt of the villains, our anxieties as the plot goes their way, and our relief as the cavalry rides in to restore what used to be referred to as "truth, justice, and the American way." Without catharsis, fiction would be totally lacking any dramatic attraction. Why would we presuppose that human viewers would miss the almost clichéd moral nature of popular entertainment, the Punch and Judy portrayal of good and evil? In my view, the failure to grasp this point has been a fatal flaw in social learning theory, and has led researchers to overlook the situational impact of even short-term media exposure on emotional volatility in the lab, something that is frequently misinterpreted as imitation. We shall return to this point later since it addresses a major theoretical inconsistency in understanding the meaning of the apparently high impact of media on behavior in lab studies of aggression.

IS SOCIAL LEARNING THEORY DISTINCTIVE?

What is the actual mechanism (or mechanisms) that contributes to social learning? Psychologists write at times as though changes in behavior occur below the threshold of consciousness. When social learning occurs, are we simply talking about absorbing cultural images as though they were normal, i.e., unnoticed? In other words, we grow up in the Shire and think as Hobbits or we grow up in Rivendel and think as Elves (Tolkien 1966). The worldviews are radically different but experienced as natural. Stereotypes are probably communicated this way. Indeed, there was some concern among psychologists that TV shows like *Amos and Andy* portrayed African-Americans in an unfavorable light. The same point is made today in the analysis of pornography as an insult to the status of women. But the concept of *selective exposure* to certain worldviews is not a specific mechanism of learning, unless we acquire conditioned responses to categories of people in the same process. In that case, this conceptualization of social learning amounts to classical conditioning. In other words, my reaction to a specific class of people (for example, a member of a racial, religious, or linguistic group) is conditioned by prior stereotypes or idealizations (favorable or unfavorable) associated with such groups in the media.

A second issue is whether the observed behavior that is mimicked must result in a reward of which we vicariously approve and pursue for our own benefit. We mimic a colleague's behavior because we see that it resulted in certain benefits. Does this happen subconsciously? Or would we be aware of consequences of action and consciously make similar choices? Is that not a case of "judgment," i.e., choosing wisely through generalization from a stimulus in our own everyday experiences? In that case, this conceptualization of social learning amounts to operant conditioning. I follow my mentor's advice because I expect to benefit from it— generalizing from his or her case to my own. Following this line of reasoning, social learning is not a distinctive form of learning. Indeed, it is arguably trivial or obvious. The argument from social learning theory amounts to the observation that we take our own culture for granted (selective exposure leading to classical conditioning) and/or we maximize our utilities as classical economics suggests (trial and error). There is nothing new or mysterious here. Perhaps the paradigm's focus on children makes such selective exposure (classic conditioning) on the one hand, and self-reflection (operant conditioning) on the other less than obvious, since we assume children are naïve and unreflective. Again, that would be an indication that social learning is premised on immaturity, or a specific theory of development as noted earlier.

Is there another approach to social learning that tacitly acknowledges the power of fiction to create arousal? When we observe that children may be acting more immaturely or impulsively in the aftermath of provocative images, are we not registering the cathartic, stimulating (i.e., plain "entertaining") effects of drama? When we "act out" in the aftermath of exposure to a "violent" cartoon, have we somehow been seduced by a subconscious mechanism of which we are only dimly aware? Is there some magical effect that sweeps us up into activities that would be terminated on a moment of mature self-reflection and/or social control? And do our individual careers evolve by such acts of magic? In either case, social learning theory would be really very novel, nontrivial, and provocative. I think that something like that does occur and that it is tied to catharsis, i.e., arousal. We shall get to the magic in due course. We began this discussion by questioning whether there really is strong consensus about harmful effects of violent fiction.

WHERE IS THE CONSENSUS ABOUT MEDIA EFFECTS?

What does the record show regarding consensus and why is that important? In 1995 Leonard Eron told a U.S. Senate hearing that "the scientific debate is over" about the harmful effects of violent TV programming, that the relationship was a settled scientific fact (Fowles 1999:20). The record suggests otherwise, both in the area of violent TV and pornography. It is difficult in the new century to appreciate the animosity associated with the debate over media effects over the last few decades. Psychologists who thought television was creating negative impacts on younger viewers besmirched the motives of the television industry experts who contested the evidence of harmful effects, as though academic researchers were impervious to their own interests. The gold ribbon panel that assembled the NIMH document wrote that "it would be no exaggeration to compare [the] attempt by the television industry [to contest evidence of harm] to the stubborn public position of the tobacco industry on the scientific evidence about smoking and health" (Chaffee et al. 1984:30–31).[3] The parallels strike me as hugely self-serving since it implies that people who work for universities have fewer career interests and ideological preferences than those in industry, a position difficult to sustain if we reflect on the previous chapters. In the case of tobacco, animal studies could be used with nicotine products to induce cancers in mice, providing evidence of a strong, direct effect. Lab studies of human violence tended to employ tests based on analogies to violence that were typically short-lived and metaphorical. Evidence from field studies was inconsistent and contradictory, and the zero order correlations (r) between media exposure and subsequent behavior were typically weak. Failures to replicate the presumably well-established findings from the lab have been common.[4] Also, the social nature of aggression studied in the lab and violence in everyday life were typically worlds apart. A methodological note is in order here regarding the experimental approach. Lab studies of aggression were conducted primarily within a research protocol called "the Buss paradigm."

The Buss paradigm was developed to explore the causes of aggression. Subjects are put into a high state of emotional discharge, typically by being insulted by a confederate (a person working for the experimenter but pretending to be just another subject). Subjects are then assigned to some kind of treatment condition (for example, one of several different kinds of film), and finally, in a supposedly unrelated third phase of the experiment, are asked to administer shocks to the person who earlier had insulted them. The experiment picks up the media effect of the intervening treatment usually only in the presence of the high state of arousal. Berkowitz puts it this way: "The observer will exhibit the highest aggressive reactions if he is emotionally aroused at the time, believes his aggressive actions will have favorable rather than unfavorable consequences, and thinks the observed victims had deserved the injury inflicted on them" (1971:18). So the evidence of harm is somewhat oblique. As in the Milgram paradigm, the subjects are encouraged to administer shocks to teach them a task, as though this were legitimate ("favorable"), and then their behaviors are equated with giving "injury."

The limited utility of the lab evidence for the impact of media on aggression is suggested by the treatment of this subject in the classic textbooks in criminology. Wilson and Herrnstein (1985:337ff.) review the case for television and the mass media impact on crime in *Crime and Human Nature*. Of the field studies they say, "The best studies come to contradictory conclusions, and even when all doubts are resolved in favor of a causal effect, they account for only 'trivial proportions' of individual differences in aggression" (ibid.:346). When experts assembled by the National Research Council reviewed the 1982 NIMH report, they concluded that televised violence "may" be related to aggression, "but the magnitude of the relationship is small and the meaning of aggression is unclear" (ibid.:353). "Even giving to existing research the most generous interpretation, viewing televised violence cannot explain more than a very small proportion of the variation in aggressive acts among young persons" (ibid.). Similarly Kaplan and Singer argued, following a review of the literature, that "this research has failed to demonstrate that TV appreciably affects aggression in our daily lives" (1976:62). Feshbach and Singer reported no evidence from field studies that violent fantasy programming aroused aggression. In fact, there was some evidence "that exposure to aggressive content on television seems to reduce or control the expression of aggression in aggressive boys from low socioeconomic backgrounds" (1971:145). In Freedman's review of the field studies, he reported that "not one study produced strong consistent results, and most produced a substantial number of negative findings" (1988:158; see also Freedman 1984, 1986). David Gauntlett reported "the search for 'direct' effects of television on behavior is over: Every effort has been made and they simply cannot be found" (1995:120). Gadow and Sprafkin: "The findings from the field experiments offer little support for the media aggression hypothesis" (1989:404). Attempts to replicate abroad earlier

work conducted in America by Huesmann et al. drew the same disappointing reactions. Wiegman, Kuttschreuter, and Baarda reported from
Australia: "These results give no support for the hypothesis that television
violence viewing will, in the long term, contribute to a higher level of
aggression in children" (1992:155).

This shows up one of the peculiar methodological directions resulting from a nearly exclusive reliance on experimentation and quasi-
experimentation. The subject matter of research is more focused on the predictor (the causes) than the outcome (the effects). This permits the
experimenter to hold onto a cause no matter how substantively trivial, and
to remain ignorant of the main contours of the phenomenon of interest that
it effects. The media effects research shed light on the programs but told us
virtually nothing about the phenomenon of violence in everyday life.
Rather than asking what are the major causes of violence, and what are the
recurrent contributions of gender, age, individual differences, and class, all
our time is devoted to a single predictor—the media. As many commenta-
tors have pointed out, this probably reflects the value orientation of the
researchers. "Social scientists tend to abhor violence and dislike much of
popular culture; it is only natural, therefore, that when the public worries
about what television may do to their children, especially when there is a
rising level of violence in society, scholars would concentrate their efforts
on showing how televised violence . . . increases the violence of television
viewers, especially children" (Wilson and Herrnstein 1985:339). One of the
costs of this approach is that it is unclear how much effect censorship policies could be expected to have even if they were adopted. If the correlation
between media and subsequent behavior is .1 to .2, the explained variance
adjusted for all the other major predictors of aggression would be about 1
to 4 percent. Liebert and Sprafkin argue in defense of the monocausal
analysis as follows: "Researchers have said that TV violence is *a* cause of
aggressiveness, not that it is *the* cause of aggressiveness. There is no *one*, single cause of any social behavior" (1988:161, emphasis in original). This is
true, but without some knowledge of the other leading causes, it is impossible to identify its *relative* importance. And without that, we cannot determine whether something that is statistically significant has any social
significance. It is noteworthy that in the most recent Surgeon General's
report on *Youth Violence* (Satcher 1999), reference to media effects is virtually absent, in spite of the views of some medical experts that violent programming is "the number one public health issue" responsible, in the
estimates of Brandon Centerwall (1993:63), for ten thousand homicides
each year in the United States.

The issue of media effects is discussed in a second leading criminology
textbook, *A General Theory of Crime*. In their review of psychological posi-

tivism, and its preoccupation with aggression, Gottfredson and Hirschi (1990:67ff.) note that psychologists sometimes stumble into the larger world of misconduct outside aggression. Huesmann, Eron, Lefkowitz, and Walder define aggression as:

> an act that injures or irritates another person. This definition excludes self-hurt ... but makes no distinction between accidental and instrumental aggression or between socially acceptable and antisocial aggression. The assumption is that there is a response class, aggression, that can include a variety of behaviors, exhibited in numerous situations, all of which result in injury or irritation to another person. This category includes both hitting and hurting behaviors, whether or not these behaviors are reinforced by pain cues from the victim or target person. This category also includes injury to or theft of property. (cited in Eron 1987:435)

How can aggression include property crimes? The inclusion of such crimes would make sense if the "response class" is a general tendency toward dysfunctional or impulsive behavior. That comes close to the criminological understanding, as we shall see. In the "Rip Van Winkle study," as it has become known, Huesmann, Eron, Lefkowitz, and Walder examined 875 subjects in grade three classes in upper New York State starting in 1960, identifying television viewing habits and peer-nominated levels of aggression. Mothers were asked to identify the children's three most popular television programs, which were then classified as either violent or nonviolent. Ten years later and again twenty-two years later, the subjects were followed up to determine their viewing habits as well as their criminal involvement. The findings suggested that early signs of aggression, especially in males, predicted patterns of aggression later in life, that the most aggressive children watched the most television, and that aggression was also related to lower IQ. Eron attributed the aggression to "continued television violence viewing" (1987:440) (although continued viewing was not observed).

However, as Gottfredson and Hirschi point out, television-viewing at age eight would equally well predict "theft, motor-vehicle accidents, trivial nonviolent offending, drug consumption, and employment instability, behaviors hard to attribute to the number of shootings or fistfights watched on television twenty years previously" (1990:69). Indeed Eron reports that childhood aggression in fact predicted "social failure, psychopathology, aggression and low educational and occupational success" (1987:440) twenty-two years later. Why? All kinds of dysfunctional behaviors tend to cluster in the same persons. Individuals who are "aggressive" do not tend to specialize in aggressiveness but exhibit a short temporal horizon or impulsiveness across whole "response classes." Gottfredson and Hirschi: "It therefore seems unlikely that the specific content of television programming viewed at age eight could contribute independently to subsequent levels of aggression" (1990:69) This is because they are all an expression of the same stable traits. This could explain why media viewing habits could be correlated with a range of dysfunctional behaviors without being an important determinant of them. Persons with a high tolerance of risk are not disturbed by provocative excitement, so the coappearance of a high-exposure threshold and a high-risk behavioral threshold is a predictable correlation. The traits that Huesmann et al. documented showed remarkable stability over the life course. "What is not arguable is that aggressive behavior, however engendered, once established, remains remarkable stable across time, situations and even generations within a family" (1984:1133). This was consistent with the earlier report of Olweus (1979:866), who showed impressive continuity in individual traits over the life cycle; over a ten-year period, the estimated coefficients were on the order of .60 for aggression and .70 for intelligence.

CAUSAL TESTING VERSUS POPULATION PROCESSES

There is one further point that must be mentioned regarding the utility of media effects in the context of criminology versus experimental psychology. As Berkowitz and Donnerstein (1982) argue, the theoretical purpose of an experiment may not be to determine a population estimate of some effect. Indeed, for some purposes it might be totally appropriate in order to test a specific causal relationship that the lab setting has little "mundane realism," i.e., little resemblance to familiar situations in everyday life. For example, the Buss paradigm may be attractive for teasing out the relative impact of an *explicit* film versus a *sexually aggressive* film. The fact that the subjects begin in a state of high emotional discharge, and that the experiment forces retaliatory aggression without permitting the subjects an opportunity to calm down may permit the estimation of the marginal differences in behavior resulting from different stimuli when all the other factors are held constant and/or when all the common restraints on aggression are eliminated. As a result, this situation may not correspond to anything found in everyday life. It may correspond to natural situations by degree, but, in some cases, it may be something found only in the lab. Henshel (1980) makes a case for this when he points out, for example, that temperatures of zero degrees Kelvin (and the effect of absolute cold on the electrical properties of magnets) are not found in nature, but can be created in a lab. Similarly, the teaching of American sign language to primates may permit scientists to learn something of primate cognitive abilities but it is not natural behavior. Berkowitz and Donnerstein recognize this possibility when they say "we are not insisting that the laboratory findings are necessarily generalizable to the world outside" (1982:255). There is a recognition that the experimentalist oftentimes exchanges ecological validity for causal control. What is difficult to determine is the extent to which the controlled world of the lab actually helps us understand the magnitude of manipulations when we want to extrapolate back from the controlled environment to everyday life.

> Even if we confine ourselves to psychological influences, the laboratory setting is not necessarily representative of the social world within which many people act. As a consequence we cannot use laboratory findings to estimate the likelihood that a certain class of responses will occur in naturalistic situations. Suppose that 60% of the subjects in a sample exhibit heightened aggressiveness over some baseline level when a weapon is present. Even if these people were representative of the persons in a larger population, we could not say, of course, that 60% of this broader group would react in the same way in a more realistic situation. Experiments are not conducted to yield such an estimate. (ibid.)

Therefore, discovering a causal relationship (which may be positive or negative) and a population estimate of its magnitude (0–1.0) are quite separate objectives. However, there is another matter raised in the title ("external validity is more than skin deep"). Berkowitz and Donnerstein stress that despite the artificiality of the learning situation, the experiment is valid because the subjects in the Buss paradigm experience an intense desire for revenge, and they administer shocks believing that they are hurting someone, someone who deserves to be punished for insulting them. In other words, the experiment has intense realism for participants that is more than skin deep. They "mean" it. However, if this is the real point of distinguishing causal-testing and a population modeling, two problems arise. First, because experiments are not based on a sampling frame, it is never possible to provide population estimates of anything with confidence. Second, the claim that the artificial manipulations still retain "realism" amounts to a claim that the *internal* validity of the experiment is sound, and that the definition of the situation (insult and subjective provocation) is credible to the subjects even if the tasks that produce such reactions are unfamiliar, i.e., in this case that the participants' conduct was sincere, and not just role-playing or following demand characteristics. But that is an empirical question the answer to which would turn on a validity check. "Appropriate questioning is vital to insure that the participants have interpreted the experimental treatments in the desired way" (ibid.). Even if the subjects defined the situation as serious, the experimenter is claiming external or ecological validity without knowing the probable ecological conditions to which the experiment applies. The causal leverage attributed to human experiments in this situation is point-less since the conditions of their ecological expression cannot be known with any confidence or precision.

THE MAGIC IN AROUSAL THEORY

Earlier we discussed the theoretical mechanisms attributed to social learn-ing explanations. We return to that issue here. In *Seductions of Crime*, Jack Katz (1988) argues that to explain the attractions of deviance you must believe in magic. *Seductions of Crime* is a phenomenological approach to deviant behavior that emphasizes the foreground of experience in the com-mission of crimes. Where the majority of criminologists stress the causal role of such background factors as family conflict, community disorgani-zation, and class conflict, Katz argues that the clue to explaining crime is the "sensory attractions of doing evil," the physical pleasures of sneaky thrills, righteous slaughter, and doing "stickup." Katz refers to "magic" as the process in which people let themselves be seduced by the criminal proj-ect. "To believe that a person can suddenly feel propelled to crime without any independently verifiable change in his background, it seems we must almost believe in magic" (ibid.:4). As a phenomenologist, Katz rejects causal explanations, but he stresses that people sometimes act as though they are forced by circumstances to behave badly. The key to the explana-tion is the powerful effects that emotions have on us. In Katz's perspective, people sometimes let themselves be seduced by their emotions. They sur-render to circumstances and situations, although he characterizes this as "an artifice" in the sense that this process involves an element of self-delu-sion. Persons are capable of resisting temptation but "give in" as though they are compelled by emotions. For example, a person who encounters humiliation can refashion it as an act of self-defensive rage, and strike out at the provocateur in "righteous slaughter." Intense emotional arousal deriving from the situation is at the core of the behavior. The impulse to kill is probably common in many of our social encounters but it is successfully stifled by self-control in most cases.

When we discussed social learning theory, I suggested that there may be a nonobvious process that operates in the cases of media exposure that is neither equivalent to classical conditioning effects nor operant condi-tioning. I would now add that it does not involve mimicry at all, but appears to result from an artifact of emotional arousal. The typical evi-dence for media effects in both TV and pornography studies discovers aggressive effects only when subjects are highly aroused (i.e., male sub-jects are insulted by a female confederate) and only when the experi-menter *requires* the angry subjects to administer shocks to their female aggressor (under the pretext of a learning exercise). Fisher and Grenier (1994) attempted to replicate some of the critical work on pornography effects from Donnerstein (1983) that purported to show how certain themes in pornography facilitated aggression against women. Donnerstein reported that films that combined both aggression and erotic elements boosted shock levels given by male subjects to female targets higher than films containing either aggressive or erotic stimuli alone. In their replication of this work, Fisher and Grenier gave the subjects the option of skipping the learning experiment (and forgoing the administration of shocks) and proceeding directly to the debriefing. The vast majority of the subjects, even if angered, opted to skip this opportunity for retaliation and proceed towards the debriefing. In other words, the link between the stimulus films and the aggressive outcome reported in earlier work was an artifact of the design, i.e., not even skin deep (see Fisher and Barak 1991).

But the nature of the aggression is far from clear. In an earlier work, Donnerstein reported that "aggressive behavior in subjects who have previously been angered has been shown to be increased by exposure to arousing sources such as aggressive-erotic films, physical exercise, drugs, and noise" (1980:279). Zillmann and Bryant (1982, 1984) used films of an eye operation and discovered that these boosted levels of aggression. Tannenbaum (1972:330) discovered that a humorous film had the same result. "Even viewing 'Sesame Street' or 'Mister Roger's Neighborhood' induced a threefold increase in aggression among preschoolers who initially measured low on aggressiveness" (Fowles 1999:28). However, the underlying process as understood by Zillmann and Bryant is called "excitation transfer." The subjects are angry because they have been insulted. The anger response tends to abate with time, but before it does so, it becomes reenergized by an intervening arouser. The pornographic films are important, not because they contain a message about women, as social learning theories suggest, but because they are highly arousing. Just as a stomach-churning film of an operation can transfer excitation to a previous source of arousal, so can an aversive noise, or a humorous film. The initial retaliatory impulses that arise from provocation are boosted by the intervening stimulus and the subjects react with more anger than they are probably aware of. But the effect is short-lived since once the anger has abated, the aggression is no longer fueled by the emotional distress at the heart of the Buss paradigm. Also, in their longer term (nine-week) study, Zillmann and Bryant suggested that pornographic films lost their ability to arouse (and fuel aggression) after repeated exposures so that the ability of the films to promote retaliatory violence became naturally self-limiting. Writing about TV, Zillmann came to the same conclusion. "It would thus appear likely that repeated exposure to dramatic portrayals of violent crime reduces rather than increases affective reactions" (1991:123).[5]

The focus on arousal may be helpful in understanding one of Donnerstein's key findings. He reports that males respond more aggressively following aggressive-erotic exposure, but only when the target (i.e., the instigator) is female, as opposed to male. The inference that social learning theorists draw is that the subjects equate the females in the film with the female confederate, but it is just as plausible that the female confederates are a *greater* source of arousal per se than male confederates. And/or that males react more powerfully to insults from a woman than another man. Either way, the mechanism is the type and level of arousal, not social learning. As for the cognitive effects of viewing the pornographic films, we return again to Fisher and Grenier's (1994) study, which sheds some light on this. This study was based on the same video that Donnerstein had used when testing for the effects of positive-outcome versus negative-outcome rape scenarios. Fisher and Grenier measured whether the various types of films (positive- and negative-outcome rape, erotica, neutral) were perceived differently in terms of the woman's apparent willingness to participate in the sexual activities and her apparent enjoyment. Perceptions varied significantly across the different film conditions as expected, but the expected change in attitudes and fantasies was not found. Even though earlier studies suggested that extremely brief exposure to violent pornography causes men to fantasize about rape, and to increase acceptance of rape myths, there was no evidence of such outcomes in this study. Fisher and Grenier measured the aggressive/violent content in self-generated fantasies, violent content in Thematic Apperception Test scores, scores in attitudes toward women, acceptance of interpersonal violence, and rape myth acceptance. There was no difference across any of the treatment groups. Fisher and Grenier concluded: "The current review on the literature on violent pornography, together with the current failures to observe effects of violent pornography on men's attitudes, fantasies, and behavior toward women, raises serious questions about the reliability of effects of violent pornography within the experimental procedures that have been used in research in this area" (ibid.:36).[6] And just as the field studies of TV violence show little consistent relationship to the acquisition of violent behaviors, the survey research on the association between violent pornography and antiwoman aggression has rarely indicated a link (ibid.:25).[7]

THE MEDIA EFFECTS RESEARCH, PUBLIC POLICY, AND LAW

The media effects research community has long lobbied for public policies to abate the harmful consequences of sex and violence in the popular culture, in comics, on TV, in pornography, and most recently in video games. However, until about 1960 social sciences did not have much to say about the systematic effects of the new media—whether TV, radio, or comics. After that point, a great deal of public money was devoted to showing just how harmful the media were, especially television. Beginning around 1970 there was a series of national commissions of inquiry, primarily in the United States, also in Britain and Canada, devoted to researching and summarizing the effects of TV violence on the one hand, and pornography on the other. But there was a remarkable lack of consensus about whether there were significant consequences to viewers from exposure to any of this material. On the TV side, there was the 1968 National Commission on the Causes and Prevention of Violence. Verdict: TV probably incites aggression, but no new research was commissioned. This was followed in 1970 by the President's Commission on Obscenity and Pornography. After two million dollars of new research, the verdict: pornography got a clean bill of health. Then the Surgeon General's Study of TV (1972) appeared with another million dollars of research. Verdict: TV causes aggression in everyday life. When the National Science Foundation reviewed the conclusions they replaced "TV causes aggression" with "TV *may* cause aggression in small numbers of individuals vulnerable to its influence." In 1979 in Britain the Williams Committee into Obscenity examined the behavioral consequences of exposure to pornography—another clean bill of health. In 1982 the National Institute of Mental Health revised the earlier Surgeon General's report, and reported "a convergence of evidence" suggesting a causal role for violent TV. In 1985 Canada's Fraser Committee of Inquiry into Pornography and Prostitution rejected the evidence of harm. The committee reported that "the research [on the effects of pornography] is so inadequate and chaotic that no consistent body of information has been established"—but a year later—1986—in the United States, Attorney General Meese's committee came to totally different conclusions. Why the differences? What appears to have made the difference was the increasing importance attached to the experimental studies and the decline in the use of field studies and criminological evidence linking media exposure to actual deviant outcomes. The experimental literature was to have a worrisome impact on the development of law.

In 1983 and 1984 Minneapolis and Indianapolis passed municipal ordinances to create liabilities for persons selling pornography that depicted "the graphic sexually explicit subordination of women, whether in pictures or words" or "in positions of servility or submission or display" (cited in De Grazia 1992:614). As Richard A. Posner (1988) noted, the law was much broader in its reach than the *Miller* test.[8] "The Bible contains many instances of what by contemporary standards is misogyny; so do *Paradise Lost* and *The Taming of the Shrew*, not to mention *Eumenides*—the list is endless" (De Grazia 1992:615). The ordinances were drafted by Catherine MacKinnon (1985) and Andrea Dworkin (1985), and supported by a coalition of

conservatives, the religious Right, and radical feminists. The logic underlying the new legal approach came from the experimental effects literature,
the literature of the Buss paradigm. It was the same literature that carried
the day in the Meese Commission in 1986. However, given the robust protection of the First Amendment, the municipal ordinances went nowhere.
The first was vetoed by the mayor of Minneapolis, the second was found
unconstitutional by the U.S. Supreme Court in 1986. It is interesting that
when the Meese Commission became an obvious pawn of the religious
Right, the media experts in psychology tried to divorce themselves from
the "overinterpretation" of the effects literature (see Linz, Penrod, and
Donnerstein 1987). In other words, those who supported MacKinnon and
Dworkin for politically correct reasons at the beginning of this policy crusade by basing their models on a concern for female victimization, divorced
themselves from the crusade for politically correct reasons as the politics of
censorship shifted to the Right (see Russell 1993).[9]

The protection accorded speech in the United States provides some protection against such acts of censorship, at least in principle. As recently as
1990, Dennis Barrie, the curator of Cincinnati's Contemporary Art's Center, was charged under Ohio obscenity law for exhibiting a collection of
Robert Mapplethorpe photographs, and 2 Live Crew was charged in
Florida for obscene song lyrics (De Grazia 1992:654–56). Both cases led to
acquittals, where charges should probably never have been laid in the first
place. What the United States and Canadian cases illustrate is the power
of interest groups to use the criminal law to advance their own values and
interests. What we have not discussed is the role of psychologists and
other media experts in assuming a role in this process. We turn to that now.

CONCLUSION: HIDDEN AGENDAS IN SCIENTIFIC
AND MORAL LEADERSHIP

Jib Fowles (1999) makes a convincing case for the idea that the academic
industry devoted to the identification of negative media effects has an
unacknowledged cultural foundation. Claims of dire consequences can be
advanced on the weakest, most inconsistent evidence because the condemnation of violence is based, not on science, but on what we called in earlier chapters "extrascientific" incentives. Media violence is, in Fowles's
term, "a perfect whipping boy" because media changes are such a large target (even if we need to exaggerate the level of violence), because hostilities
in fact or fiction are provocative, and because "the issue attracts no supporters. Virtually no one speaks out in defense of television violence . . . as
a whipping boy, television violence could hardly be improved" (ibid.:55).
Television violence represents the culture of the plebeians, society's cruder

elements, the great unwashed face of unruly youth. Fowles points out that real class antagonisms have diminished tremendously in the last century, without disappearing entirely. Borrowing from Bourdieu, Fowles argues that the preoccupation with material comfort has been overcome with by a new kind of capital—cultural capital, the sense that what sets individuals off in contemporary society is their acquisition of refinement, an ability to make distinctions based on taste and a heightened moral sensibility. A condemnation of physical or sexual violence, especially based on expertise regarding its effects, socially elevates those who make it, and reinforces their cultural capital. "Television violence [is] an issue in the largest social struggle—that of the privileged (the baccalaureates, the dominant) against the rest (the dominated). Television violence is the rhetorical issue of choice in the dominants' efforts to demean and control the dominated" (ibid.:58). But the dominant and the dominated are not real classes—they are postures created by defining the social good effectively. The academy creates a social momentum for its visions through its ability to legitimize knowledge and define the good, and set an authoritative perspective for the rest of society.

> As keepers of the Academy and as those who make actual its mission, professors are highly valued, almost revered, members of society. They are coddled, given fewer duties than most employed people, and granted time off for one third of the year. Their autonomy (they are little accountable) replicates the autonomy of the Academy; their privileged position replicates the lofty status of the institution. Although their rewards in terms of Bourdieu's financial capital are middling, the cultural capital they accrue cannot be surpassed. . . . They may devote their entire careers to demonstrating the dangers of television violence and are bound to receive approbation from the dominant class as a result. No wonder the position of the television-effects researcher has proven so attractive. (ibid.:59–60)

The prestige of the academy is further enhanced by setting the pace for normative controls in the legal order, redefining the kinds of images that harm, the forms of control that are "justified," and making the social development of children and women dependent on a scientifically grounded agenda. Besides law, the prestige of the academy grows further by creating alliances with elites in other influential professions such as medicine. Recall the epigraphs at the start of this chapter. This explains the academy's interest in having its views certified by the Surgeon General and such institutions as the American Medical Association, thereby expanding a psychological question of media effects into a question of "public health."[10]: Recall that the anticomic crusade mentioned earlier was led by Dr. Frederic Wertham, chief of psychiatry at New York Hospitals in the 1940s. Two decades earlier, the stories of Jesse James and Dead Eye Dick were condemned as a threat to public "health" because of their popularity among younger readers.[11] This is highly consistent with the findings we have reported in previous chapters. Much of what passes for science is morality in other clothes. Few areas in social psychology have received such massive levels of funding over such a long period of time with so little reliable knowledge to show for it. Bad science often makes for popular public policy.

The view is reflected in several issues raised in this chapter. First, the study of the media only became academically fashionable when it was a way of theorizing about violence in society. Concern for other bad "effects" such as racial and gender stereotyping and for the potentially positive influence of educational programming was always overshadowed by this morally loaded, but universally attractive agenda. The study of advertising and its influence never got off the ground. Hence the link between advertising for tobacco products and population health trends received little scientific attention, so that when governments today are wrestling with the health costs arising from nicotine addiction, there is no way of determining the probable effect of changing or controlling advertising to encourage smokers to quit, and to prevent youth from starting to smoke. Likewise, the effects of mass media on political opinions and the utilization of media in political propaganda, something that dearly concerned psychologists like Solomon Asch, were simply not part of the mainstream research agenda. From the start, the agenda was ideologically biased, and the academy, as a bastion of high culture, flourished as a critic of popular culture. To condemn popular culture as bad taste would simply be a matter of opinion. To show that it was dangerous required scientific expertise. Second, the expertise was fashioned around the politics of victimization. In the first wave (TV), children were identified as the *cause célèbre* due to their heightened vulnerability. In the second wave (pornography), women were added to the mix in what will be remembered as the generation of *victimization feminism*. In both waves, this agenda amounted to advocacy research, and while this is morally defensible in politics and social movements, it is problematic when it is presented as neutral or value-free science, a posture that in psychology has been associated with the adoption of the experimental method. The downside of this kind of orientation is that we have learned little from psychology about the nature of drama, about the suspension of belief associated with it, about the way in which stories create deeply arousing cognitive involvement and emotional affect, and about how the mind moves across different frames of reference keeping real life separate from fiction and fantasy. Also, we have learned little about human sexuality and how erotic fantasies and sexual images function in the love lives of ordinary people. Instead we learn: pornography is the theory, rape is the practice. My point here is that much has been lost through the unacknowledged subscription to this moral agenda. We pile up annual tallies of the percentage of programming defined as "violent" without a scintilla of understanding of the nature of entertainment per se, and the role of conflict in such entertainment.

Two further points. First, because the entire approach has been experimental or quasi-experimental, psychologists have been preoccupied with methodological questions. The contribution of psychology to the "explanandum," the outcome, has been stifled: psychology has not shed much light on the actual nature of violence in everyday life since the outcome was taken for granted or taken as unproblematic. Everything the psychologist needed to know about violence could be learned in a newspaper. Issues such as gender differences, the age-crime curve, the role of social marginalization, family conflict, and individual differences were unexamined. Criminology could learn nothing from a psychology preoccupied with explanations deriving from the effects of media. Also, from the start, experimental studies were premised on a theory of mimicry. This presupposition of mimicry turned the "tests" of theory into demonstrations. The designs were premised on the idea that a child exposed to Bobo-bashing will bash in like fashion if given the opportunity. Rather than asking what occurs when a child watches cartoons (what is the nature of drama) and exploring a range of options as potential outcomes, the orthodoxy underlying the social learning paradigm forged a link between exposure and mimicry. However, as we have stressed in this chapter, the effect at stake may have nothing to do with mimicry as much as arousal or excitation transfer. None of the experiments in the media effects paradigm were designed to determine which underlying process was responsible for the observed behaviors. This means that the experiments were predicated on adoption of a specific theory. The potential of theoretical complexity was forestalled and practitioners acted as though it did not matter that fundamentally different processes might account for the observations. However, the admission of theoretical heterodoxy in terms of effects, while desirable from a scientific perspective, would not have served the ideological agenda that drove the study of media effects in the first place.

NOTES

1. The Naples museum accessioned frescoes of nude females, couples making love, satyrs having sex with goats, phalluses in relief in paving stones and on the walls of houses, statues with oversized penises and phallic ornaments in household appliances and birdfeeders, to name a few items. In addition, Pompeii apparently had hundreds of brothels but the erotic artifacts were found throughout the city. Childhood in such a city must have been a Roman psychologist's nightmare.

2. For example, in the Zamora case, a youthful Ron Zamora had burglarized an elderly neighbor's home and shot the occupant when she threatened to call the

police. At his trial for murder he raised the defense that he had become addicted to violent TV shows, and suffered a conditioned response when confronted with threats of police apprehension that triggered the shooting involuntarily. The jury failed to buy the defense. In an earlier case, a suit was brought against NBC on behalf of a nine-year-old San Francisco girl who was sexually assaulted with a bottle by a gang of older girls. The family sought damages arguing that the assault had imitated an episode in a NBC crime drama. That case ultimately failed on first amendment grounds. The liability of NBC could only be established if the network *intended* the viewers to act in a similar fashion (Liebert and Sprafkin 1988:127ff.).

3. Diana Russell cites Edward Donnerstein to the effect that "the relationship between pornography and violence against women is even stronger than the relationship between smoking and lung cancer" (Backhouse 1996:280). Contrast this statement to Linz et al. (1987) on the criticism of the Meese Commission for overstating the claims of harm.

4. See Linz and Donnerstein (1988) with comments by Zillmann and Bryant in the *Journal of Communication* colloquia section. The former focused on the Buss paradigm to study the incitement to violence following exposure to *aggressive* pornography. The latter focused on the decline in sensitivity in attitudes toward women following exposure to *explicit* pornography. Donnerstein's students report that they could replicate his work, but not that of Zillmann and Bryant, although Weaver, their student, could! Even people who reported dramatic changes in attitudes found inconsistent results across their own studies. This is reviewed by Fisher and Grenier (1994:24–25), who examined twenty-seven refereed reports dealing with conflicting estimates of the prevalence of violence in pornography, conflicting findings about the ability of pornography to create antiwoman thoughts as well as antiwoman acts.

5. This suggests that the effects of pornography in a lab study with subjects who are largely naïve would overstate the effects of exposure. As a consequence, the generalization from reactions in naïve subjects in the lab to those more familiar with the arousing material in everyday life is fatuous. Berl Kutchinsky once suggested to me that any aggressive reactions studied in the lab might be attributable to the fact that male subjects exposed to pornography did not masturbate— defeating the very purpose of sexual arousal with pornography in the first place.

6. Edwin Boyd and I attempted to replicate the changes in attitudes arising from adult-rated sexually aggressive materials on some 450 subjects at the University of Calgary. We were also interested in determining whether we could discover any evidence for changes in attitudes in films that endorsed violent robbery. If sexually violent fiction promotes rape myth acceptance and callousness toward victims of rape, we hypothesized that social learning theory would predict that robbery films would have the same influence in regard to victims of robbery. We could find no differences across three film conditions (rape, robbery, and neutral films) on any of the rape, robbery, or altruism measures (Boyd and Brannigan 1991).

7. There is a large criminological literature that attempts to examine the relationship between "decensorship," the circulation of pornography and the changes in the rates of sex crimes: Kutchinsky (1991), Abramson and Hayashi (1984), Becker and Stein (1991), Langevin et al. (1988), Baron (1990), Scott and Schwalm (1988),

Diamond and Uchiyama (1999), and Fisher and Barak (2001). The purportedly positive relationship has not been established.

8. In the United States, the definition of obscenity was laid down in the U.S. Supreme Court in the 1973 case of *Miller v. California*. Miller held that to be obscene the material must (a) appeal to a prurient [or obsessive] interest in sex; (b) contain "patently offensive depictions or descriptions of specific sexual conduct," as judged by a local grand jury in light of the contemporary standards in the community; and (c) when taken as the whole, have "no serious literary, artistic, political or scientific value." The scope attached to the third criterion has made convictions for obscenity difficult to sustain. In Canada, the definition of obscenity was laid down in the Supreme Court's decision in *Regina v. Butler* (S.C.R.) 1 432 (1992). Canadian law forbids "the undue exploitation of sex"—implying that exploitation that is "due" is legal. The determination of what is "due" is a question of national community standards of what individuals would tolerate their neighbors to see. The *Butler* case built on a series of lower court cases that allowed expert social science evidence about the harmful effects of pornography. The new decision suggested that materials that were harmful would not meet the community standard test. That would be the case even if such works had any serious literary or other value as in the United States. U.S. constitutional law places an extremely important role on protection of free speech that borders on treating it as an absolute good while Canadian law is designed to balance competing interests (free speech and individual security). These ordinances were defeated in Minneapolis and Indianapolis, but the same logic of harm was accepted in the Canadian obscenity law in *Butler*.

9. In Canada, feminists were successful in importing some of the logic of the ordinances into Canadian obscenity law. During a Calgary obscenity case [*Regina v. Wagner*, (A.Q.B.) 43 C.R. (3d) 301 (1985)], members of a feminist antipornography group persuaded the prosecutor to retain an experimental psychologist as an expert witness on the question of media harm. This trial set a trend in decisions that ultimately made its way to the Canadian Supreme Court in the case of *Regina v. Butler*. The new doctrine held that the criminal law would not tolerate violent pornography because it was thought to incite violence against women (following Donnerstein), second that it would not tolerate degrading pornography because it undermines attitudes to women (following Malamuth, and Zillmann and Bryant), and third, it would tolerate erotica, no matter how explicit, since this was thought to be harmless. Among the first victims of the new common law rule were a feminist bookstore in Toronto, an art gallery displaying paintings dealing with child sexual exploitation, also in Toronto, and a gay and lesbian store in Vancouver.

After publication of the *Regina v. Butler* decision, complaints were made about the availability of pornographic materials in the city of Calgary that had become forbidden as a result of the new ruling. The police Vice Unit had not received any complaints from the public so the activists generated complaints to the police on behalf of the public. Several dozen volunteers from the Legal Education Action Fund, mostly female law students at the University of Calgary rented hundreds of videos with financial support from the police, and screened the materials for evidence of violence and/or degrading or dehumanizing portrayals of sex. This was an educational first—a "field school" in obscenity. It resulted in the largest single seizure of pornographic videos in the city's history in May 1993. This raid raised some obvious questions. Should a vigilante group administer the criminal law? Should the justice system have tried to educate the merchants about the nature of the *Regina v. Butler* decision—as opposed to charging them? Has the law become so technical that it takes a law degree to apply it? If the materials are harmful, how could anyone justify exposing students to them by the dozens? If they are not, what was the point of the raid? The moral of the case, as I see it: junk science, junk law!

10. In 1986 the U.S. Surgeon General issued a report on pornography as a public health concern (see Mulvey and Haugaard 1986). The conclusions were arrived at by a consensus created in the absence of contrary, critical, or dissenting voices. The claims of each psychological school were honored. This was largely a political exercise to ensure that the Attorney General and the Surgeon General were on the same page.

11. See the following report about the adolescent books depicting the lives of Jesse James and Dead-Eye Dick. The quote is from the editorial in the *Public Health Journal* (Toronto: 1923): "This filth purveying medium . . . is filled with stories of a dangerous character, most of them relating incidents, which not only have to do with sex, but which are told in such a way and from such an angle as to make any sensible reader conclude that the only safe method by which one can dispose of such muck, is to ban it from the mails altogether. One's determination will not be lessened in the least by the information that these magazines are commonly snapped up with avidity by young school girls. A fine school for moral training they provide!"

6

Gender and Psychology
From Feminism to Darwinism

This book records different modes of thinking about relation-
ships and the association of these modes with male and
female voices in psychological and literary texts and in the
data of my research.

— Carol Gilligan, *In a Different Voice*

Whereas modern conditions of mating differ from ancestral
conditions, the same sexual strategies operate with unbridled
force. Our evolved psychology of mating remains. It is the
only psychology we have.

— David M. Buss, *The Evolution of Desire*

INTRODUCTION

In this chapter we will explore the contributions of both Gilligan and Buss to the psychological explanation of gender differences. Some of the same extrascientific dimensions that we found in experimental work are found here as well, suggesting that moral agendas are never far below the surface in social psychology. To some degree we move away from experimental psychology to examine issues of gender that have emerged in recent years. We focus on two developments. The first is associated with the work of Carol Gilligan, and the suggestion that moral development is quite different in males and females, with the result that men and woman differ significantly in how they make moral choices. The second involves the evolutionary psychology of David Buss and others, which makes equally radical claims about how parental investment in human reproduction and sexual selection pressures have differently shaped the preferences and morals of human males and females. Both perspectives have

115

generated a great deal of debate over the question of whether such differences actually exist, and if they do, whether they are innate, socially acquired, or a conjoint outcome of each. Both perspectives suggest that they may provide the basis for fundamental changes to society. Gilligan writes:

> The rash of questions about relationship and difference which become inescapable once women enter the conversation are now *the most urgently pressing questions* on the local, national and international scene. The political has become psychological in the sense that men's disconnection and women's dissociation perpetuate the prevailing social order. ([1982] 1993:xxvii, emphasis added)

As women recover their distinctive voice, their resistance argues for, in Gilligan's words, "potentially revolutionary" change, and threatens the demise of patriarchal societies that are based on men's disconnection from women and women's dissociation from their own distinctive moral voice, a voice based on their sense of connectivity.

On the side of evolutionary psychology, Buss writes that

> we are empowered now, perhaps more than at any previous time in evolutionary history, to shape our future. . . . We are the first species in the known history of three and a half billion years of life on earth with the capacity to control our own destiny. The prospect of designing our destiny remains excellent to the degree that we comprehend our evolutionary past. . . . Only by understanding why these human strategies have evolved can we control where we are going. (1994b:220, 222)

Although lacking the specific initiatives associated with feminist psychologies, Buss's claim is no less grandiose in its scope. We begin our work with an examination of the recent debate over the crisis in development in young males and females in American society.

GILLIGAN, SOMMERS, AND *THE WAR AGAINST BOYS*

Throughout the 1990s, the American Association of University Women (AAUW), with assistance from the Ms Foundation and other women's interest groups, mobilized a widespread and media-savvy campaign to communicate the message that female students were being seriously undermined by the nation's educational institutions. The AAUW published a study, *How Schools Shortchange Girls* (1991) that suggested girls were being disadvantaged in teaching processes, and that this was resulting in a diminished sense of self-esteem as adolescent girls reached adulthood. Advocacy "experts" suggested that teachers were biased in favor of males in the classroom, and that boys were permitted to "cry out" responses in class, "eight times" as often as girls, according to the Sadkers, while girls who did likewise were told to raise their hands if they wanted to speak. Clinical psychologists reported that there was a dramatic shift in adolescent female suicide, suggesting that the popular culture was "girl-destroying." The image conveyed by the campaign was that little girls showed self-confidence, insight, and sparkle in their eyes in their formative years but faced a downward spiral in self-worth as they entered adolescence. The exuberant girl of primary school became the shrinking girl of high school.

The media took to the release of such provocative "information" like sharks to bait. The story of the shrinking girl was reported uncritically in many of the leading newspapers and magazines. The initial study that cost $100,000 was publicized by AAUW with a budget of $150,000. The U.S. Congress passed the Gender Equity in Education Act (1994). "Millions of dollars in grants were awarded to study the plight of girls and learn how to cope with the insidious bias against them" (Sommers 2000a:23).There was a backlash against boys since a subtext of the campaign was that the psychological deficits faced by girls were a result of the advantages conferred unfairly on boys. These advantages were presumably one of the devices that guaranteed "the reproduction of patriarchy." Gradually, part of the pedagogical agenda to restore the equal treatment of girls was to reconstruct boyhood, to render boys "less competitive, more emotionally expressive, more nurturing—more, in short, like girls" (ibid.:44). Ironically, those who argued that boys were being advantaged in the socialization process subsequently argued that the boys were being poisoned by their masculinity since the latter was equated not merely with competition, but with violence, indifference to others, and lack of connectivity to women. The impression created by this line of thinking was that gender is essentially a caste system with two qualitatively different kinds of human beings, males and females. The system is grounded in different patterns of psychological development that provides the lynchpin that confers systematic advantage to the upper caste, males, and that stifles the growth of the lower caste, females. This analysis implies that masculine and feminine identities are no more than social constructs that can be changed by policy, although, as we shall see, there is ambiguity on all sides in regard to this perception, a point to which we shall return later.

The evidence of the marginalization of girls in American education was first criticized at length in Christine Hoff Sommers's *Who Stole Feminism* (1994) and later in Judith Kleinfeld's *The Myth That Schools Shortchange Girls* (1998). In a spirited attack on the empirical evidence in the 1991 AAUW report, Kleinfeld argued that

the findings in this report are based on a selective review of the research.
. . . Findings contrary to the report's message were repressed. These contrary
findings indeed appear in studies the AAUW itself commissioned, but the
AAUW not only did not include these findings in their media kits but made
the data difficult to obtain. . . . Major assertions in the AAUW report are
based on research by David and Myra Sadker that has mysteriously disap-
peared. Evidence which contradicts their thesis that the schools shortchange
girls is buried in supplemental tables obtainable only at great difficulty and
expense. Such shady practices undermine public confidence in social science
research.

Expanding on her earlier research, Christina Hoff Sommers in *The War
Against Boys* (2000a) argues at length that the evidence for the educational
deficits faced by girls is contradicted by the facts:

Data from the U.S. Department of Education and from several recent university studies show that far from being shy and demoralized, today's girls
outshine boys. Girls get better grades. They have higher educational aspirations. They follow a more rigorous academic program. (ibid.:24)

Sommers reports that girls read more books, show higher levels of artistic and musical ability, are more likely to study abroad and join the Peace
Corps. By contrast boys were far more likely to leave school prematurely,
to receive discipline at school for misconduct, and to receive "special education" for learning deficits and to show signs of hyperactivity and attention deficit disorders. The National Center for Education Statistics (NCES)
reported in 1994 that boys were more likely to go to school unprepared,
i.e., arrive at school without books or paper and pencils, and to appear
without completing homework. The NCES reported in 1996 that girls were
more likely to devote longer periods of time to homework, and to do so at
every level of schooling. Hardly surprisingly, it is estimated that female
attendance at university is increasingly higher than male attendance and
will outstrip male attendance by an estimated 33 percent in the United
States by 2007.

A similar picture was painted by a 1997 study sponsored by the Metropolitan Life Insurance Company in a survey conducted by Harris and
Associates. *The American Teacher 1997: Examining Gender Issues in Public
Schools* was based on a survey of 1,300 students and over 1,000 teachers in
grades seven through twelve. It discovered that girls were more likely to
have higher educational aspirations than boys, more likely to value a good
education, and less likely to believe that their teachers didn't listen to them
(19 percent) compared to boys (31 percent). Similarly a survey of some
99,000 students in grades six through twelve undertaken by the Search
Institute in Minneapolis found that "on almost every significant measure

of well-being, girls had the better of boys: they felt closer to their families, they had higher aspirations and a stronger connection to school—even superior assertiveness skills" (ibid.:37). As Sommers points out, the Search Institute with a sample thirty-three times as large as the original AAUW survey was significantly more reliable.

In 1998 the National Council for Research on Women published *The Girl's Report: What We Know and Need to Know about Growing Up Female*. The report dismissed the problem of self-esteem differences across gender, bringing into question the very utility of the concept. The report failed to replicate earlier studies of female's diminished self-esteem in adolescence (Kleinfeld 1999:18). The report was based, in part, on the research of University of Denver psychologist, Susan Harter, who studied 900 male and female students in grades six through twelve. She found no evidence for "loss of voice" for female adolescents, nor any evidence for gender differences favoring females.

One of the more worrisome pieces of evidence that Kleinfeld and Sommers present is a 1990 survey of gender roles and self-esteem conducted by the AAUW. This survey provided evidence that, in the views of the girls and boys themselves, girls were systematically favored by their teachers. Both girls and boys believed that teachers thought girls were smarter than boys, were more likely to get complimented by teachers, less likely to get disciplined, more likely to be called on in class, more likely to get the teachers' attention, and more preferable in terms of whom teachers preferred to be around. In other words, while lobbying the public on the image of the "shortchanged girl" drowning in a sea of sexism and facing educational deficits at every turn, the AAUW had in its possession survey information that suggested quite the contrary. Not only were girls outperforming boys in terms of academic achievements, they were experiencing greater levels of self-esteem as indicated by these survey items.

What about the patterns in adolescent suicide? In 1997 there were approximately 4,500 suicidal deaths in the United States; 84 percent were males. As for the Sadler "evidence" that boys were permitted to "call out" eight times as often as females, this claim was based on an unpublished paper that never made it to the refereed literature. The original research commissioned for the National Institute of Education either could not be found or failed to corroborate the claim of gender bias in "call-outs" (Sommers 1994:164ff.). The advocacy claim of the "shortchanged girl" was in Sommers's words, "politics dressed up as science."

What is the harm of this bias? Surely, advocacy on behalf of females by women's organizations can only do good. Kleinfeld argues that the campaigns of the AAUW and similar groups actually insult women by understating their accomplishments. On the positive side, they identified the lag of female accomplishments in science and mathematics, but this gap is

narrowing, while the gap between male and female language and compo-
sition is not. "Unfortunately, the feminist agenda, because it is pushed so
strongly and receives so much attention from media elites, distracts us
from the real problem of low educational achievement among African-
American males and boys more generally" (Kleinfeld 1999:19).

Sommers argues that the ideological foundation for the "shrinking-
girl" thesis is found in the psychological research of Harvard psychologist,
Carol Gilligan. Gilligan is a student of Lawrence Kohlberg, a leading proponent of the theory of moral development. Kohlberg argued, following
Piaget, that as children grow older, they not only show signs of more complex levels of cognitive skills, but become increasingly sensitive in terms
of *moral* development. Gilligan discovered what she claimed to be gender
differences in patterns of moral development. Unlike most of the theories
examined in social psychology, this perspective had roots that grounded
developmental patterns, not in behaviorism or cognitive theory, but in
psychoanalysis.

KOHLBERG'S MORAL DEVELOPMENT THEORY

Kohlberg originally thought he could identify six discrete levels of moral
development, although recent work suggests that there are only four
major levels that reflect clear developmental progression (Greeno and
Maccoby 1986:311). As with Piaget, such levels were thought to be tempo-
rally sequential and hierarchical. Level three, which marks a movement to
adult reasoning, is characterized by a preoccupation with bonds with others and the development of trusting relationships. This is the level at
which females were alleged to "top out." Level four reflects more societal
concerns for the rule of justice and law, and maintenance of the collective
interests of society. Level four, for Kohlberg, reflected a more global sensibility that transcended obligations and attachments idiosyncratic to individuals and their personal ties. As a student of Kohlberg, Gilligan
departed from the master by identifying the coding system which relegated women to a lower level of moral development as "androcentric,"
and by postulating that women progress on a path of moral reasoning different from men. The differential experiences and obligations of women as
caregivers in contemporary society heighten the importance of connectivity for them in a way that overshadows the more abstract male concerns.
"This different construction of the moral problem by women may be seen
as the critical reason for their failure to develop within the constraints of
Kohlberg's system" ([1982] 1993:19). The key mechanism for gender differentiation was not genetic predisposition, but patterns of identity formation in girls and boys raised by their mothers. According to this theory,

girls more closely identify with mothers than do their brothers, and presumably experience greater interconnectedness with them. Boys, being more aware of their separate identity, differentiate themselves more completely from their mothers and experience generational power imbalances that valorize the importance of justice and equality as opposed to an ethical sense based on attachment and care (see Chodorow 1978). In the result, female children bond and connect while male children individuate and isolate.

Gilligan's research was based on a handful of small-scale studies: the college student study designed to study identity and moral development in early adulthood ($n = 25$), the abortion decision study designed to explore the reasoning of young women facing unplanned pregnancies ($n = 29$), and the rights and responsibilities study designed to explore moral conflicts, individual choices, and judgments of hypothetical moral dilemmas at different ages over the life cycle ($n = 144$). The results of her work are reported in a discursive manner, citing suggestive quotations from the subjects but there are never any explicit hypotheses, clear design features appropriate to testing them, or tests of statistical significance to determine whether measurable differences exist.

The social science literature contains many studies of gender differences on such traits as empathy and altruism (Eisenberg and Lennon 1983; Hoffman 1977). In addition, there are striking differences in social relationships in male and female peer groups and how they engage in play (Maccoby 1985). There are also tremendous differences in childhood aggression in males and females at every age. However, the evidence of differences in moral reasoning fails to substantiate Gilligan's claim of a distinctive moral voice. Lawrence Walker (1984) reviewed sixty-one studies that tested for gender differences of the sort Gilligan suggested. They failed to establish that males scored higher than females on Kohlberg-type scores.

> In adulthood, the large majority of comparisons reveal no sex differences. In the studies that do show sex differences, the women were less educated than the men, and it appears that education, not gender, accounts for women's seemingly lesser maturity. . . . There is no indication whatever that the two sexes take different developmental paths. (Greeno and Maccoby 1986:312)

In a review of Gilligan's book in the *Merrill-Palmer Quarterly* (1983), Colby and Damon came to similar conclusions. "There is very little support in the psychological literature for the notion that girls are aware of other's feelings or are more altruistic than boys" (ibid.:475). Colby and Damon recount the differences in children's play. Boys like games with organized rules and competition. Girls like "dyadic intimate exchange and turn-taking games." But it is not clear why. The organized games may lend themselves to dominance displays and bullying, but it is impossible in naturalistic observations to determine whether such differences are a natural gender trait or whether these are the molds into which the children are shoehorned by parents. There are also many other differences in such areas as occupational choices, aggressiveness, and competitiveness but these may reflect little more than opportunities and restraints, and they are differences that are increasingly being narrowed in contemporary society.

What about Gilligan's supposition that Kohlberg's system artificially privileges "justice" thinking over "relationship" thinking? This would seem to be a credible concern if in fact the empirical evidence corroborated such gender differences, but the more systematic tests of gender differences failed to corroborate the claim. In the alternative, Gilligan treated the readers to reports from her handful of qualitative studies. However, as Colby and Damon pointed out, such reports were based exclusively on *anecdotes* that appear to have been chosen to illustrate the differences on which the research was premised. *In a Different Voice* contains no information on how the respondents' views were coded to determine whether the "evidence" was selectively cited to confirm Gilligan's views. The abortion study was particularly problematic since it is unclear that a small sample of young single women ($n = 29$) facing unplanned pregnancies and contacted via a counseling service designed to deal with the potential stress or trauma of confronting abortion—sometimes for a second and third time (and sometimes with the same married man)—is a valid source of general gender differences in moral reasoning. In particular, a specific gender comparison is, at one level, out of the question, since men cannot have abortions. But the study also ignored information from the *potential* fathers whose views on aborting potential offspring might have provided a measure of difference in moral reasoning. It also overlooks the potential bias that arises from sampling exclusively in an abortion-counseling clinic. The absence of comparative data undermines the entire claim to unearthing gender differences of all but the most trivial kind. "Although Gilligan's abortion interviews yield some interesting data on real-life decision making processes, they do not provide support for her thesis of sex bias in Kohlberg's theory" (Colby and Damon 1983:478). Colby and Damon conclude by warning about the irony of Gilligan's position. The idea that men and women reason in qualitatively different ways may tend to justify gender stratification by relegating social differences in opportunities and achievement to innate differences: it is "important to guard against reinforcing gender stereotypes that in themselves contribute to the maintenance of women's oppression" (ibid.:480). Sommers (2000) went further. After repeated attempts to obtain copies of the original research protocols and raw data, she charged that the data did not exist.

Gilligan herself qualified the relevance of the abortion study. Since the focus of the study was the relationship between judgment and action,

> No effort was made to select a sample that would be representative of women considering, seeking or having abortions. Thus the findings pertain to the different ways in which women think about dilemmas in their lives rather than to the ways in which women in general think about the abortion issue. ([1982] 1993:82)

Gilligan seems to think that this ameliorates the methodological limitations of her research design. But it does not. Her position amounts to the claim that abortion decisions can be used to throw light on women's *general* moral dilemmas. On the one side, many women refuse to consider abortion at all under such circumstances (see Luker 1984). And on the other, in her study, it is not clear that abortion automatically presented a traumatic dilemma for the women in counseling.

Furthermore, if no care was taken to grasp how women thought about a particular dilemma, abortion, on the strength of what would we be permitted to make valid inferences about the larger topic of the "different ways" in which women think about dilemmas in general? Gilligan seems to imply that shoddy research has more power when it comes to larger questions. Luria, writing in *Signs*, thinks otherwise: "In general, Gilligan's sample specification is inadequate to justify her group characterizations" (1986:317). In other words, women's thinking about abortion, particularly contacted in this context, cannot be used to gauge important gender differences in moral thinking or moral dilemmas. Gilligan's analysis also failed to shed light on the *different* responses among the women, some of whom chose abortion while others did not. Her analysis fails to explain the determinants of choosing abortion versus alternative courses of action. A constant, "female connectivity," cannot explain a variable.

Gilligan's work appeared with Harvard University Press in 1982. It was a tremendous academic *cause célèbre,* but it also spawned a torrent of empirical criticism from many quarters in the immediate years after its release, including criticisms from feminist psychologists and gender theorists sympathetic to women's political and economic advancement. It was reissued in 1993 without a hint that anything important had occurred in the discipline in the intervening years to raise questions about Gilligan's theory. In 1986, Thoma had written: "There is now considerable evidence that justice defined measures of moral reasoning are not biased against females. Further, there is little support for the notion that males are better able to reason about hypothetical dilemmas [than females]" (1986:176). Systematic reviews of the moral dilemma literature found no support for her claims about different moral voices (Brabeck 1983; Friedman, Robinson, and

Friedman 1987; Gibbs, Arnold, and Burkhart 1984). Martha Mednick wrote: "There seems to be general agreement among moral development researchers that the presumed sex differences have not been supported" (1989:1119). The subtitle of her paper was instructive: "Stop the Bandwagon, I Want to Get Off." Luria came to similar conclusions: "When usual summary techniques are applied to add all the studies together, the data do not support any finding of a statistically significant sex difference" (1986:318). Gilligan reported in the "Letter to Readers" in the 1993 edition that she did not revise the study "because it has become part of the process that it describes." Which was what? "The ongoing historical process of changing the voice of the world by bringing women's voice into the open, thus starting a new conversation." But were Mednick's, Maccoby's, Luria's, or any other of the women's voices even acknowledged? Not a word. The book has become part of the process it describes by indifference to criticism, not by conversation.

   Gilligan's indifference to the empirical evidence brings us back to a theme that we have found throughout social psychology: the moral lesson frequently embedded in psychological research outweighs its empirical foundations. In our review of the classic group influence studies from Sherif to Asch to Milgram to Zimbardo, we showed how the key studies at the heart of the tradition were *not* careful experiments in the model of the natural sciences. They were demonstrations, typically undertaken without the identification of specific hypotheses, and derived with little benefit from psychological theory. So in that respect, the current work *demonstrates* the differences Gilligan attributes to her subjects through impressionistic storytelling. Just as the classic work had for various reasons a powerful moral appeal, similar processes are operative here. What are they?

MEDNICK'S BANDWAGON HYPOTHESIS

Writing in 1989, Martha Mednick argued that the three most prominent bandwagons in psychology in the previous two decades surrounded issues of gender: women's fear of success, the emergence of androgyny as an alternative to typical gender constructions and "different voices" in the moral thinking of males and females. Mednick argues that the staying power of the bandwagon is "quite independent of scientific merit" (ibid.:1120). The concept of distinctive moral voices in men and women has tremendous appeal because it plays into familiar gender stereotypes, the belief that distinctive female perspectives are excluded by male-dominated sciences, that women's more sensitive moral compass is stifled by the harsh realities of patriarchy, and that important social change will only be possible when women assume political dominance. As Greeno and Maccoby observed regarding Gilligan's evidence, "many women readers find that the comments by women quoted in Gilligan's book resonate so thoroughly with their own experience that they do not need any further demonstration" (1986:315). Kohn reports on the back cover of the 1993 edition: "[Gilligan's] thesis is rooted not only in research but in common sense." However, as Mednick notes, the stereotypes are stronger than the real gender differences, and in fact, are more debilitating since they often tend to undermine the goal of gender equality. Mednick summed up as follows: "the simplicity of such ideas is appealing; such gender dichotomy confirms stereotypes and provides strong intuitive resonance" (1989:1122)—even while playing into conservative politics.

A large part of Gilligan's following is not in traditional empirical psychology, but in women's studies and literary disciplines, disciplines that are indifferent to, if not actually hostile to, the scientific project and the use of systematic evidence and tests of significance. Here Gilligan's case studies are less informative than her exploration of "voice" through her rich literary allusions to the characters created by Virginia Wolfe, Toni Morrison, and Joseph Conrad. Her imaginative juxtaposition of fiction and qualitative descriptions blurs the lines between convincing proof and suggestive exploration. Her own form of exposition, particularly in the 1993 preface, adds to the mystique of her writing by invoking the categories of "voice," "difference," and "development" that have few of the concrete referents found in her earlier work. She formally disavows a biological foundation for gender differences (which suggests a repudiation of gender essentialism) but continues to condemn "powerful men" for silencing women and lacking connection (which makes her a darling of cultural feminists). Much can be said of this, but I will keep my remarks brief. To the extent that this discourse makes strong claims about the social realities of males and females, it has been shown to be patently untrue. To the extent that the claims are simply poetic, it is, in Mednick's terms, all bandwagon. And to the extent that it motivated a decade of antimale propaganda in education and failed to grasp the vulnerability of boys, particularly young African-Americans in contemporary learning environments, it was myopic and harmful. In the summer of 2002, Gilligan received $12.5 million in research donations from Jane Fonda to examine the plight of boys (Owens 2002:A3). This was the largest private donation to Harvard in its history. Gilligan departed Harvard's educational faculty in 2002 for New York University's school of law. Harvard returned Fonda's gift.[1]

GENDER AND THE RISE OF EVOLUTIONARY PSYCHOLOGY

There are some ironic parallels between the feminism of Gilligan and the Darwinism of David Buss and the new generation of evolutionary psychologists. Both treat gender differences in sexual orientation as real, although the mechanisms underlying them are quite different. Unlike most psychology, neither work is experimental nor borrows primarily from experimental evidence. Both speak to fundamental questions of how sexuality structures other elements of social life. And evidence, the stock and trade of scientific life, in both cases, tends to raise more questions than it answers. Evolutionary psychology is one of the most important new intellectual developments in postexperimental psychology in the past decade, and requires a close examination to evaluate its potential for the intellectual development of social psychology.

Evolutionary theory in biology and medicine is the foundation for intellectual growth in those areas. It is materialistic, nonteleological, and nonessentialist. Evolutionary models explain changes in species over time as a function of biological variability, often the result of chance variations in traits, and selection pressures that result in a greater or lesser reproductive success. The *fitness* of an organism is the degree to which the organism's inherited characteristics contribute to the organism's reproductive success. Evolution is nonteleological in the sense that adaptive changes are not directed a priori toward some state of perfection or transcendence. The theory is nonessentialist inasmuch as it denies that there are specific rigid traits that define a species. The evidence suggests instead that there is variability in traits within a species, greater variability between related species even though related species share many of the same genes, and that the form of the organism is constantly evolving under changing environmental pressures.

Arguments of this sort in respect of the evolution of the *physical* characteristics of species such as teeth, bones, muscles, organs such as eyes, stomachs, fingers, and toes are universally accepted in contemporary science. And arguments to explain the *social* behaviors of insects and animals are standard in the curriculum of biology, entomology, and zoology. The attempt to explain *social* characteristics (altruism, the sense of justice, jealousy), particularly in the human species, has often met with resistance, particularly in the social sciences (Gould 1978). It is assumed that the basic adaptive mechanisms in human experience derive from two major sources: Pavlovian classical conditioning and Skinnerian operant conditioning. It is often assumed that the understanding of human social life requires no knowledge of human evolution, as though human social evolution stopped with the natural selection of the capacity to learn. This assumption often coappears with the related assumption that human traits are either biological (genetically determined) or environmental (the results of socialization), either nature or nurture.

Evolutionary psychology is premised on the idea that human *social* behavior has evolved under natural selection pressures, and that human conduct has large instinctual foundations or elements. The approach to analyzing the mechanisms that influence social behavior is the same sort of "reverse engineering" that applies to the analysis of the physiological properties of the organism. We examine, for example, the teeth of a species as well the realities of the food supplies. Where the ecology supports savannahs and prairies of vast grasslands, molars for grinding grains, seeds, and other plant foods show "design features" that exploit the food resources efficiently, as in elephants and bison. Over millennia of variations in tooth morphology, those animals best able to exploit the resources would tend to enjoy higher levels of fitness through a process of natural selection since such morphological traits are preserved across generations in the species' genes. By contrast, animals with highly developed canines evolve in environments that favor predatory consumption of other animals, as in lions and tigers. An analogous form of reasoning (i.e., reverse engineering) is applied to *social* traits such as "altruism." Altruism seems at the outset an unlikely candidate for a natural selection argument since "good Samaritans" who lay down their lives for others would seem to be selected against in the long run. Unless they reproduced before their acts of self-sacrifice, they would become as rare as hen's teeth. However, under some conditions, altruistic behavior may be adaptive (i.e., genetically selfish). The whistling marmots that let loose their shrill whistles as predators approach the colony may be exposing themselves to individual predation, and indeed those closest to the predator may be more liable to be eaten. However, if the majority of the colony survives, natural selection will favor "altruism." This is premised on the condition that members of this closely related group all share the same genetic disposition (to be altruistic), and that in the long run such self-sacrificial behavior permits more marmots to survive than are lost to predators. Biologists acknowledge that such processes probably occur at the level of "kin groups," i.e., initially small, relatively homogeneous, interrelated family groups. Evolutionary psychology is premised on the idea that the selection process described for altruistic behaviors in animals provides grounds for inferring how distinctive *social* behaviors could evolve in humans.

Evolutionary psychology is also premised on the idea that human social behavior may have evolved as a result of *sexual* selection pressures. Sexual selection is the evolution of traits that confer advantages in *intra*specific reproduction. Individual organisms not only compete with pressures arising from competition *between* species for control of ecological resources, but often compete with one another *within* the species for reproductive success. The fact that the elaborate feathers and ornamentation of peacocks may make them vulnerable to stalking by predatory cats and hawks is less relevant than the success that such secondary sexual characteristics contribute to their ability to compete for peahen mates. And here too the evolutionary perspective notes that adaptive pressures not only shape the *morphologies* of body parts, but the *social* behaviors of insects and animals as well. Elaborate courtship rituals in the animal kingdom, whether the dancing of birds or food offerings of spiders suggest that courtship behavior is frequently genetically programmed, i.e., a reflex triggered by changes in the seasons and opportunities to mate.

RESISTANCE TO THE DARWINIAN APPROACH TO HUMAN SOCIAL BEHAVIOR

Students of human nature identify a cluster of difficulties in accepting the plausibility of natural and sexual selection pressures when it comes to human social behaviors. Human societies are thought to structure social behavior through cultures that consist of historical as opposed to genetic memories. It is argued that culture differentiates humanity from nonhuman species, so that the major determinants of human social behavior arise from ontogenetic experiences, not phylogeny. In addition, human behavior is voluntaristic, i.e., based on free will and agency. Evolutionary psychology implies in the minds of some people that we are automatons, or puppets whose behaviors are determined by our genetic programming. Genetic determinism contradicts the entire rational choice foundation of the social sciences from Aristotle to Hobbes to contemporary learning theories. And finally, the combination of the historical accumulation of beliefs and values captured in cultures at the macro level and the processes of socialization and indoctrination at the micro level makes a science based on genetic mechanisms appear irrelevant or redundant. But are these criticisms well founded? I will argue that they misrepresent the Darwinian approach to human social behavior.

I return to an observation from Carol Gilligan that strikes a chord with the Darwinian approach. As I mentioned earlier, Gilligan formally disavows a biological foundation for gender differences. What I did not mention is that she was equally critical of sociological determinations of gender differences. "I find the question of whether gender differences are biologically determined or socially constructed deeply disturbing. This way of posing the question implies that people, women and men alike, are either genetically determined or a product of socialization—that there is no voice—and without voice, there is no possibility for resistance, for creativity, or for a change whose wellsprings are psychological" ([1982] 1993:xix). She goes on to say that biological reductionism as well as sociological reductionism pave the way for totalitarianism, because they both conceive of social action without reference to "voice." Voice is the expression of individual aspirations and responsibilities. It is the core of the "classical tradition," i.e., the idea that individuals are responsible for their own actions. For Gilligan, neither genetic conditioning nor cultural conditioning captures the field of action negotiated by individuals as they muster their resources, opportunities, and desires in everyday life. This position is ironically shared by the evolutionary psychologist. How could that be so?

CHOICES AND APPETITES

Evolutionary psychology does not supersede agency. It does not ignore the role(s) of culture nor does it replace learning theories with behavioral genetic mechanisms that are indifferent to experience. It deepens our understanding of choice behavior by focusing on the things that characterize our appetites. Bentham ([1789] 1970) allows human actors free will, but the expression of that will is tempered by two masters: pain and pleasure. Various systems of control inhibit the individual's acquisition of pleasure and self-interest: the physical, the moral, the religious, the state, etc. The physical system, for example, inflicts costs on persons who pick fights with opponents larger than themselves. Sexual excesses are inhibited by STDs, gluttony by heart disease, etc. The informal moral system attaches costs in the forms of pains of "conscience" and loss of status in the eyes of the reference group. The formal legal system attaches penalties to transgressions in terms of arrests, fines, and confinement. In the terms of classical economics, people "maximize their utilities" by calculating the balance between costs and benefits, or, in Bentham's terms, between pain and pleasure, as experienced within these systems of constraint (Gottfredson and Hirschi 1990). Evolutionary psychology enlarges this picture by suggesting that human desires do not materialize out of thin air. We have evolved highly discerning taste buds to identify salt, sugar, and protein, and have become more successful foragers as a result. In a parallel way, we have evolved social preferences that we retain as "intuitions" or "instincts" that guide our choices in everyday life. So that in exercising our choices, evolution may have shaped the things we desire and enjoy.

In *The Evolution of Desire*, David Buss explores gender differences in preferences for a mate. These differences appear to have evolved to deal with the differential costs to males and females that arise from mating behavior. The parental investment of males and females is significant but not equal. The females carry the fetus for nine months, suckle the newborn for several years, and assume parental responsibility for raising the offspring. Pregnancy has significant and unavoidable opportunity costs for the female but less so for the male, who could choose to father many offspring simultaneously with different mates. There are many potential evolutionary solutions to this cost differential. Buss argues that in *Homo sapiens* this has resulted in female preferences for older, taller, higher status, economically successful, generous, and faithful mates. Buss's evidence was based on a number of cross-cultural surveys "in thirty-seven cultures on six continents. . . . Women across all political systems . . . , all racial groups, all religious groups, and all systems of mating (from intense polygyny to presumptive monogamy) place more value than men on good financial prospects" (1994:24–25). In fact, women valued financial resources twice as much as men. "These findings provide the first extensive cross-cultural evidence supporting the evolutionary basis for the psychology of human mating" (ibid.:25). The same pattern emerges in analysis of personal ads placed by men and women looking for partners: women seek older, financially secure partners. The preference for older and higher status males is, according to Buss, a marker for economic security and success. Height is a marker for dominance, which is also related to social and economic success. The fact that women want men who are successful, more mature, ambitious, intelligent, dependable, tall, healthy, and faithful will strike many people as "common sense." After all, are not these favorable attributes in people in general? Buss's point is that the shaping of desires will result in choices that are "no brainers" *because* they are instinctual. But what is more persuasive is that male priorities are so different. Where women value conditions associated with material security (presumably due to maternal investment), men value youthful women, physical attractiveness (a proxy for health and fertility), a hip to waist ratio of about 0.7, chaste premarital behavior, and postmarital fidelity—all of which are elements that enlarge male fitness. The older males become, the more they desire increasingly younger women, indeed, "trophy" wives who enlarge their status. As a result, males are more interested in casual sex, have different expectations as to at what point an emotional relationship should become physically intimate, have an inflated view of the ideal number of sexual partners, and have a lower threshold for engaging in casual sex.

> Imagine that an attractive person of the opposite sex walks up to you on a college campus and says: "Hi, I've been noticing you around town lately, and I find you very attractive. Would you like to go to bed with me?" If you are like 100% of the women in one study, you would give an emphatic no. . . . But if you were a man, the odds are 75 percent that you would say yes. (Buss 1994b:73)

If women are by nature "coy" and men by nature "randy," this derives from the costs of casual sex for each gender. Buss also argues that jealousy has an important evolutionary origin. While female baboons undergo external changes when they become fertile, human female ovulation is "cryptic" or nonobvious. Because the male cannot monitor his mate during ovulation, this makes it somewhat more difficult for human males to be certain of the paternity of their mate's offspring. In evolutionary history, men whose mates copulated with other males would have undermined their own fitness if they had spent years investing in nonprogeny. Buss argues that the emotion of jealousy evolved as a (potential) solution to this problem. Both males and females have a proprietary interest in the fidelity of their mates, but how they experience the loss of bond exclusivity is quite different. Buss reports that when male and female subjects are asked to imagine different kinds of infidelities ranging from spending time with a sexual rival, giving that rival gifts, or actually engaging in sex with the rival, males were far more agitated by their mates having sex with their rivals, while women were more agitated by their mate's *emotional* attachment to the rival. Women's jealousy "is triggered by cues to the possible diversion of their mate's investment to another woman, whereas men's jealousy is triggered primarily by cues to the possible diversion of their mate's sexual favors to another man" (1994b:128). This was also reflected in differences in physiological distress measured by changes in heartbeat, skin conductance, and other measures of arousal. Men reacted far more to thoughts of *sexual* infidelity than women, and women reacted far more to thoughts of *emotional* infidelity than men. These patterns were investigated cross-culturally and the same differences in fears of jealousy emerged. "These sexual differences in the causes of jealousy appear to characterize the entire human species" (ibid.:129).

Buss analyzes specific strategies that reflect each step in the mating game. Under "attracting a mate" he describes how individuals display their resources, commitment, and physical prowess, how they try to enhance appearance, and convey sexual signals to express interest. He also outlines strategies for "staying together" and dealing with "sexual conflict and competition," and the contribution of fitness concerns in "breaking up" (infidelity, infertility, withdrawal of support, withdrawal of sexual access, etc.). In each case he describes the differences in strategies for males and females, differences that arise primarily from differences in parental investment, and differences in fitness value over the life cycle. It is clear that each specific strategy that he identifies is not hardwired in the sense that Parkinson's disease is hardwired, expressing itself ineluctably after the age of fifty and proceeding through a set of steps that ruin the nervous system and make premature death unavoidable. Fitness pressures and differences in parental investment shape desires sometimes in vivid ways—intense male insecurities over infidelity—and sometimes in more generalized ways—where, for example, women come to find attractive a range of social traits because of their *indirect* linkage to the material security that evolution has mandated as a priority. Even though they are thought to have a position somewhere in the human genome (to be determined), these feelings and desires are not impervious to cultural pressures, nor are they totally removed from influences of learning and reinforcement. I will return to these issues momentarily.

The point that I wish to emphasize here is that evolutionary psychology does not retire "utilitarianism" or "rational choice theory" or learning theories. It attempts to shed light on the contribution of selection pressures to the evolution of our social priorities in the choices we exercise. In other words, it tries to make intelligible what are for Bentham merely *generic* "pains" and "pleasures." And it makes intelligible many social behaviors that seem to be patently irrational. Buss's explanations for human strategies for mating sometimes strike us as all too obvious or commonsensical. The analysis of crime within a Darwinian perspective is another matter.

EXPLAINING MURDER: "TRIVIAL ALTERCATION," POLYGYNY, AND STATUS

Jack Katz describes in detail the paradoxical behaviors of the "hard-man" robber. These individuals frequently weave "stick-up" into a fabric of other criminal activities that include pimping, assault, narcotics, and gambling (1988:165–66). They cut a flashy figure in criminal circles, buying new clothes and giving gifts to friends, partying at length, and cyclically finding themselves broke as a result. They are also far more likely than other career criminals to spend a great deal of time in jail before they "square up"—typically half their adult lives. They often cultivate fearsome reputations because of their employment of what some have dubbed "recreational violence"—a fact that makes them threatening not only to victims but to other perpetrators. Ironically, the average take from a non–bank robber is small—two hundred to three hundred dollars. Bank robberies, which have an extremely high clearance rate, net about two thousand dollars. So "hard-men" into the robbery game go on sprees of stickup, followed by sprees of partying, alcohol and drug consumption, gambling, and whoring. Katz asks, What is the rationality of this life style? It's not about the money, since no one has anything to show for it at the end of the day. It's not that crime has become a form of work since the offenders spend half their adult lives in prison. Katz points to the emotional attractions of the lifestyle, but notes that it does not appeal to everyone; indeed, statistically, it's most prevalent among young black men. I will return to why this pattern emerges.

The first attempt to understand the emotional appeals of robbery and violence from a Darwinian psychological framework was made by Daly and Wilson in *Homicide* (1988). They point out that the most prevalent form of male-to-male killing in contemporary Western societies starts from "trivial altercations." This has been noted by criminologists for a generation, but no one offered a credible explanation beyond identifying gender and age as behavioral hazards. Trivial altercations are fights that start over "stupid little incidents," arguments, insults, even accidents. Often the combatants are egged on by their associates and friends, and often the violence escalates to the point where someone produces a knife or revolver and conducts a lethal attack, or has the knife or gun taken from him by an assailant who uses it on him. No one planned the killing beforehand. Usually it is a toss-up as to who will win and who will lose. And typically the matter that results in a homicide is "a little old fight over nothing at all." Daly and Wilson point out that the fights mean a great deal to those who pursue them. What is at stake is "face," reputation, or credibility in the eyes of one's associates. Daly and Wilson point out that in preindustrial societies, violence is an important social commodity that is associated with respect and power in village society, and that men who gain prestige through their willingness to kill, often on the smallest pretext, in fact enjoy greater status as well as greater fitness, i.e., more wives, and more children.

How do we get from violence to fitness? Daly and Wilson argue that *Homo sapiens* is essentially a polygynous species. In fact, in the anthropological record, over 80 percent of societies practice polygynous marriage. Many argue that European societies practice serial polygyny. Polygyny is important in understanding the problem of *fitness variance*. In a polygynous species such as the fruit fly, every fertile female will have offspring, but some male flies will breed a great many times, and some not at all. The female's fitness is limited by the number of eggs she carries. The male is limited by the number of mates. Daly and Wilson draw a parallel between the predicament of people and fruit flies:

> A man—like a fruit-fly—could always increase his expected fitness by gaining sexual access to one more fertile female, regardless of whether he presently has no mates or fifty, whereas a woman—like a female fruit-fly—typically would not enhance her expected fitness by gaining sexual access to every fertile male on the planet (ibid.:139).

As a result, female fitness is guaranteed, but not male fitness. This has consequences. In many polygynous species, males fight one another to establish dominance. Elk and deer develop large racks of horns, not for defense against predators, but to establish their dominance over the male competitors in their own herds, and hence their right to breed. Where a dominant male establishes exclusive reproductive control of the females, his control is subject to challenge from younger males, often in bloody and deadly contests. Polygynous species are characterized by sexual dimorphism, higher rates of male mortality due to intraspecific conflict as well as differences in male-female rates of senescence (longevity), traits that are found in our species.

If *Homo sapiens* is essentially polygynous, this would explain the cross-cultural patterns of male overrepresentation in homicide and other violent crimes. Men, but not women, find the resort to violence attractive to establish status. And it appears to be the intangible aspect of homicidal altercations and the ostentatious quality of the robber lifestyle that matters. As Daly and Wilson note, if the explanation for robbery were penury, most robbers would be women (ibid.:178). But most robbery, robbery-homicide, and homicidal altercations are male-dominated activities if not a male monopoly. Why?

> Men's minimum needs for survival and sustenance are hardly greater than those of women. And the men . . . are certainly no more likely to be desperately poor than their female counterparts. But in a paternally investing species such as our own, males gain reproductive success by commanding and displaying resources that exceed their own subsistence needs. (ibid.:179)

Their account does not end here. Violence is not the only way to acquire status, indeed, it is among the least feasible in industrial societies. In their examination of homicide statistics Daly and Wilson point out that males kill other males at a rate ten times that of females killing other females, that they tend to kill persons of the same age as themselves (i.e., their competitors), that the age of highest risk occurs during the period of most intense family formation (the early twenties), and finally, that those who engage in such activities are far more likely, compared to the population at large, to be unmarried and unemployed. The appeal of homicide is greatest for those whose fitness is most precarious: young, poor, and unattached males. This analysis also explains Katz's findings about gender, race, and age in his study of robbery. Just as escalating a trivial altercation to the point of homicidal violence only appeals to males lacking other resources to establish reputation, the appeal of robbery only makes sense to young men living in communities lacking access to the legal avenues of wealth and status acquisition. Note in all this that we are not contesting the fact that these individuals are free agents, or that they are not responsible for their actions. Evolutionary theory is explaining the appetites for ostentatious and violent displays and why they have the distinctive gender, age, and social configurations we find in contemporary studies of murder and robbery. This analysis provides a nonobvious explanation of the underlying rationality of behaviors that are otherwise inexplicable.

LEARNING THEORIES AND CULTURE IN EVOLUTIONARY PSYCHOLOGY

Many students of social psychology view the evolutionary perspective as redundant because, they say, gender differences are learned. "It's all a matter of socialization," and as such, it can be easily changed if people simply choose to raise their children differently. This view falsely juxtaposes nature and nurture. When we try to "shape" a behavior in animals through operant or Pavlovian means, learning theorists point out that there already exists an *unconditioned* reflex (Breland and Breland 1966). Gender socialization is the *modification* of existing dispositions, which are not learned but which appear developmentally. The infant is not a *tabula rasa* at birth but comes equipped with certain dispositions that are natural and that can be reinforced. The learning of language is the paradigm example. People have a genetic disposition to acquire speech. Cultures may differ in which language is imparted, but the underlying ability to acquire speech is genetic. And it is also developmentally sensitive—if the child fails to receive instruction in the first decade of life, the ability to acquire speech subsequently is severely impaired. There are parallels to gender. Gender differences occur as early as we can measure them. Boys are far more likely to be born prematurely, to show deficits in motor and social behavior, difficult temperament, hyperactivity, emotional disorder, and aggressiveness relative to girls. They are also *more* likely to have parents who are hostile and depressed. Socialization is not a one-way street, and it does not work on a blank slate. Evolutionary psychology acknowledges that pain and pleasure can help *shape* behavior, but learning theory is falsely seen as a substitute for a Darwinian approach to the understanding of behavior. Skinner's rats learned to press bars and run mazes to get fed, but feeding was already an innate trait, and the experiment capitalized on its evolved versatility. As Breland and Breland (ibid.) point out, Skinner's experiments reflected the innate abilities of his experimental subject, the white rat, and reflected the behavioral repertoire found in the rat's ecology. But all the reinforcement in the world could not make the skill sets of rats interchangeable with those of cows, dolphins, pigs, or cats, a lesson the Brelands, who were students of Skinner, learned in the course of careers trying to condition some eight thousand animals representing sixty different species. The point is that learning theory is not an alternative to the evolutionary perspective. The social construction of reality is erected on a biological foundation.

What about culture? Buss explicitly acknowledges that cultures have an enormous influence on the expression of evolved appetites. "Cultural conditions determine which strategies get activated and which lie dormant" (1994b:15). Accordingly, when there is a surplus of males to females in the population, despite a vestigial preference for polygyny, monogamy is the rule. However, in social scenes like bars, where more men than women are seeking casual relationships, there is a premium on deceptive practices in respect of commitment (ibid.:122). Where social welfare programs cover costs of child care, maternity benefits, and material support as in Sweden, the value placed on premarital chastity declines. "Women's economic independence from men lowers the cost to them of a free and active sex life before marriage, or as an alternative to marriage. Thus, practically no Swedish women are virgins at marriage" (ibid.:69). For Buss, the evolutionary legacy of human desires is context-sensitive. Whatever the "default setting" in terms of desires, individual actors tailor their actions in the face of external conditions (culture) that modify how they are expressed. Again, the point is that culture does not replace evolved appetites, any more than evolutionary psychology replaces utilitarianism. It determines which appetites enjoy expression, and which are conditioned toward extinction.

PROBLEMS WITH THE EVOLUTIONARY APPROACH TO GENDER DIFFERENCES

One of the virtues of Gilligan's theory of vivid differences in male and female moral outlooks was that it made it easy to expose it to evidence to determine whether it had empirical validity. The problem outlined in this chapter was that she persisted in her views in the absence of objective evidence and enjoyed professional celebrity because of her extrascientific appeals. The situation with evolutionary psychology is more complex due to the nature of the arguments found in this area. There are four major points to raise.

First, the nature of the explanations of the instinctual basis of human social behaviors is explicitly a post hoc argument. This derives from the reverse engineering approach that is unavoidable when we move from the deductive nature of evolution in the *general* sense to the more inductive application of fitness models in the case of *specific* social traits or instincts.[2] For example: "*If,* over evolutionary time, generosity in men provided these benefits repeatedly and the cues to a man's generosity were observable and reliable *then* selection would favor the evolution of a preference for generosity in a mate" (Buss 1994b:21, emphasis added). Or, sperm count in male ejaculate increases significantly if a couple spends time apart. "This increase in sperm is precisely what would be expected *if* humans had an ancestral history of some casual sex and marital infidelity" (ibid.:75, emphasis added). The presumption is that the trait actually enhanced fitness and was heritable. This leads the theorist to speculate on how such an advantage would work. But this is clearly speculation. Stephen Gould (1978) compared such accounts to Kipling's "just-so" stories, like how the leopard got its spots or how the tiger got its stripes.[3] The psychologist's reconstruction trades on prehistorical ecological histories that are imagined since usually the only clue to the fitness pressures are the outcomes and their "design features," i.e., the thing we are trying to explain.[4] Sometimes good use is made of comparative methods as in the examination of "sperm wars," where it is possible to relate the size of primate testes (in chimps, gorilla, and humans) to differential patterns of mating, but often this comparative evidence is lacking. The method of "reverse engineering" requires us to accept the conclusion first, and search for the evidence later. In organic evolution, we start with the morphological peculiarities of a bone, feather, or hair specimen and conjure the ecological pressures that would be necessary to create them, but in the realm of social behaviors we are not even sure that that the peculiarities we identify (in contrast to organic traits) are heritable.

This leads to my second point. The theory of truth in such explanations is quite different in this area of psychology than elsewhere. The experimental method in principle is based on a test of the null hypothesis. Statements of relationships are made in hypotheses, and evidence is marshaled to determine if the relationships are as predicted. The evolutionist proceeds by putting together pieces of a puzzle without knowing what the original pattern looked like and without necessarily having all the pieces. The test of the theory is its coherence or integrity. It makes sense of things that otherwise strike us as unconnected or incoherent. The problem is that it is logically possible for several alternative puzzle solutions to be equally coherent. One is reminded of Sigmund Freud's ([1957] 2001) psychoanalysis of Leonardo da Vinci. Freud saw in Leonardo's painting of the Madonna and Child with St. Anne a disturbing subliminal image: a vulture disguised in the folds of the mother's clothing that threatened the child. Leonardo had recalled from his youth that he was attacked by a bird, specifically a kite, whose tail brushed his lips. In Freud's sources this was mistranslated as a vulture. From these fragments Freud deduced Leonardo's aversion to his mother, his homosexuality, and other themes of his paintings, including the ambiguity of Mona Lisa's smile. He wove together a coherent account of Leonardo's life that reconciled the tensions and contradictions in Leonardo's life. I for one cannot see the vulture that Freud detects, and his detection appears to be premised on a mistranslation in any case. The other major problem with the analysis was that the painting Freud analyzed was not actually finished by Leonardo but probably by his students or another artist. Typically master painters would compose the main subjects and leave details such as clothing to their assistants, but in this case the master appears to have lost interest in the work before it was completed. So the story Freud pulls together may be coherent, but its empirical premises may be dubious. Coherence may be a necessary condition of truth, but it is not sufficient.

The third, and really worrisome aspect of an evolutionary account of social behaviors, is that cultures can *mimic* traits that may have an instinctual basis. This is a point advanced by Daniel Dennett (1995), a philosopher highly sympathetic to Darwinian thinking. Just as sexual selection, for example, can create an appetite for status through escalation of violence as discussed earlier, this "trait" can be reinvented by *observers* of trivial altercations, and embedded in social histories that effectively influence people who are unaffected by heritable dispositions for face-saving violence escalation. In the result, young men may adopt violent ego contests that result in violence to establish reputation. In effect, an inherited trait may be independently reengineered in a cultural group as an adaptive strategy that is wholly cultural. Machismo cultures may shape male appetites for violence by rewarding conflict with status, which may in turn influence fitness. "With the human species, as Dan Dennett observed, you can never be sure that what you see is instinct, because you might be looking at the result of a reasoned argument, a copied ritual, or a learned lesson" (Ridley 2003:55). The implications of this cannot be overstated. What it suggests is that the entire field of evolutionary psychology consists of the *identification* of hypotheses, often through brilliant "reverse engineer" reasoning. Establishing the evidence for a hypothesis to choose between a model of culturally based fitness as opposed to organic fitness is another matter. I am unaware of any principled attempts to put "paid" to Dennett's position.

The final point concerns the moral ambiguities in the evolutionary psychology perspective. Sometimes the authors write as though the social behaviors they explain are *vestigial*, in the way that the human appendix is a vestige of a second stomach and functions quite differently from the "main" stomach. For example: "The man who hunts down and kills a woman who has left him has surely relapsed into futile spite, acting out his vestigial agenda of dominance to no useful end" (Daly and Wilson 1988:219). Or consider Buss's reflections on whether he should have published the bad news about men's preoccupation with young, fertile females. "Suppression of this truth is unlikely to help, just as concealing the fact that people have evolved preferences for succulent, ripe fruit is unlikely to change their preferences. . . . Telling men not to become aroused by signs of youth and health is like telling them not to experience sugar as sweet" (1994b:71). Buss also holds that "whereas modern conditions of mating differ from ancestral conditions, the same sexual strategies operate with unbridled force" (ibid.:14). If they operate with *unbridled* force, why should we have any optimism that "only by understanding our evolved sexual strategies . . . can we hope to change our current course" (ibid.:14–15). Or, "We are the first species in known history of three and a half billion years of life with the capacity to control our destiny" (ibid.:222). If the sexual strategies are Dawkins-like cultural patterns (memes),[5] this may be so, but if they are instinctual (heritable), we are no more able to deny the "unbridled force" of such appetites than we are able simply to decide that sugar is *un*sweet. Evolutionary psychology appears to classify harmful instincts as *vestiges* that can be rooted out by an act of will while the other instincts—our sense of empathy, our ear for music, talent for numbers, linguistic ability—can be preserved at will because, by implication, they represent our good nature. But Mother Nature is indifferent to this kind of romantic thinking: one species' vestige is another species' true nature. It is all the same to the DNA.

FINAL WORDS

In previous chapters, we have seen that social psychology is awash in extrascientific agendas lurking behind the experimental design. In our discussion of gender—from Gilligan to Buss—the experiment per se has receded from view to be replaced by anecdotal evidence, but the political agendas have not. In neither case can the science that each advances contribute positively to scientific progress. Where Gilligan has claimed that the political has become the psychological, the evidence reviewed here is quite the opposite: the psychological has become political. Mednick captures this in her analysis of the gender bandwagon in contemporary psychology, as does Sommers in her report on the academic war against boys. Gilligan's case fails because the evidence for differences in moral outlook is all gainsaid. Ironically, evolutionary psychology acknowledges these kinds of gender differences. It acknowledges further that gender conflicts, if not normal, are virtually unavoidable if we recognize the competing interests of men and women, but for different reasons. Men are disconnected because they are competing for fitness. Yet both proponents write in romantic terms about deciding to "make it all right." Both Gilligan and Buss are optimists. If on self-reflection one realizes that society and history have structured one's experience, one can choose to act differently. One can recover one's "voice." One can say "no" to polygyny.[6] One can say "no" to patriarchy. These may be interesting moral points, but they are not very compelling scientific points.

NOTES

1. Harvard agreed in 2003 to return most of the Fonda donation. There were several difficulties including poor stock market performance of the securities funding the gift, as well as delays at Harvard in implementing the provisions of the gift (see MassNews Archives Internet June 7, 2002). However, the original gift appeared to initiate a new cultural form in gender studies: celebrity science. Celebrity science is to real science what the Fonda Foundation is to the National Science Foundation. The former is a caricature of the latter.

2. In the general explanation we suggest that traits (unspecified) vary to some extent randomly, and that, if these confer reproductive advantages, they are pre-

served in the organism's genetic legacy. When we move from the general case to arguing for the adaptive advantages of specific traits, the explanation becomes historical, since we are looking for evidence of changes in the fossil record, peculiarities in biogeographic distributions of fauna and flora, and homologies across related species. Goudge (1961) refers to "historical explanations in evolutionary theory" and the role of narratives in framing the conditions found in the historical record. For example, explaining how amphibians developed limbs that allowed them to evolve into land creatures consists "in proposing an intelligible sequence of occurrences such that the event to be explained 'falls into place' as the terminal phase of it. . . . Thus the explanation proposed is an historical one" (ibid.:72). Desmond offers a similar narrative to explain how hot-blooded dinosaurs evolved into birds. In *Archaeopteryx* it is argued that the feathers evolved as a means of trapping insects in a species that was initially ground-living, fleet of foot, and large brained. "The bird-dinosaur, complete with endothermy, feathers, wings and a brain able to coordinate intricate manoeuvres, was *completely* 'preadapted' to flight" (1975:175).

3. This was clearly unfair inasmuch as the explanation of any specific organic trait would require the sort of narrative explanation of the kind Goudge describes in the previous note. Gould's position is paradoxical since, as a paleontologist, he clearly subscribed to evolutionary theory, although the variant he proposed as one of "interrupted equilibria"—based on his analysis of the Burgess Shales, and the stunningly varied forms of life in the Precambrian period (Gould 1989).

4. Logically, this is the fallacy of affirming the consequent. See Hempel (1965: 310).

5. The idea of "memes" was first introduced by Richard Dawkins in the *Selfish Gene* ([1976] 1990) and elaborated by Daniel Dennett in *Darwin's Dangerous Idea* (1995). Memes are basically memories that reproduce something that confers an advantage. They are the cultural equivalent of genes, but permit the replication of a structure dramatically faster than organic reproduction and permit the acceleration of cultural evolution with increasingly diminishing input from genetic information.

6. It is ironic that evolutionary psychology posits an optimistic future while simultaneously asking us to acknowledge as science what we repudiate morally— polygyny. While the vast majority of societies in the cross-cultural files of anthropology are polygynous, the leading European industrial nations, after two millennia of Christianity, are monogamous, as are the leading Asian nations (largely without the influence of Christian teachings).

7

The End of Experimental
Social Psychology

"I don't see how you can write anything of value," the great anthropologist Marvin Harris told me years ago, "if you don't offend someone." Skeptical inquiry is endangered when those who are offended or threatened by knowledge are able to silence those who have something valuable to say.

—Carol Tavris, "The High Cost of Skepticism"

Suppose tomorrow that all these scholarly efforts of the psychologists should disappear from the collective knowledge of mankind. . . . Would it really make a difference? I suggest not.

—Rod Cooper, "The Passing of Psychology"

WHY HAS SOCIAL PSYCHOLOGY FAILED?

In this work we have reviewed some of the classic studies of social influence in the early days of the field from Sherif to Milgram and Zimbardo. We have examined the application of social psychology to industrial production (Hawthorne), school performance (Pygmalion), and mass media effects (aggression). And we have most recently reviewed some of psychology's recent contributions to the study of gender. These do *not* represent an exhaustive sampling of the developments of the field, but they cover materials that would have a very high recognition factor among serious students of the field, and they touch on many of its classic contributions, and include studies that are viewed as the foundations on which the field has developed. My point in this book is to suggest that the scientific achievements in the field, as represented in these studies, are rather modest, frequently misleading, and sometimes downright wrong. Social psychology has failed as a science, not because it has made mistakes but because it appears incapable of recognizing them as such. What is alarming is that the devotees of social psychology either do not seem to attach much gravity to this situation or do not know what to do about it. Carey, in questioning the acceptance of the Hawthorne effect in the absence of any credible evidence supporting it, suggested that the answer lay in the occupational and professional attractions of the idea. He wrote:

> How is it that nearly all authors of textbooks who have drawn material from the Hawthorne studies have failed to recognize the vast discrepancy between evidence and conclusions in those studies, have frequently misdescribed the actual observations and occurrences in a way that brings the evidence into line with the conclusions, and have done this even when such authors based their whole outlook and orientation on the conclusions reached by the Hawthorne investigators? Exploration of these questions would provide salutary insight into aspects of the sociology of social scientists. (1968:416)

In his discussion of the debate over operationism in the history of the cognitive dissonance, Rosenwald wrote:

> The main objective of this paper is to explore the incentives of a scientific strategy which delivers a scanty theoretical yield and which lacks firm philosophical supports. The premiss [sic] underlying the present discussion is that, whereas operationism can be criticized (or defended) on logical grounds, its persistence in the face of methodological critique and of its disappointing theoretical yield cannot. We must seek answers outside the philosophy of science, for instance, in the sociology of professions and in the explicit and implicit missions which learned disciplines set for themselves. (1986:303–4)

Mednick argued that *bandwagons* have characterized a great deal of the research on gender and, I might add, media effects. I have argued that in all these cases the scientific agenda has been drawn below the threshold of critical radar by a powerful "tractor beam," i.e., by unacknowledged moral and political agendas. These have frequently dictated the scientific agenda and sabotaged the prospects of scientific progress. Ironically, they have also kept the field alive. The idea of the failure of the field of social psychology has to be taken with a grain of salt. The failure that I refer to borrows from previous reports of psychologists discussed in earlier chapters who recognize that the scientific project has gone off the rails. Recall Zajonc's remarks, looking back over the past four decades, that social psychology has not developed any consensus about what is central to the field, nor accumulated any evidence to establish important, nonobvious lawlike statements about human behavior. Recall Buss's characterization of the field as in "theoretical disarray," or G. A. Miller's characterization of the field as "an intellectual zoo" without any standard method or technique. Cooper concluded that psychology's failure to progress was to be attributed "not to immaturity but to retardation." Ferguson characterized the history of psychology as decades of "useless research." These rather grim assessments of the discipline come from people who have enjoyed successful careers in the field. In spite of the concerns I have outlined, the field flourishes as a popular undergraduate subject, and its publications, journals, and conferences proceed as though none of what I argue is valid or relevant. This motivates me to clarify what I mean when I argue that social psychology has failed. My concerns lie in three areas: methods, theory, and ethics. We shall examine each in turn.

METHODS

In the area of methods, there are three issues. The first has to do with the logic of experimentation. Psychology's purchase on the scientific community has been made on the basis of its scientific methodology, particularly its emphasis on experimentation. As every student of methodology knows, the gold standard in terms of empirical inquiry is the true experiment: random assignment of subjects to treatment groups, identification of correlations between treatments and outcomes, temporal precedence of the causes over effects, and an ability to rule out spurious relationships. The reality was rather different. At the heart of the discipline covering the period from Sherif to Asch to Milgram to Zimbardo, the "experimental" projects carried on in the labs were primarily "demonstrations." They were undertaken without the intent of explicitly testing specific theories. Sherif *simulated* how norms evolved. Asch *mimicked* resistance to propaganda. And Milgram *dramatized* obedience to authority. The demonstrations were inductive or exploratory. There were no tests of significance. They attempted to paint a picture of realities that were already, to some extent, well understood, at least in a commonsense way. The studies of media effects of violent TV and pornography through the use of Milgram-type shock designs were not studies of the actual effects of media on sexual and physical aggression but the imagined *parallels* or *analogs* to what such effects on aggression might look like *if* they were real. So rather than exposing ideas to the potential of falsification that derives from explicit theory testing, classical social psychology replaced the scientist with a dramatist. It made for memorable stories, but little in the way of theory development.

The second major issue follows directly. Because demonstration was so central to the academic culture of experimental social psychology, there was little evidence of disconfirmation. Indeed, without any explicit theory, the idea of disconfirmation was almost foreign to the research culture. This was also noted by Pepitone in his reflections noted earlier, when he recalled that the vast majority of published research articles findings confirmed their hypotheses, and that progress through falsification was rare. As we observed, Festinger explicitly questioned the logic of falsification, and in his own work on cognitive dissonance, the field "progressed" despite the profoundly ambiguous empirical results that it generated. Rather than conclude that the underlying model was problematic, experimenters bent themselves into pretzels to preserve it (Cooper and Fazio 1984).

The final point is that the field appears to have handicapped itself by a virtually exclusive devotion of its research methods to experimentation. The crisis literature that emerged in the 1970s returned to this point repeatedly. The field became wedded to the belief that complex social events could be examined causally in the lab, even though such experiments of necessity were of short duration, low impact, and typically drew from a restricted sector of the population—the undergraduate psychology majors. This limitation was noted, but no serious movement to broaden fundamentally the methodological scope of social psychologists ever proved successful.

THEORY

Given the preoccupation with methods, it is hardly surprising that social psychology has failed to develop substantial headway in the development of a theory of action. The situation is exacerbated further by the legacy of commonsense psychology, i.e., the idea that, at the meso level, most actors already have a relatively sophisticated understanding of interpersonal interaction. Commonsense knowledge and scientific knowledge claim the same territory. By contrast, evolutionary psychology theory has made great strides in our understanding of the foundation of appetites that otherwise strike us as perplexing (i.e., "trivial altercations"), but its insight is not based on methodological premises, as much as a larger Darwinian explanation of adaptation—a much-needed strong theoretical basis. However, this promising development has yet to attract much attention in the core of social psychology because it does not lend itself readily to experimental testing, any more than Darwinism does in zoology or paleontology. Also, psychology has yet to sort out all the mechanisms of sense-making that are attributed to the evolved brain—cheater detection, nepotism toward blood relatives, altruism, moral compulsions, retributive justice, etc.—and to determine their relative importance vis-à-vis the long-standing mechanisms of adjustment—classical and operant conditioning.

In social psychology this avenue of theory development has been over-shadowed by the moral agendas that have grounded the demonstrations of the classical tradition. The most important theoretical development in the field, cognitive dissonance, did not prove successful, but rather than scrubbing the agenda and moving on, a generation has attempted to rede-fine and finesse it, as though incapable of acknowledging that not every new idea is scientifically sound. The demonstrations of Asch, Milgram, and Zimbardo, as well as the field studies in industry (Hawthorne) and schools (Pygmalion) were landmark *moral* achievements, but they did not advance psychological theory. George Miller (1992:40) warned that "pan-dering to public interest" would destroy the scientific integrity of psy-chology. While this may be an overstatement, in my view, the classical tradition, because of its "relevance" and extrascientific agendas has suf-fered in theoretical development.

ETHICS

The final area of concern is ethics. As recounted in previous chapters, many of the classical studies were quite provocative and, in some cases, traumatic for the human subjects. Let us examine some cases. Zillmann and Bryant (1982, 1984) recruited 160 students for a study of the effects of pornography on attitudes toward women. One group viewed a menu of sexually explicit films for one night per week for a period of six weeks. Subjects were tested in three further weeks for evidence of calloused atti-tudes toward rape, rape myth acceptance, tolerance of censorship, and sympathy for the "female liberation movement." Changes in attitudes were found in both male and female subjects. The authors suggested that participation in the experiment had produced "nontransitory" shifts in attitudes toward rape myth acceptance, increasing indifference to victims of rape, etc. If we accept that changes for the worse were "nontransitory," were subjects' attitudes "injured" as a result of this study? I do not believe that the changes were permanent, contrary to what the authors suggest, but as experimenters, are we not simply gambling that the risks associated with experiments are always tolerable? To their credit, Zillmann and Bryant suggested that there should be an embargo on future pornography effect studies since the harm to subjects had been established in their eyes. Ironically, this would have the effect of curtailing the replications that were so unsuccessful in corroborating their findings.

Consider the drug emotion studied undertaken by Stan Schachter with his students in the early 1960s. In order to control levels of arousal to a film that was calculated to produce emotion (i.e., laughter—the film was Jack Carson's *The Good Humor Man*), subjects were injected with a powerful sedative—chlorpromazine. Ladd Wheeler explains that the graduate students had to experiment on themselves to determine a suitable dose to administer (blind) to undergraduate subjects.

> We pretested the chlorpromazine doses at 50 mg on ourselves and other graduate students, and Stan had us make notes of our feelings. Chuck Hawkins wrote that he had decided he was definitely going to die, after he checked his pulse at 32 and falling. Bibb Latané came out of the testing room and promptly fell on his head, knocking over the coffee pot. Stan consulted all sorts of experts and finally decided to halve the dosage, in the face of overwhelming ignorance on the part of the experts. Mental hospital patients are given extreme dosages, but no one knew what it might do to an undergraduate. Even then, we had a cot available for the chlorpromazine subjects, and it was used with some frequency after the experimental session. (1987:48)

Wheeler goes on to say that they had the welfare of the subjects as a first priority and that a physician was always on hand. But how could anyone determine a "reasonable" dosage when *expert* knowledge could provide little guidance, and when the primary clinical use of the drug was to treat schizophrenics? And what sort of human experiment requires a *frequently used* cot to help subjects recover? Again, I have no reason to believe that anyone suffered serious injury in these experiments, but were the psychologists not simply taking risks with the adjustments of their graduate and undergraduate students? Zimbardo (1999) argued that the Institutional Review Boards (IRBs) had *over*acted to the treatment of human subjects in psychological experiments. When we see the nature of the interventions undertaken in this period, can we honestly claim this was overreaction? Milgram's subjects sweated, trembled, stuttered, bit their lips, groaned, dug their fingernails into their flesh, and experienced uncontrollable nervous laughing fits and full-blown, uncontrollable seizures. This was the most important "experiment" in the classical tradition.

Some sense of the lack of concern over ethical treatment of subjects is suggested indirectly in Leon Festinger's reflection on the issue of deception and ethical treatment of human subjects. He refers to the Tuskegee syphilis study in which 399 American black men, poor sharecroppers, in Macon County, Alabama, were misled by the U.S. Public Health Service about their illness. They were not treated for their infections, but were simply monitored over a period of four decades (1932–1972) and developed grotesque symptoms that could have been eliminated by antibiotics and sulfa drugs. As Festinger notes:

> one group was treated; the other was also followed in time but not treated. Was this an ethical violation? Is it "harming" someone, who would have had

no medical attention anyway? . . . *I'm not so sure about this*. These persons
were not harmed by the research in the sense that they were no worse off
than if the research had not been done at all. (1980:249, emphasis added)

This opinion seems ethically challenged on several counts, not the least
of which was the secrecy that made the subject participation uninformed,
and the medical experimenters' abandonment of the Hippocratic oath—*do
no harm*—even by omission. One has to wonder not whether, but to what
extent, the current restrictions on the protection of human subjects owe
their origin to the insensitivity of earlier "masters" to issues of ethical
treatment of human subjects.

Having said that, social psychologists quite properly note the overreach
that has accompanied the new ethical environment that holds psychological researchers to the same standards that governs medical research. The
only justification for exposure of human subjects to an experimental drug
therapy is that it is undertaken to improve their health. A social psychologist trying to replicate Milgram or Zimbardo would secure no approval by
justifying the research on the basis of identifying the capacity for "evil" in
ordinary persons. As a consequence, obtaining approval in the new ethical environment is quite difficult. Despite what I think were dubious practices in the past, I am not certain that this new regime is wholly desirable.
For example, because of the IRBs, a student who writes a story about
coaches and sports violence for the student newspaper is less encumbered
than the individual who investigates the same issues for a research paper.
A professional researcher is more encumbered by ethical strictures than a
professional journalist who may be working on the same story. The professional researcher faces significant limits of action from committees
struck in the first instance to review *medical* experiments on human
subjects.

Consider the predicament of Elizabeth Loftus and Mel Guyer. A clinical
case reported in *Child Maltreatment* by David Corwin in 1997 was cited in
a court decision to establish the reliability of "recovered memories" of
childhood sexual abuse. Loftus (1993; Loftus and Ketcham 1994) had previously established the difficulty of crediting the veracity of repressed
memories, and wanted to investigate the case of "Jane Doe" to determine
if her recovered memories were as reliable as had been reported. Loftus
and Guyer succeeded in identifying the case in court records and interviewing Jane Doe's mother, who, in their view, had been *falsely* accused of
sexual assault, and subsequently lost custody of her child. Guyer contacted the IRB at the University of Michigan to establish that their work
constituted a comment on a forensic issue that was beyond the framework
of the IRB committee. Initially, in 1998 the committee agreed but subsequently it informed Guyer that his research was "disapproved" and that

he faced a reprimand for conducting it. After a year of appeals and reviews, the IRB determined it lacked jurisdiction because it was not "human subjects research." Just as they thought they had the "all clear" signal, Jane Doe sent an e-mail to the University of Washington complaining that Loftus's inquiry into her case was invading her privacy. Carol Tavris picks up the story:

> On September 30, 1999, having given Loftus 15 minutes' advance notice by phone, John Slattery of the University of Washington's "Office of Scientific Integrity" arrived in Loftus' office, along with the Chair of the psychology department, and seized her files. She asked Slattery what the charges against her were. It took him five weeks to respond, and when he did he had transformed Jane Doe's "privacy" complaint into an investigation of "possible violations of human subject research." (2002)

Loftus was eventually cleared but not before her institution had reprimanded her for employing methods inconsistent with ethical principles of professional psychologists, i.e., journalism. She was also forbidden to make further contact with the principals in the Jane Doe case. Despite the U.S. Supreme Court's vigilant protection of first amendment rights, the IRB bureaucracy undertook a campaign of secret accusation, professional harassment, obstruction, and intimidation of leading scholars to suppress their free speech in the name of protecting human subjects. A journalist would have faced none of these obstructions, and would have been better equipped to publish the truth. In my view, this situation is absurd, and it materially threatens the future growth of social psychology. If unchallenged, budding young social scientists would be better counseled to seek a career in journalism.

OUTCOMES

I have reviewed three areas where social psychology has disappointed—methods, theory, and ethics. The field continues to enjoy great popularity in university courses, but the rise of the IRBs threatens to curtail future research activities, both experimental and, if the Loftus-Guyer episode is any guide, nonexperimental. The result of this situation is a lack of progress in the field, recurrent crises that are never convincingly resolved, no basic change in methodological outlook, no theoretical resolution, and volumes of writing that, in the words of Rod Cooper, lead to no new knowledge.

> Every year psychologists turn out thousands of books and articles. I find it difficult, however, to see much in the way of fruits from these labors. . . . In

spite of the tremendous publishing record of the psychologists I can see no psychological contributions that I can call marvelous. Think about it. Suppose tomorrow that all these scholarly efforts of the psychologists should disappear from the collective knowledge of mankind. . . . Would it really make a difference? I suggest not. (1982:264)

When a crisis emerges, it results in professional fragmentation as new subdisciplines of "humanistic" psychologists, feminists, Darwinians, and poststructuralists depart from the experimental core. The field loses its grasp on the larger picture of how all the elements fit together and there is no sense of unity or integrity that forges a coherent discipline. This brings us back to Zajonc's reflections in an earlier chapter: there is no consensus about the key contributions of the field, textbook chapters can be reshuffled randomly without costs because there is no inherent order in the subject matter. Indeed, textbook authors appear unconstrained in representing profoundly important deficiencies in the works they report. Any fair-minded observer would conclude that this marks the fall of social psychology as a distinct academic enterprise, and the obituary has been written by its practitioners.

THE END OF SOCIAL PSYCHOLOGY

One could leave off here, the matter settled, and retire to sociology on the one side and biology on the other. But out here on the ledge, I may be starry-eyed in looking beyond "the end" and thinking about what "the end" means. We need to reflect on the very idea of an intellectual field coming to its "end" and a philosophical reflection may be in order here. Our capacity to envision the end of social psychology, in the sense of failure and termination, is only possible because of our intuitive sense of "the end" or "ends" in that *other* sense: the *telos* or driving objective that we are trying to achieve through our discipline. What is "the end" (*telos*) of social psychology? In other words, what is the purpose that it serves? What role does the science of social psychology play in human life? If we can clarify these questions, then a "postsocial psychology" future may become achievable. In my view, there are three end-points that animate the field. Social psychology is intimately associated with *our sense of identity* in a way that economics, sociology, and demography are not. Social psychology is about our understanding of ourselves. It is not an intellectual pursuit indifferent to human aspirations. It is grounded in a quest for where our species, nations, groups, families, and circle of friends fit into the larger Darwinian universe. In addition, we look to social psychology, not only to learn "facts" about ourselves, but to assist us in determining how to act and behave in society.

In other words, the objective of our knowledge is deeply intertwined with our moral and political imaginations, and our projection of how we plan our futures. And, finally, we seek to undertake our investigations and applications of knowledge with integrity and objectivity. We cannot wish our way to a utopian tomorrow. We have to know more about our social and biological natures to plan the future. These observations suggest three specific end-points or social goals through the pursuit of social psychology. The first goal of social psychology must be self-knowledge and self-fulfill-ment. As we have noted earlier, social psychology is the "preoccupation of all mankind"—and meso-level knowledge is *already* sophisticated, even in the absence of our discipline. As Rod Cooper suggests, humankind would not miss a heartbeat if today's psychology were to disappear tomorrow. We ought not to be trying to replace commonsense knowledge with a scientific version of the same thing. Our objective ought to be the identification of levels of knowledge that *elude* common sense. And the purpose of achiev-ing such knowledge ought to be to permit us to fulfill our nature with insight based on our understanding of the *limits* of our commonsense understanding.

The second objective is implied in the concept of self-fulfillment. We seek self-governance. It would be absurd to have a science based on our self-knowledge that did not have some insight into social relevancies, social problems, and public policies. But our self-government should *fol-low* the advances of our research. The research conclusions should not sim-ply derive from our political aspirations. This appears to have been the subtext of studies of industry, schools, and the media.

The final objective of social psychology ought to be to build a discipline based on intellectual integrity—defensible ethics, appropriate methods, and a search for a genuine consensus about what really matters in the dis-cipline. Although it is premised on the search for objective knowledge that is not driven by unacknowledged extrascientific agendas, integrity does not come automatically from the experiment. In the epilogue, I explore the implications of this interpretation of "the ends" of social psychology in the areas of theory, methods, and ethics. Perhaps here, an iconoclast finds hope.

Epilogue

Looking Forward

*The conventional wisdom speaks of ethology, which is the nat-
uralistic study of whole patterns of animal behavior, and its
companion enterprise, comparative psychology, as the central
unifying fields of behavioral biology. They are not; both are
destined to be cannibalized by neurophysiology . . . from one
end and sociobiology and behavioral ecology from the other.*

—Edward O. Wilson, *Sociobiology*

PSYCHOLOGICAL THEORY AND THE LIMITATION
IN SELF-KNOWLEDGE: MAKING SENSE
OF THE INEXPLICABLE

If we accept that commonsense knowledge is already more or less a sound
foundation for our self-understanding, the work of theory development in
social psychology takes on a special focus. We ask *not* how we make sense
of reality (since this is done extremely effectively by most persons most of
the time), but under what conditions our intuitive or "unschooled" sense
of reality fails us, and how social psychological research can establish how
this comes about. I will sketch a potentially fruitful direction of theory construction by identifying several research areas that point to processes of
self-misunderstanding or self-mystification, and that question our commonsense ability to make the inexplicable explicable. In my view, these are
not the future of social psychology, in the sense that they describe the specific chapter titles of a future *Principia Psychologia*. But these suggest what
the next social psychology might look like, if my critique is valid. I explore
three areas in which self-understanding is a poor guide to self-knowledge,
and where we need to better integrate social and biological conditions of
social development.

IS GENDER IDENTITY MORE THAN SKIN DEEP?

Identical twin brothers were born to a Winnipeg couple, the Reimers, in August 1965. When they were seven months old they were diagnosed with phimosis, a condition that makes urination difficult. The family pediatrician recommended circumcision. In April 1966, they entered hospital for the procedure, but a terrible accident ensued. The electrocautery needle used to remove the foreskin malfunctioned and Bruce Reimer's penis was horribly burned. The flesh literally fell off within days. The parents were devastated. Medical experts predicted that the boy would never be able to consummate marriage or have normal sexual relations resulting in children. After examining the baby, experts at the Mayo Clinic in Rochester, Minnesota, came to the same conclusion. The parents had no one to turn to for medical guidance until December 1966, when they saw a television interview with Dr. John Money of the Johns Hopkins University Medical Center. Money had pioneered the study of hermaphrodites, i.e., intersexed children, or children whose physiologies showed evidence of both male and female sexual organs, or "ambiguous" genitals. Johns Hopkins University had opened one of the first sexual reassignment clinics to refashion genitalia surgically to produce unambiguous males and females. In a study of 105 intersexed children and adults, Money claimed that 95 percent were reassigned successfully, and that it did not matter whether they were raised as boys or girls (Colapinto 1997:60; see also Colapinto 2000). For Money, gender identity is created through experience, and it follows from the child's sexual self-perception, and parental reinforcement. Since Money claimed that it was possible to reassign sexual identities in hermaphrodites, this gave the Reimers a glimmer of hope that their son's condition could be treated.

The Reimers contacted Dr. Money early in 1967 and he invited them to Johns Hopkins for a consultation. Money explained that reassignment was possible if undertaken within the first thirty months of life. He also pointed out that the vast majority of reassignments involved removing the male genitalia since it was surgically easier to refashion female genitalia. However, it was essential that the child be castrated to minimize the effects of male hormones, that the male scrotum be reconstructed through a series of operations throughout childhood to fashion a vaginal canal, that the child be treated as a girl and not told that she was born as a boy, and that at the age of puberty the child go on a regime of hormone replacement to induce the growth of breasts and other secondary sexual characteristics. Also, the child would be dressed as a girl and encouraged to play with female toys and games. When Money encouraged the Reimers to agree to the intervention, and when he pressured them for delaying the start of the changes, it is not clear that he communicated to the family that the reassignment had never been done with a normal XY child with a normal nervous system. The procedure was purely experimental. Nonetheless, the family agreed to return to Johns Hopkins in July 1967 for surgical castration when baby Bruce was twenty-two months old.

The parents complied with the plan. Bruce was renamed Brenda, her mother sewed dresses for the little girl, her hair was encouraged to grow long, as she got older she was encouraged to wear makeup, and the family bought her toy sewing machines, skipping ropes, and other "feminine" toys. Both Brenda and her twin brother, Brian, were required to return annually to Johns Hopkins for an interview and examination with Money and his team. In 1972 John Money published a book with Anke Ehrhardt celebrating the experimental reassignment as an unqualified success. The story was covered in *Time* magazine and Kate Millett cited the case in her *Sexual Politics* (1970) as proof positive that gender differences were a function of the environment and were mutable, i.e., that gender differences were only skin deep.

However, the case presented by Money was wholly misleading. The children dreaded visiting Money, and were affronted by his exposure of them to explicit pornography, and by his requests for them to undress and examine each other's genitalia. At home Brenda walked and acted like a boy, hated wearing dresses, and played with Brian's toys. From the very first day she attended kindergarten, she was rejected by the other girls. Even her female teacher detected that her behavior was aberrant for a girl. And in spite of repeated parental directions, Brenda preferred to stand up to urinate. Throughout her school years, she was a social outcast, poorly adjusted, isolated, and profoundly unhappy. She showed interests in building treehouses, go-carts and model airplanes, and was more aggressive and competitive than her brother (Colapinto 1997:70). She fantasized about being a young male with a mustache, a sports car, and admiring male peers. In grade one she reported that when she grew up she wanted to become a garbage man: "easy work, good pay." By grade two she had come to the realization that she was not really a girl at all. When Dr. Money tried to encourage her to undergo further surgery, she refused. She reported at age nine that she would prefer a female partner when she got older, leading Money to infer that she would become a lesbian. At age twelve she was started on estrogen therapy, and within months her breasts began to develop. By age fourteen, because of residual male hormones, her voice deepened, and she was becoming even more of a spectacle. Her classmates referred to her as "cavewoman" and "sasquatch." Indeed, she had lived her entire existence at school as an outcast, and received ongoing counseling from the Child Guidance Clinic for depression and conflict. At fourteen she refused to wear female clothing, preferring a jean jacket, pants, and work boots. When encouraged repeatedly to cooperate in further surgery and asked whether she wanted to become a "real woman," she replied with an emphatic no. However, she had now reached the age when her consent was necessary for any further sexual reassignment surgery.

In March 1980, her father came to the realization that the experiment on his child had been an awful mistake. He explained her past medical history to her, the hospital accident, and the treatment prescribed by Dr. Money. Her primary reaction appears to have been one of *relief*. Now her whole history of maladjustment, her feelings of discomfort in the skin of a girl, the history of rejection by other children, all began to make sense. She determined almost immediately to live as a boy, and adopted the name David (as in David and Goliath). Later in 1980 David Reimer had a double mastectomy and subsequently surgeons began to fashion a penis. However, the road to recovery was not easy. David was repeatedly suicidal, and isolated himself for months at a time. Eventually, he associated with his brother's friends, and was accepted as a male. At twenty-three he met a woman who had three children from previous relationships, and married her two years later. In 1994, when David was twenty-nine, he agreed to meet with psychiatrist Keith Sigmundson and biologist Milton Diamond to discuss his case. At first he refused their approaches because his childhood memories were so traumatic. However, he changed his mind when he was told that his case had been cited in the medical and psychological literature for twenty-five years as a remarkable success, and that, because of its success, thousands of similar operations were being undertaken annually. It took Diamond and Sigmundson two years to find a journal willing to publish their exposition of the experiment, and a further seven months before it appeared in March 1997 in the *Archives of Adolescent and Pediatric Medicine*. Other medical journals were reluctant to print it because it condemned a quarter-century of surgical practice premised on a dubious theory of sexual development. The publication of this article was an intellectual bombshell that changed our understanding of gender differences and our surgical ethics regarding sexual reassignment.

Diamond's reluctance to accept Money's claims about the ease with which gender could be reassigned after birth was based on his earlier work with animal models. Female rats and guinea pigs exposed artificially *in utero* to testosterone not only displayed evidence of intersexed organs once born, but they also behaved like males, and tried to mount other females sexually. For Diamond, testosterone changes the male brain during pregnancy. Until the mid-1990s, there had been no long-term follow-up to determine the adjustment of sexually reassigned patients as they grew older. In one of the first studies of its kind, William Reiner of Johns Hopkins University reported results consistent with the outcome in the Reimer case. A significant number of XY boys reassigned and raised as girls behaved interpersonally as boys (rough and tumble play), had male career aspirations (astronauts, race car drivers), and showed signs of clinical depression and suicidal ideation when treated as girls. In a retrospective sample of several dozen cases, "twenty-two of the patients who were raised as girls have reassigned themselves as males" (Hendricks 2000). So there is growing evidence that Diamond's model of *in utero* brain changes limits the ability of society to arbitrarily reassign gender identity.

Indeed Roger Gorski identified a distinct anatomical difference in the brains of male and females rats labeled the *sexual dimorphous nucleus (SDN)*—a bundle of cells in the hypothalamus that is overdeveloped in males. However, *in utero* injection of female rats with male hormones led them to develop an SDN similar to that in male rats. A similar anatomical picture was reported in humans by Dick Swaab (Swaab et al. 2001). Swaab and his colleagues believe that sex differences in the brain account for sex differences in reproduction, as well as gender identity and sexual orientation. Edward O. Wilson had predicted in the first chapter of *Sociobiology* (1975:6) that the study of animal behavior, including human behavior, would be cannibalized on the one side by neurophysiology and on the other by sociobiology (or what today we call evolutionary psychology). The developments in the understanding of gender in human and other species appear to bear this out, although at this point in time we do not understand how the SDN operates, when it develops, and the full range of effects that can be traced to it.

The Reimer case is important on a number of levels. It reverses the swing of the pendulum back to the study of biological mechanisms at the foundations of human social behavior. It raises questions about the propriety of surgical interventions when subsequent social adjustment could only be hypothesized and where the surgeries themselves were essentially experimental. It raises questions about the propriety of parental and professional decisions that affect the lives of children whose consent cannot be obtained, and who are typically raised on deception about their biological identity. It also seems to convey the idea that differences in anatomical development make those who possess them something less than human, a point raised by the Intersex Society of North America, a support group that lobbies against surgical intervention for intersexed people. Studies of people with anatomically ambiguous genitalia (e.g., microphallus) increasingly suggest that they can live relatively well-adjusted lives without reconstructive surgery, can enjoy normal sex lives, and can raise families (Nova 2001).

However, the key issue that this case raises in a renewed social psychology is that psychologists trying to understand gender have to learn a great deal about the development of the brain. The way that testosterone contributes to the masculinization of the brain is immeasurably consequential, and results in consequences that commonsense psychology could hardly fathom. It represents the paradigm shift away from under-standing the mind as a *tabula rasa* influenced by nothing but "socializa-tion" to a new science that links subjective experiences to underlying mechanisms and neurophysiological factors as Wilson suggested.

HYPNOSIS: FROM ROLE THEORY TO NEURAL IMAGING

Hypnosis has a very mixed reputation in contemporary Western culture. Stage hypnotists bank on the "Svengali" myth of the hypnotist's "power" to charm audiences into believing that volunteers can be reduced through suggestions to automatons who submit to commands, however ridiculous it makes them look on stage. In 1784, the report of the French Commission of Inquiry into "animal magnetism" concluded that "such practices may have an injurious reaction upon morality"—chiefly that women could be seduced or compelled to do something without their conscious consent while in a trance (Conn 1972). In the nineteenth century, James Braid, a British physician, regarded hypnosis as a physiological phenomenon, and a Scots doctor, James Esdaile, used hypnosis as an analgesic during oper-ations and amputations in his medical practice in India. In the 1890s, French neurologists Jean Martin Charcot and Hyppolyte Bernheim used hypnosis to treat psychiatric disabilities, and attracted the attention of Viennese psychoanalyst Sigmund Freud, who used the technique to relieve symptoms of hysteria. Freud later abandoned hypnosis because he thought the ailments relieved by hypnosis simply "migrated" to other symptoms. In the twentieth century, clinical and legal practitioners became aware of the perplexing changes in subjective awareness, motiva-tion, and memory associated with the induction of hypnotic trances. Med-ically, hypnosis has been enlisted to combat a range of afflictions from obesity, cigarette addiction, alcoholism, migraine headaches, hyperten-sion, asthma, and even cancer (Wadden and Anderton 1982). In the legal realm, hypnosis has been used in criminal investigations to aid witness recall of crime scenes, and is credited with helping police solve a number of important crimes. The production of hypnosis has been associated with subjective experiences of dissociation (the zombielike trance), posthyp-notic suggestion (autonomic behavior), subjective distortions in percep-tion (visual and auditory hallucinations), changes in subjective tolerance for pain (anesthesia), memory distortions (amnesia), as well as memory enhancements (hypermnesia). There appears to be significant individual difference in the subject's capacity to exhibit these "symptoms" and even disagreement over the importance of a formal induction process.

Many authorities argue that hypnosis, far from being an occult phe-nomenon, is common in everyday life. We drift in and out of a reverie as we stare out a window while traveling on a train and lose all sense of time.

Or we pick up a crying child who has injured her knee and comfort her by kissing the scrape "to make the pain disappear." Altered states of consciousness are produced in preindustrial societies by rhythmic dances and chanting at seasonal festivals, a phenomenon also experienced by citizens of industrial nations at "raves" and music concerts. The generality of the phenomena associated with hypnosis has produced some controversy as to its status. At one of end of the continuum is the belief that it is simply role-playing, i.e., situational responses to cues provided by a hypnotist that is little more than a variant of the game, Simon-says. Indeed, Martin Orne produced different responses in hypnotized subjects depending on whether they were led to believe such conduct was expected in the state of hypnosis. Where they believed "catalepsy of the dominant hand" was expected (suggested in a lecture prior to solicitation of volunteers), the subjects experienced catalepsy (Orne 1959). Where they expected subjective distortions in perception, they reported distortions. So, however, did subjects recruited to "fake" hypnosis—suggesting that the effect was simply a function of demand characteristics.

However, far from viewing hypnosis as mere humbug, Orne noted that some of the "best" hypnotic subjects, i.e., "somnabulists," demonstrated evidence of expectations (posthypnotic suggestions) *outside* the experimental setting, where, presumably, demand characteristics would not explain their behavior (Orne, Sheehan, and Evans 1968). Orne was also instrumental in outlining how hypnosis could assist in criminal investigations (Orne 1979). Criminal courts have become wary of "hypnotically enhanced evidence." Accused persons under oath have asked to be hypnotized to aid in their recovery of criminal events only to "recall" that they had witnessed someone else committing the crime, thereby exonerating themselves. Other people have been led to make false confessions under hypnosis. Hypnosis is no guarantee of the truth for it both can be faked to manufacture exculpatory testimony and, in the hands of a skilled interrogator, can lead to false inculpatory testimony. Orne (1961) also reports that it is possible for deeply hypnotized subjects to willfully lie. Criminal courts typically disallow evidence that has been hypnotically enhanced because, without corroboration, it is impossible to determine its reliability and validity. Even so, in criminal investigations, it has a role as an *aide memoire* to assist investigators in the development of criminal leads, e.g., to assist in the recollection of a license plate number or the way certain individuals were dressed. In these cases hypnosis is simply harnessing an existing human capacity. In the past, more weight was attached to such recollections than was warranted because there was a "halo effect" since hypnosis was associated with what were presumed to be "expert powers."

Kirsch and Lynn (1995) reviewed the dominant alternative perspectives that have emerged on hypnosis in recent years. Is it mere role-playing? Is it a specific altered *state* or *trance* that most people can enter and leave, and that is distinctive from both sleep and the normal waking state? Or is it a specific *trait* that is more common among some people than others ("susceptibility"). Kirsch and Lynn concluded that these perspectives are not mutually exclusive and that "positions on these issues can more accurately be described as points on a continuum" (ibid.:846). Clinically, a review of the literature on the medical use of hypnosis ruled out its relative efficacy in treating compulsive conduct (obesity, cigarette dependency, and alcoholism)—which we would expect if hypnosis was merely role-playing. But there is more to hypnosis than "social construction." In a thorough review of the clinical use of hypnosis, Wadden and Anderton (1982) looked specifically for the *marginal* benefits of hypnosis over and above more common therapeutic techniques such as verbal counseling, group support, and visual imagery and desensitization. Hypnosis did *not* assist in the control of compulsive behaviors, probably because the incentives to their persistence (calories, nicotine, intoxication) were so strong. But a number of researchers had documented and replicated the ability of hypnosis to curtail clinical pain, asthma, and warts.

The clinical pain control studies examined the management of migraines, dental interventions without anesthetics, and burn recovery. In some designs, patients were permitted to alter their level of painkillers while in hospital. Hypnosis permitted them to reduce their dependency on chemical analgesics compared to nonhypnotized patients. The analgesic effect of hypnosis has been recognized as one of its longest-standing consequences. Asthma management was positively effected by the use of hypnosis to produce relaxation and to relieve stress. Although the causes of asthma are not entirely understood, they are thought to be a combined effect of psychological, and infective and/or allergic factors. Asthma attacks are often triggered by stress. Hypnosis appears to aid in the control of such precipitating conditions. As with the management of migraines, it is thought that hypnosis plays a role in wart reduction by conveying control over blood vessel constriction that permits the body's immune system to attack warts naturally by shunting blood to the affected area. This means that the autonomic nervous system is capable of significant activation by human volition—which suggests an intriguing link between role-playing and neurophysiology.

People who accept and "act out" the injunctions and suggestions of the clinical hypnotist may be tapping into control systems that operate below the threshold of consciousness. In the past this was characterized as "mind over matter," but developments in neural imaging in the past three or four years have actually captured changes in brain physiology associated with hypnotic induction. For example, Kosslyn et al., using positron emission tomography (PET) to measure brain changes during an experiment in which subjects were asked to perceive color when presented with a black and white stimulus, concluded: "Among highly hypnotizable subjects, observed changes in subjective experience achieved during hypnosis were reflected by changes in brain function similar to those that occur in perception. These findings support the claim that hypnosis is a psychological state with distinct neural correlates and is not just the result of adopting a role" (2000:1279). Rainville et al., also using PET, monitored changes in blood flow in specific regions of the brain associated with hypnosis. They concluded: "These results provide a new description of the neurobiological basis of hypnosis, demonstrating specific patterns of cerebral activation associated with the hypnotic state and with the processing of hypnotic suggestions" (1999:110). Rainville et al. replicated these findings and extended them in a further study: "Basic changes in phenomenal experience produced by hypnotic induction reflect, at least in part, the modulation of activity within brain areas critically involved in the regulation of consciousness" (2002:887; also see Raz and Shapiro 2002). These findings establish the existence of specific mechanisms in the brain that link the prior induction of the role, trance, or trait (i.e., volitional behavior) with subsequent clinical and legal outcomes (for example, pain control on the one hand and memory improvement on the other). This moves the study of hypnosis from the realm of the occult to the world of neurophysiology. Correspondingly, the identification of the neural mechanisms that underlie hypnosis moves social psychological theory beyond common sense. Comprehension of how the brain works makes the socially inexplicable neurologically intelligible. As a consequence, social psychology no longer occupies the territory of common sense.

EXCITATION TRANSFER, MISATTRIBUTION, AND FAILURES IN SELF-KNOWLEDGE: FURTHER ILLUSTRATIONS

The theory of excitation transfer is premised on the idea that human neurophysiology is often less precise than we believe—and that human culture sometimes exploits this imprecision for hedonistic reasons, although, as in the previous cases, this typically escapes the self-awareness of those affected by it. How does excitation transfer work? And what is its theoretical significance? The theory was advanced by Dolf Zillmann. Zillmann argues that the neural pathways that excite the central nervous system are relatively nonspecific as to the sensations they report. The same neural bundles may carry happy feelings one moment and sad feelings a moment later. Given that a social definition has been established and accepted as the source of arousal, the physiological component can be boosted in ways to which the person is insensitive and may lead the person to *misattribute* the reasons for changing levels of arousal. Recall the Buss paradigm from Chapter 5. Retaliatory aggression against subjects insulted by a confederate at the start of a media-effects experiment can be maintained at the initially high levels by use of an intervening arousing stimulus—exposure to explicit pornography, for example. But other arousing stimuli work just as well—films of an eye operation, physical exercise, exposure to aversive noise, and so on. It is not the process of social learning by exposure to the films that causes inflated aggression, it is excitation transfer from the intervening stimulus to the initial arousal that is key.

Research conducted in Vancouver by Dutton and Aron extended this idea into an analysis of romantic attraction. It involved a test of how a mixture of sexual attraction *and* fear could combine to boost arousal. Unaccompanied males were approached by a person described as "an attractive female experimenter," who asked the males to volunteer for an experiment that consisted of filling out a questionnaire. The subjects were approached on two separate bridges—a narrow suspension bridge that crossed a deep canyon and that tended to tilt, bounce, sway, and wobble high above roaring rapids, "creating the impression that one is about to fall over the side." The other bridge was a wide, low wooden structure, solid and immobile. Crossing the suspension bridge provoked anxiety and fear, while crossing the second bridge had no comparable arousing effects. The questionnaire was the Thematic Apperception Test, which examined sexual imagery and personal attraction. In the control group the same approaches were undertaken by a male experimenter. The experimenters in each case gave the subjects their phone numbers and asked them to call later if they had any further questions about the experiment. Subjects approached on the suspension bridge exhibited much higher scores on sexual imagery than the solid bridge—but only when the experimenter was female. Also, more subjects from the suspension bridge called the female experimenter afterward than those from the solid bridge. When the test was administered by a male experimenter, the bridges failed to result in any differences.[1] Zillmann summarized Dutton and Aron's conclusions:

> Subjects who presumably were in acute fear because of the threat of painful stimulation exhibited more sexual imagery and increased sexual attraction to the female confederate than did less apprehensive Ss. The effect was independent of whether or not the female was believed to be in distress. The distress treatment was without consequence altogether. Again, the findings are consistent with an arousal explanation. (1984:141)

Why is this interesting? Here we have a social situation that lends itself to mild sexual fantasy *and* that is boosted in ways in which the subjects appear to be unaware. The physiological excitation has been elevated by stimuli below the threshold of perception. The mechanisms that lead to these forms of misattribution are either powerful *consecutive* stimulations or *simultaneous* stimulations. The key appears to be the fact that emotional reactions to stimulation do not decay very quickly and become confused with one another. The higher functions of the brain sort them out but sometimes integrate different sources of arousal under a single cognitive entity.

This social psychology shows how everyday experiences get mixed up in the minds of people in ordinary settings through processes such as *misattribution*. For example, people who are already sexually aroused can intensify their lovemaking by spanking, bondage, and other "perversions." Aggression, within limits and trust, can intensify sexual catharsis. Another application of misattribution theory concerns what is called *sexual hypoxia*. As every coroner's office knows, accidental deaths are sometimes wrongly attributed to suicide. People sometimes die accidentally through "erotic strangulation." Strangulation or asphyxiation triggers intense physiological arousal, which signals imminent life-threatening circumstances designed to motivate the person to restore normal "inhalation and expiration" of air. These are the classic "flight/fright" symptoms—heightened adrenal action, shunting of blood to the core, intense anxiety, flushing, pupil dilation, etc. In a sexual context, erotic strangulation boosts sexual arousal to more intense plateaus. It can lead to accidental death if asphyxiation is prolonged. In the context of torture, the use of asphyxiation intensifies fear and intimidation in a situation already designed to extract confessions and cooperation from prisoners during questioning. Interrogation techniques by police sometimes employ "dry submarining" where police asphyxiate subjects with a plastic bag that is pulled over the head and removed as the subject is interrogated. The asphyxiation boosts anxiety already created by interrogation. The phenomenon of misattribution is evident in a whole range of other social settings.

The consumption of *fugu* fish (puffers) by Japanese involves a confusion between self-poisoning and high cuisine (Davis 1985). *Fugu* fish stimulate the appetites of their consumers by exposing them to low levels of natural neurotoxins. The gourmands report the dish makes them ecstatic. The flesh of the fish produces mild numbing and tingling in the mouths of its consumers. Rather than an emotion here, we have an altered set of sensations arising from the effects of neurotoxins ingested in small amounts. These changes in subjective feelings are labeled positively when ingested in exotic meals prepared by carefully trained chefs. However, some people cannot get enough of a good thing, and every year in Japan, many succumb to the feast.

Consider a more common pastime—gambling. What is the point of this if not economic? It appears people gamble not so much for the money as the excitement. But what is the excitement based on? It is a combination of risky behavior—putting money at stake, intense emotional suspense, and either *elation or disappointment*, depending on the outcome. So both losing and winning create high levels of emotionality—and the alternation over the course of a hand of cards or a game of dice takes the players to peaks and troughs of emotions, both of which flood the other feelings. In some people, the emotional attachment takes on obsessive qualities and may become addictive, and highly dysfunctional for the compulsive gambler. The mechanism appears to be excitation transfer and the emotional peaks and troughs that it creates. This creates a seductive emotional structure that few gamblers understand cognitively.

Narcotics is another area in which there may be some application of misattribution theory. All that is required is that the user take a compound that alters the subjective state—and acquire a cultural repertoire to learn how to label the effects positively. Certain powerful tranquilizers—like cocaine—appear to have their effects by directly stimulating receptor sites in the brain. Others require a greater social definition, particularly hallucinogens like LSD and marijuana. If someone administered a powerful dose of LSD to an unsuspecting other, the victim might well develop the sense that he or she was going crazy and losing his or her mind. However, if the drug was taken purposely to produce hallucinations of "psychic flying," and the like, then the user's expectations would come into play. The cultural preparation provides an expectation effect, and the drug produces cognitive irregularities by interfering with normal synaptic transmissions in the neuroreceptors. In some cultures, licking the skin of poisonous toads (i.e., the cane toad) has the same effect (Davis 1985; Becker 1963).

Consider another experience: the intense religious activities of the "Holy Ghost people." The Holy Ghost people are a sect in Appalachia who are descendants of some of the first American pioneers. They follow the scriptures of Mark 16:17: "And these signs follow them that believe; In my name shall they cast out devils; they shall speak with new tongues." And Mark 16:18: "they shall take up serpents; and if they drink any deadly thing, it shall not hurt them, they shall lay hands on the sick and they shall recover." What is unusual about the services is that the congregation passes around poisonous snakes—they come to pray with boxes of them—timber rattlers, copperheads, even cobras. They drink strychnine. They handle fire. They speak in tongues and practice faith healing. How does the misattribution theory apply here? First, they have a basic religious conviction—a conviction that also tells them to look for *signs* that their faith is strong. Passing of snakes intensifies the emotional quality of their religious experiences by displacing their natural apprehension about being bitten into religious ecstasy. And should they be bitten, or quaff a glass more of poison than their bodies can stand, the religious imagery gives them a cognitive map that explains why things have gone adversely: they are unworthy. We observe misattribution of the grounds of arousal combined with a cognitive principle that reinforces their understandings of who they are no matter what the outcome.

In recent years psychologists have become familiar with a serious form of misattribution that arises in the context of therapy. Because of the prevalence of incest and child sexual abuse and interference, clinicians have frequently queried their patients about recollections of childhood abuse. These patients typically present with a range of diffuse dysfunction symptoms: sleeplessness, amnesia, inability to sustain normal personal relationships, generalized lack of motivation, feelings of self-doubt, and so on. Where childhood sexual trauma has occurred, the adult may react by blocking recollection of such traumatic events as a means of coping. However, the tensions that the trauma produced in the child may continue to call attention to the situation at a subconscious level. In psychiatric circles it is believed that the adult patient can begin to deal with the symptoms by "working through" the childhood trauma. However, it is also the case that the therapist can make an *incorrect* diagnosis of childhood sexual abuse—and can nonetheless induce in the patient the conviction that the cause of the presenting symptoms lies in childhood traumatic events that never occurred. This is what is known as false memory syndrome (FMS). The patients may accept the attributions and sometimes confront innocent parents with unfounded charges of incest. The notion of FMS is controversial. When incest has occurred, FMS amounts to *incest denial*. When incest has not occurred, FMS is *clinical malpractice*. In 1997 the Royal College of Psychiatrists in Britain banned the recovery of lost memories of incest (*London Daily Telegraph,* October 1, 1997) following the recommendation of the Brandon Report. Psychiatrists who persist face penalties for professional misconduct. The crux of the matter is that psychiatry cannot tell the difference between valid reconstruction of memories and false memories.

Here again we see a special role for social psychology that does not reiterate common sense. Social psychology has identified a model of "arousal overload" that implicates the brain's *limited* ability to effectively manage the sources of arousal. By sorting out the way sensory transfers or arousals get decoupled cognitively from things that cause them, social psychology provides a nonobvious, noncommonsensical insight into human experience. This covers a huge range of human experience as attested by our examples. But at core, the role it identifies for social psychology is making sense of the inexplicable.

METHODS: PLEA FOR A FEW MORATORIA

There are several points to explore in the area of *methods* when we contemplate the ends of social psychology. The first point almost goes without saying: there should be a moratorium on the use of experimentation. The most important issues in social psychology are theoretical. Psychologists have to take stock of what we already know as a matter of experience—"Bubba psychology"—versus those things that perplex us and that defy commonsense psychology: Why do ordinary people commit genocide? Why do we dream? Why do we gamble? Why are men more aggressive than women? How does hypnosis affect pain? As I have argued, the most important theoretical questions are the ones that arise from problems in the life world where self-knowledge is not reliable. We need to start by examining the issues of *inexplicable behavior* found in situ in the life world. It is a mistake to jump from observations in the life world immediately into the lab to model such behaviors experimentally according to a priori suppositions. There is no merit in premising the future with a devotion to a method that has impeded progress in the past. Social psychology must become pluralistic in its methods—as are the other social sciences.

What distinguishes the social sciences is not their methodologies, but the part of the social life they investigate. In our discussion of theoretical issues, we emphasized the need to link human experiences to the mechanisms that underlie them. This means that social psychology as described here will be inherently interdisciplinary. The situational logic that has marked the classical period is a dead end. When social psychology is "cannibalized" (following Wilson) the one side goes methodologically to positron emission tomography (PET) and other digital brain assessments (MRI, EGG, etc.) to tap neurophysiology and brain behavior, and the other side goes to ethology: display of emotions, fitness theory, depth psychology, etc. None of this limits the field, as in the past, to experimentation.

Another observation is relevant regarding experimentation. During the classical period, the need for double-blind designs became emphatic. Persons who were told they were part of a control group might behave differently than if they were told they were part of the experimental or treatment group. Similarly, assistants analyzing the results from experiments might be inclined (subconsciously) to code the results differently if they knew whether they were recording the outcomes of a treatment or a control group. To avoid bias, neither the subjects nor the analysts could be briefed on their specific roles. The double-blind design was implemented to eliminate bias arising from both sources. Are these precautions sufficient? When one considers some of the reports from the pornography effects research, we are advised that Team A finds massive levels of rape fantasy in male subjects following an extremely short visual exposure. Team B finds levels that fail to come even remotely close. Alternatively, an experimenter finds stunning levels of teacher expectations in one site but fails in several others, but only reports the positive outcome experiment. What are we to make of this? My point is not to impugn motives or to raise the specter of data manipulation, but to point out that the procedures implemented for the purposes of bias control in double-blind designs may be insufficient. In physics, there is a division between experimentalists and theoreticians. The questions are raised by the theoreticians but the methods of testing the theories fall to individuals with access to complicated astrophysical and earth science methods. Hypothesis testing is separate from theoretical advances. Important findings can be reproduced independently without relying exclusively on the authors of the ideas for their corroboration. My point is that confidence in social psychological findings would improve significantly if this "triple-blind" level of control were adopted. The wholesale return to experimentation would be reckless without this professional division of labor and/or a more rigorous ethic of replication. The field would also benefit by a more sympathetic attitude toward the publication of negative findings.

This brings us to the issue of textbook pedagogy. Social psychology is probably among the three or four largest textbook markets in the undergraduate curriculum. Textbooks make controversies disappear. Textbooks repair the methodological deficiencies of classic studies by treating these as though they were separate from the basic studies themselves. Textbooks celebrate the moral attractions of the research so that the reader can apply the lessons to everyday life without worrying about the ecological validity of what is done in the labs. The textbooks in social psychology are among the fattest, longest, and most expensive volumes a student will purchase, and create the impression that the field comprises a mountain of knowledge. Is progress better assured by treating students' brains as garbage cans that have to be filled with content by textbooks, or by exposing the students to ideas of crisis and controversy through the same monographs and primary sources that their professors read? A moratorium on textbooks at this point in history would, in my view, better serve the goals of scientific progress. I would ask the reader to reflect on how the textbooks reported the Pygmalion study as indicated earlier and contrast it to its actual intellectual history. The same applies to Hawthorne, media effects, cognitive dissonance, and the classic influence studies. Thomas Kuhn (1970) argued that in normal science the function of textbooks is to create consensus by socializing recruits into an orthodox view of the science. Their purpose is little different from propaganda or indoctrination. This may expedite pedagogical ends where there is consensus in a field by shortening the learning curve. In a field marked by deep intellectual dissensus and lack of progress, instructors use textbooks the way parents use a pacifier.

ETHICS

The final area to reflect on is ethics. In this book, we have noted repeatedly the invasiveness of some research practices, particularly in experimental settings designed to heighten mundane realism in the laboratory. If social psychology is more encumbered by the IRBs than other disciplines, this is owed to its overreliance on experimentation, and particularly reliance on experimental deception. The disciplinary changes advocated here would lessen that dependence. But we have also registered opposition to the *over-reach* of the IRBs, and the material dangers they pose to the freedom of inquiry in social psychology, both experimental and otherwise. In some cases, the IRBs have become part of the culture of political correctness of North American universities, and the race and gender speech codes implemented to promote "inclusiveness." Just as such speech codes frequently stifle legitimate criticism and political dissent—things that are especially valued at universities—the IRBs may be becoming part of "the shadow university" (Kors and Silvergate 1998) that puts the moral mission of the institution above the quest for knowledge, making the university society's *second* church. While the need to respect the integrity of human subjects must be acknowledged, this cannot be equated with a denial of the right to study them. Injunctions on inquiry that are more restrictive than those that face journalists are intolerable. Is free scientific inquiry any less necessary for democracy than a free press? If not, why should it be more severely restricted?

THE FUTURE

In thinking about the end of social psychology, that is, thinking about the future, it has been imperative to maintain the role of empirical inquiry as the *desideratum* while renovating this science. These reflections are not a prologue to a poststructural psychology that equates scholarship with the study of linguistic representation. A social science that is seduced by the linguistic turn in philosophy has lost its empirical bearings. It has no prospect of scientific progress. Representation does remain a primary consideration for postclassical social psychology but largely as a question of how the brain represents information, and how those mechanisms explain social behaviors, and channel human choices and appetites. Dramaturgy is over. Bring in the PETs and the field studies!

NOTE

1. It might be that different kinds of bridges attract different kinds of people—people who like to take risks may have higher levels of sexual imagery as a matter of course. Dutton and Aron returned to the field with their female experimenter once more, but in this case the control group consisted of people approached some ten minutes away from the bridge. Here the levels of arousal were lower, the Thematic Apperception scores declined, and fewer subjects called the experimenter later to talk. This implicated the bridge (arousal), not self-selection of the people.

References

Abramson, Paul R. and H. Hayashi. 1984. "Pornography in Japan: Cross-Cultural and Theoretical Considerations." Pp. 173–83 in *Pornography and Sexual Aggression*, edited by N. M. Malamuth and Edward Donnerstein. Orlando, FL: Academic Press.

Abse, D. 1973. *The Dogs of Pavlov*. London: Valentine, Mitchell and Co.

Allport, Floyd H. 1924. *Social Psychology*. Boston: Houghton Mifflin (Johnson Reprint Corporation 1967).

American Association of University Women. 1992. AAUW Report: "How Schools Shortchange Girls." Washington, DC: AAUW.

Anderson, D. F. and R. Rosenthal. 1968. "Some Effects of Interpersonal Expectancy and Social Interaction on Institutionalised Retarded Children." *Proceedings of the 76th Annual Convention of the American Psychological Association* 3:479–80.

Arendt, Hannah. 1964. *Eichmann in Jerusalem: A Report on the Banality of Evil*. New York: Penguin Books.

Aronson, Elliot. 1999. "Adventures in Experimental Social Psychology: Roots, Branches, and Sticky New Leaves." Pp. 82–113 in *Reflections on 100 Years of Experimental Social Psychology*, edited by A. Rodrigues and R. Levine. New York: Basic Books.

Asch, Solomon. 1951. "Effects of Group Pressure Upon the Modification and Distortion of Judgements." Pp. 177–90 in *Groups, Leadership and Men*, edited by H. Guetzkow. Pittsburgh: Carnegie Press.

Asch, Solomon. 1952. *Social Psychology*. Englewood Cliffs, NJ: Prentice-Hall.

Asch, Solomon. 1955. "Opinions and Social Pressure." *Scientific American* 193(5, November):31–35.

Asch, Solomon. 1956. "Studies of Independence and Conformity: A Minority of One Against a Unanimous Majority." *Psychological Monographs: General and Applied* 70(146):1–70.

Asch, Solomon. 1958. "Review of *A Theory of Cognitive Dissonance* (Leon Festinger)," *Contemporary Psychology* 3:194–95.

Backhouse, Connie. 1996. Review of *Against Pornography* (Diana Russell), *Canadian Review of Law and Society* 11 (1):277–80

Baker, J. P. and J. L. Crist. 1971. "Teacher Expectancies: A Review of the Literature." Pp. 48–64 in *Pygmalion Reconsidered*, edited by Janet D. Elashoff and Richard E. Snow. Worthington, OH: Jones.

Bandura, A., D. Ross, and S. A. Ross. 1963. "Imitation of Film–Mediated Aggressive Models" *Journal of Abnormal and Social Psychology* 66:3–11.

Bandura, Albert. 1973. *Aggression: A Social Learning Analysis*. Englewood Cliffs, NJ: Prentice Hall.

Bannister, D. 1966. "Psychology as an Exercise in Paradox." *Bulletin of the British Psychological Association* 19(63):21–26.

Banuazizi, Ali and Siamak Movahedi. 1975. "Interpersonal Dynamics in a Simulated Prison." *American Psychologist* (February):152–60.

Baron, Larry. 1990. "Pornography and Gender Equality: An Empirical Analysis." *Journal of Sex Research* 27(3):363–80.

Baumrind, Diana. 1964. "Some Thoughts on Ethics of Research: After Reading Milgram's 'Behavioral Study of Obedience.'" *American Psychologist* 19(2):421–23.

Baumrind, Diana. 1985. "Research Using Intentional Deception: Ethical Issues Revisited." *American Psychologist* 40(2):165–74.

Becker, Howard. 1963. *Outsiders: Studies in the Sociology of Deviance*. London: Free Press.

Becker, J. and R. M. Stein. 1991. "Is Sexual Erotica Associated with Sexual Deviance in Adolescent Males?" *International Journal of Law and Psychiatry* 14:85–95.

Bentham, Jeremy. [1789] 1970. *An Introduction to the Principles of Morals and Legislation*. London: Athlone.

Berkowitz, Leonard. 1971. "Sex and Violence: We Can't Have It Both Ways." *Psychology Today* (December):14–23.

Berkowitz, Leonard. 1999. "On the Changes in U.S. Social Psychology: Some Speculations." Pp. 158–69 in *Reflections on 100 Years of Experimental Social Psychology*, edited by A. Rodrigues and R. Levine. New York: Basic Books.

Berkowitz, Leonard and Edward Donnerstein. 1982. "External Validity Is More Than Skin Deep." *American Psychologist* (March):245–57.

Blass, Thomas. 1992. "The Social Psychology of Stanley Milgram." *Advances in Experimental Social Psychology* 28:277–329.

Blum, Milton L. 1949. *Industrial Psychology and Its Social Foundations*. New York: Harper.

Boyd, J. Edwin and Augustine Brannigan. 1991. "Attitudes towards Sexual Aggression, Robbery and Altruism: Contributions of Media Exposure versus Sociological Variables." *Aggressive Behavior* 17(2):61–62.

Brabeck, M. 1983. "Moral Judgement: Theory and Research on Differences Between Males and Females." *Developmental Review* 3(3):274–91.

Breland, Keller and Marian Breland. 1966. *Animal Behavior*. New York: Macmillan.

Browning, Christopher R. 1998. *Ordinary Men: Reserve Police Battalion 101 and the Final Solution in Poland*. With New Afterword. New York: Harper Collins Books.

Buss, David. 1994a. "Evolutionary Psychology: A New Paradigm for Psychological Science." *Psychological Inquiry* 6(1):1–30.

Buss, David. 1994b. *The Evolution of Desire: Strategies of Human Ratings*. New York: Basic Books.

Buss, D. M. and K. H. Craik. 1980. "The Frequency Concept of Disposition: Dominance and Prototypically Dominant Acts." *Journal of Personality* 48:379–92.

Campbell, Donald T. and Julian C. Stanley. 1963. *Experimental and Quasi-Experimental Designs for Research*. Chicago: McNally.

Carey, Alex R. 1967. "The Hawthorne Studies: A Radical Criticism." *American Sociological Review* 32:403–16.

Cattell, Raymond. 1966. "Psychological Theory and Scientific Method." Pp. 1–18 in *Handbook of Multivariate Experimental Psychology*, edited by Raymond Cattell. Chicago: Rand McNally.

Centerwall, Brandon S. 1993. "Television and Violent Crime." *Public Interest* (Spring):56–71.

Chaffee, Steven H., George Gerbner, Beatrix A. Hamburg, Chester M. Pierce, Eli A. Rubinstein, Alberta E. Siegel, and Jerome L. Singer. 1984. "Defending the Indefensible." *Society* (September/October):30–35.

Chapanis, N. P. and A. Chapanis. 1964. "Cognitive Dissonance: Five Years Later." *Psychological Bulletin* 61(1):1–22.

Chase, Stuart. 1941. "What Makes the Worker Like to Work?" *Reader's Digest* February, 38:15–20.

Chodorow, N. 1978. *The Reproduction of Mothering: Psychoanalysis and the Sociology of Gender*. Berkeley: University of California Press.

Cicourel, Aaron. 1964. *Method and Measurement in Sociology*. New York: Free Press.

Clark, K. B. 1963. *Prejudice and Your Child*. Boston: Beacon.

Cohen, S. and E. Nagel. 1934. *An Introduction to Logic and Scientific Method*. New York: Harcourt.

Colapinto, John. 1997. "The True Story of John/Joan." *Rolling Stones Magazine* (December):56–96.

Colapinto, John. 2000. *As Nature Made Him: The Boy Who Was Raised as a Girl*. New York: Harper Collins.

Colby, A. and W. Damon. 1983. "Listening to a Different Voice: A Review of Gilligan's in a Different Voice." *Merrill-Palmer Quarterly* 29(4):473–81.

Conn, J. H. 1972. "Is Hypnosis Really Dangerous?" *International Journal of Clinical and Experimental Hypnosis* 20:61–79.

Conn, L. K., C. N. Edwards, R. Rosenthal, and D. Crowne. 1968. "Perception of Emotion and Response to Teacher's Expectancy by Elementary School Children." *Psychological Reports* 22:27–34.

Cooper, J. and R. H. Fazio. 1984. "A New Look at Dissonance Theory." *Advances in Experimental Social Psychology* 17:229–66.

Cooper, R. M. 1982. "The Passing of Psychology." *Canadian Psychology* 24(2):264–67.

Crist, Judith. 1948. "Horror in the Nursery." *Collier's Magazine* (March 27):22–23, 95–97.

Cronbach, L. J. 1975. "Five Decades of Public Controversy over Mental Testing." *American Psychologist* 30:1–14.

Daly, M. and M. Wilson. 1988. *Homicide*. Hawthorne, NY: Aldine de Gruyter.

Davis, Murray. 1971. "That's Interesting! Towards a Phenomenology of Sociology and a Sociology of Phenomenology." *Philosophy of the Social Sciences* 1(4): 309–44.

Davis, Wade. 1985. *The Serpent and the Rainbow*. New York: Simon and Schuster.

Dawkins, Richard. [1976] 1990. *The Selfish Gene*. Oxford: Oxford University Press.

De Grazia, Edward. 1992. *Girls Lean Back Everywhere: The Law of Obscenity and the Assault on Genius*. New York: Random House.

Dennett, Daniel. 1995. *Darwin's Dangerous Idea: Evolution and the Meanings of Life*. New York: Simon and Schuster.

Desmond, Adrian J. 1975. *The Hot-Blooded Dinosaurs*. London: Futura.

Deutsch, Morton. 1999. "A Personal Perspective on the Development of Social Psychology in the Twentieth Century." Pp. 1–34 in *Reflections on 100 Years of Experimental Social Psychology*, edited by A. Rodrigues and R. Levine. New York: Basic Books.

Dewey, John. 1901. *Psychology and Social Practice*. Chicago: University of Chicago Press.

Dewey, John. [1922] 1950. *Human Nature and Conduct: An Introduction to Social Psychology*. New York: Modern Library.

Diamond M. and H. K. Sigmundson. 1997. "Sex Reassignment at Birth: A Long term review and clinical implications." *Archives of Adolescent and Pediatric Medicine* 151(3):298–304.

Diamond, M. and A. Uchiyama. 1999. "Pornography, Rape, and Sex Crimes in Japan." *International Journal of Law and Psychiatry* 22(1):1–22.

Donnerstein, Edward. 1980. "Aggressive Erotica and Violence Against Women." *Journal of Personality and Social Psychology* 39:269–77.

Donnerstein, Edward. 1983. "Erotica and Human Aggression." Pp. 53–81 in *Aggression: Theoretical and Empirical Reviews*, edited by R. Geen and E. Donnerstein. New York: Academic Press.

Dworkin, Andrea. 1985. "Against the Male Flood: Censorship, Pornography and Equality." *Harvard Women's Law Journal* 8(Spring).

Eisenberg, N. and R. Lennon. 1983. "Sex Differences in Empathy and Related Capacities." *Psychological Bulletin* 84(4):712–22.

Elashoff, J. D. and R. E. Snow. 1971. *Pygmalion Reconsidered*. Worthington, OH: Jones.

Elms, Alan C. 1975. "The Crisis of Confidence in Social Psychology." *American Psychologist* (October):967–76.

Eron, Leonard. 1987. "The Development of Aggressive Behavior from the Perspective of a Developing Behaviorism." *American Psychologist* 42:435–42.

Evans, J. T. and Robert Rosenthal. 1968. Unpublished data, Harvard University (as cited in Worchel et al. 2000).

Evans, J. T. and Robert Rosenthal. 1969. "Interpersonal Self-Fulfilling Prophecies: Further Extrapolation from the Laboratory to the Classroom." *Proceedings of the 77th Annual Convention of the American Psychological Association* 4:371–72.

Ferguson, K. G. 1983. "Forty Years of Useless Research?" *Canadian Psychology* 24(2):153–204.

Feshbach, S. and R. D. Singer. 1971. *Television and Aggression: An Experimental Field Study*. San Francisco: Jossey-Bass.

Festinger, Leon. 1954. "Laboratory Experiment." Pp. 136–54 in *Research Methods in the Behavioral Sciences*, edited by Leon Festinger and Daniel Katz. London: Staples.

Festinger, Leon. 1980. "Looking Backward." Pp. 236–54 in *Retrospections on Social Psychology*, edited by Leon Festinger. New York: Oxford University Press.

Festinger, Leon. 1987. "A Personal Memory." Pp. 1–9 in *A Distinctive Approach to Psychological Research: The Influence of Stanley Schachter.* edited by Neil E. Grunberg, Richard E. Nisbett, Judith Rodin and Jerome E. Singer. Hillsdale, NJ: Lawrence Erlbaum Associates.

Festinger, Leon and J. Carlsmith. 1959. "Cognitive Consequences of Forced Compliance." *Journal of Abnormal and Social Psychology* 58:203–10.

Festinger, Leon, Henry W. Riecken, and Stanley Schachter. 1956. *When Prophecy Fails.* Minneapolis: University of Minnesota Press.

Festinger, Leon, Stanley Schachter, and Kurt Back. 1950. *Social Pressures in Informal Groups.* New York: Harper and Row.

Fisher, William and Azy Barak. 1991. "Pornography, Erotica, and Behavior: More Questions than Answers." *International Journal of Law and Psychiatry* 14:65–83.

Fisher, William and Azy Barak. 2001 "Internet Pornography: A Social Psychological Perspective on Internet Sexuality." *Journal of Sex Research* 38(4).

Fisher, William and Guy Grenier. 1994. "Violent Pornography, Antiwoman Thoughts and Antiwomen Acts: In Search of Reliable Effects." *Journal of Sex Research* 31(1):23–38.

Fowles, Jib. 1999. *The Case for Television Violence.* London: Sage.

Frankford-Nachmias, Chava. 1999. *Social Statistics for a Diverse Society.* Thousand Oaks, CA: Pine Forge.

Freedman, Jonathan L. 1984. "Effects of Television Violence on Aggression." *Psychological Bulletin* 96:227–46.

Freedman, Jonathan L. 1986. "Television Violence and Aggression: A Rejoinder." *Psychological Bulletin* 100:372–73.

Freedman, Jonathan L. 1988. "Television and Aggression: What the Research Shows." Pp. 144–62 in *Television as a Social Issue,* edited by Stuart Oskamp. Newbury Park, CA: Sage.

Freud, Sigmund. [1957] 2001. *Leonardo DaVinci: A Memoir of His Childhood.* Translated by Alan Dyson. London and New York: Routledge Classics.

Friedman, W. J., A. B. Robinson, and B. L. Friedman. 1987. "Sex Differences in Moral Judgments?" *Psychology of Women Quarterly* 11(1):37–46.

Gadlin, Howard and Grant Ingle. 1975. "Through the One-Way Mirror: The Limits of Experimental Self-Reflection." *American Psychologist* (October):1003–9.

Gadow, Kenneth D. and Joyce Sprafkin. 1989. "Field Experiments of Television Violence with Children: Evidence for an Environmental Hazard?" *Pediatrics* 83(3):399–405.

Garfinkel, Harold. 1967. *Studies in Ethnomethodology.* Englewood Cliffs, NJ: Prentice Hall.

Gauntlett, David. 1995. *Moving Experiences: Understanding Television's Influences and Effects.* London: J. Libbey.

Gerard, Harold. 1999. "A Social Psychologist Examines His Past and Looks to the Future." Pp. 47–81 in *Reflections on 100 Years of Experimental Social Psychology,* edited by A. Rodrigues and R. Levine. New York: Basic Books.

Gibbs, J. C., K. D. Arnold, and J. E. Burkhart. 1984. "Sex Differences in the Expression of Moral Judgment." *Child Development* 55:1040–43.

Gillespie, Richard. 1991. *Manufacturing Knowledge: A History of the Hawthorne Experiments.* Cambridge: Cambridge University Press.

Gilligan, Carol. [1982] 1993. *In a Different Voice: Psychological Theory and Women's Development.* Cambridge, MA: Harvard University Press.

Ginsberg, Morris. 1942. *The Psychology of Society* (5th ed.). London: Methuen.

Glueck, Sheldon and Eleanor Glueck. 1950. *Unraveling Juvenile Delinquency*. Cambridge, MA: Harvard University Press.

Goffman, Erving. 1961. *Asylums*. Chicago: Aldine.

Goldhagen, Daniel. 1997. *Hitler's Willing Executioners: Ordinary Germans and the Holocaust*. New York: Random House.

Gottfredson, Michael R. and Travis Hirschi. 1990. *A General Theory of Crime*. Stanford, CA: Stanford University Press.

Goudge, T. A. 1961. *The Ascent of Life: A Philosophical Investigation of the Theory of Evolution*. Toronto: University of Toronto Press.

Gould, Stephen J. 1978. "Sociobiology: The Art of Story-Telling." *New Scientist* 16:530–33.

Gould, Stephen J. 1989. *Wonderful Life: The Burgess Shale and the Nature of History*. New York: Norton.

Greeno, C. G. and E. E. Maccoby. 1986. "How Different Is the 'Different Voice'?" *Signs* 11:310–16.

Haney, C., W. C. Banks, and P. Zimbardo. 1973. "Interpersonal Dynamics in a Simulated Prison." *International Journal of Criminal Penology* 1:69–97.

Haney, Craig and Philip Zimbardo. 1977. "The Socialization into Criminality: On Becoming a Prisoner and a Guard." Pp. 198–223 in *Law Justice and the Individual in Society: Psychological and Legal Issues*, edited by J. Levine. New York: Holt, Reinhart and Winston.

Hempel, C. G. 1952. *Fundamentals of Concept Formation in Empirical Science*. Chicago: University of Chicago Press.

Hempel, C. G. 1965. "The Logic of Functional Analysis." Pp. 297–330 in *Aspects of Scientific Explanation*. New York: Macmillan.

Hendricks, Melissa. 2000. "Into the Hands of Babes." *Johns Hopkins Magazine* 52(4) on-line, September).

Henshel, Richard L. 1980. "The Purpose of Laboratory Experiments and the Virtues of Deliberate Artificiality." *Journal of Experimental Social Psychology* 16:416–78.

Herrnstein, Richard J. and Charles Murray. 1996. *The Bell Curve: Intelligence and Class Structure in American Life*. New York: Free Press.

Hewstone, Miles, Antony S. R. Manstead, and Wolfgang Stroebe (Eds.). 1997. *The Blackwell Reader in Social Psychology*. Oxford: Blackwell.

Hoffman, M. L. 1977. "Sex Differences in Empathy and Related Behaviors." *Psychological Bulletin* 84(4):712–22.

Hopkins, P. 1938. *The Psychology of Social Movements: A Psychoanalytic View of Society*. London: Allen & Unwin.

Houston, John. 1983. "Psychology: A Closed System of Self-Evident Information?" *Psychological Reports* 52:203–208.

Hovland, Carl. 1959. "Reconciling Conflicting Results Derived from Experimental and Survey Studies of Attitude Change." *American Psychologist* 14:8–17.

Huesmann, L. R., L. D. Eron, M. M. Lefkowitz, and L. O. Walder. 1973. "Television Violence and Aggression: The Causal Effect Remains." *American Psychologist* 28:617–20.

Huesmann, L. R., L. D. Eron, M. M. Lefkowitz, and L. O. Walden. 1984. "Stability of Aggression over Time and Generations." *Developmental Psychology* 20:1120–34.

Hunt, Morton. 1993. Pp. 396–434 in *The Story of Psychology*. New York: Doubleday.

Jones, Stephen. 1992. "Was There a Hawthorne Effect?" *American Journal of Sociology* 98(3):451–68.

Kaplan, R. M. and R. D. Singer. 1976. "Television Violence and Viewer Aggression: A Re-Examination of the Evidence." *Journal of Criminal Psychopathology* 3:112–37.

Karpf, Fay B. 1932. *American Social Psychology: Its Origins, Development and European Background*. New York: McGraw-Hill.

Katz, Daniel. 1967. "Editorial." *Journal of Personality and Social Psychology* 7:341–44.

Katz, Daniel and Richard L. Schanck. 1938. *Social Psychology*. London: Chapman & Hall.

Katz, Jack. 1988. *Seductions of Crime: The Sensual and Moral Attractions of Doing Evil*. New York: Basic Books.

Kelley, H. H. 1992. "Common Sense Psychology and Scientific Psychology." *Annual Review of Psychology* 43:1–23.

Kelley, H. H. 1999. "Fifty Years in Social Psychology: Some Reflections on the Individual-Group Problem." Pp. 35–46 in *Reflections on 100 Years of Experimental Social Psychology*, edited by A. Rodrigues and R. Levine. New York: Basic Books.

Kendrick, Walter. 1988. *The Secret Museum: Pornography in the Modern Culture*. New York: Viking Penguin.

Kirsch, I. and S. J. Lynn. 1995. "Altered State of Hypnosis: Changes in the Theoretical Landscape." *American Psychologist* 50(10):846–58.

Kleinfeld, J. 1998. *The Myth That Schools Shortchange Girls: Social Science in the Service of Deception*. Washington, DC: Women's Freedom Network.

Kleinfeld, J. 1999. "Student Performance: Males vs. Females. *Public Interest* 134:3–20.

Klineberg, Otto. 1948. *Social Psychology*. New York: Holt.

Koch, Sigmund. 1969. "Psychology Cannot be a Coherent Science." *Psychology Today* 14(September):64, 66–68.

Koch, Sigmund. 1969. "Wundt's Creature at Age Zero—and as Centenarian: Some Aspects of the Institutionalization of the 'New Psychology.'" Pp. 7–35 in *A Century of Psychology as Science*. Edited by S. Koch and D. E. Leary. Washington, DC: American Psychology Association.

Kors, A. C. and H. A. Silvergate. 1998. *The Shadow University: The Betrayal of Liberty on America's Campuses*. New York: HarperCollins.

Kosslyn, Stephen M., William L. Thompson, Maria F. Costantini-Ferrando, Nathaniel M. Alpert, and David Spiegel. 2000. "Hypnotic Visual Illusion Alters Color Processing in the Brain." *American Journal of Psychiatry* 157:1279–84.

Krech, David and R. S. Crutchfield. 1948. *Theory and Problems of Social Psychology*. New York: McGraw-Hill.

Kuhn, Thomas. 1970. *The Structure of Scientific Revolutions*. Chicago: Chicago University Press.

Kutchinsky, Berl. 1991. "Pornography and Rape: Theory and Practice?" *International Journal of Law and Psychiatry* 14(1/2):47–64.

Langevin, R., R. A. Lang, P. Wright, L. Handy, R. R. Frenzel, and E. L. Black. 1988. "Pornography and Sexual Offenses." *Annals of Sex Research* 1:335–62.

174 References

LaPiere, Richard T. and Paul R. Farnsworth. 1949. *Social Psychology* (3rd ed.). New York: McGraw-Hill.

Latour, B. 1983. "Give Me a Lab and I Will Raise the World." Pp. 141–70 in *Science Observed,* edited by K. Knorr-Cetina and M. Mulkay. London: Sage.

Latour, Bruno and Steve Woolgar. 1979. *Laboratory Life.* London: Sage.

Lazersfeld, Paul. 1941. "Repeated Interviews as a Tool for Studying Changes in Opinion and Their Causes." *American Statistical Association Bulletin* 2:3–7.

Leamer, Edward E. 1990. "Let's Take the Con out of Econometrics." Pp. 29–49 in *Modeling Economic Series,* edited by C. W. J. Granger. Oxford: Clarendon.

Leibert, Robert M. and Joyce Sprafkin. 1988. *The Early Window: Effects of Television on Children and Youth* (3rd ed.). New York: Pergamon.

Levy, Leon. 1974. "Awareness, Learning and the Beneficent Subject as Expert Witness." Pp. 187–97 in *The Experiment as a Social Occasion,* edited by P. Wuebben, B. Straits, and G. Schulma. Berkeley: Glendessary.

Lewin, Kurt. 1951. *Field Theory in Social Science.* New York: Harper.

Lindesmith, Alfred R., and A. L. Strauss. 1949. *Social Psychology.* New York: Dryden.

Linz, Daniel, Steven Penrod, and Edward Donnerstein. 1987. "The Attorney General's Commission on Pornography: The Gap Between 'Findings' and Fact." *American Bar Foundation Research Journal* 713.

Linz, Daniel and Edward Donnerstein. 1988. "The Methods and Merits of Pornography Research," *Journal of Communication* 38(2): 180–84.

Loftus, E. 1993. "The Reality of Repressed Memories." *American Psychologist* 48(5):518–37.

Loftus, E. and K. Ketcham. 1994. *The Myth of Repressed Memory: False Memories and Allegations of Sexual Abuse.* New York: St. Martin's.

Lord, Charles G. 1997. *Social Psychology.* Harcourt Brace College Publishing.

Lowy, Samuel. 1944. *Man and His Fellowmen: Modern Chapters on Social Psychology.* London: Kegan Paul, Trench, Trubner & Co.

Luker, K. 1984. *Abortion and the Politics of Motherhood.* Berkeley and Los Angeles: University of California Press.

Luria, Z. 1986. "A Methodological Critique." *Signs: Journal of Women in Culture and Society* 11:316–21.

Maccoby, E. 1985. "Social Groupings in Childhood: Their Relationship to Prosocial and Antisocial Behavior in Boys and Girls." Pp. 263–85 in *Development of Antisocial Behavior and Prosocial Behavior: Theories, Research and Issues,* edited by Dan Olweus, Jack Block, and Marian Radke-Yarrow. San Diego: Academic Press.

MacKinnon, Catherine A. 1985. "Pornography, Civil Rights and Speech." *Harvard Civil Rights-Civil Liberties Law Review* 20.

Malamuth, N. M. and J. V. P. Check. 1981. "The Effects of Mass Media Exposure on Acceptance of Violence against Women: A Field Experiment." *Journal of Research in Personality* 15:436–46.

Mannheim, Karl. 1954. *Ideology and Utopia.* Translated by Louis Wirth and Edward Shils. London: Routledge and Kegan Paul.

Mantel, David Mark. 1971. "The Potential for Violence in Germany." *Journal of Social Issues* 27(4):110–11.

Mayo, Elton. 1933. *The Human Problems of an Industrial Civilisation.* New York: Macmillan.

Mayo, Elton. 1939. "Preface." Pp. xi–xiv in *Management and the Worker*, F. J. Roeth-lisberger and William J. Dickson. Cambridge, MA: Harvard University Press.

McDougall, William. 1919. *An Introduction to Social Psychology* (14th rev. ed.). London: Methuen.

Mead, G. H. 1934. *Mind, Self and Society from the Standpoint of a Social Behaviorist.* Chicago: University of Chicago Press.

Mednick, M. T. 1989. "On the Politics of Psychological Constructs: Stop the Bandwagon, I Want to Get Off." *American Psychologist* 44(8):1118–23.

Merton, R. K. 1948. "The Self-Fulfilling Prophecy." *Antioch Review* 8:193–210.

Metropolitan Life Insurance Company. 1997. "The American Teacher 1997: Examining Gender Issues in Public Schools." New York: MetLife.

Milgram, Stanley. 1963. "Behavioral Study of Obedience." *Journal of Abnormal and Social Psychology* 67(4):371–78.

Milgram, Stanley. 1965. "Liberating Effects of Group Pressure." *Journal of Personality and Social Psychology* 19:137–43.

Milgram, Stanley. 1974. *Obedience to Authority.* New York: Harper and Row.

Mill, J. S. [1843] 1965. *On the Logic of the Moral Sciences*, London: John Parker West Strand.

Miller, Arthur G. 1986. *The Obedience Experiments: A Case Study of the Controversy in Social Science.* New York: Praeger.

Miller, Arthur G., B. E. Collins, and D. E. Brief. 1995. "Introduction" to *Perspectives on Obedience: The Legacy of the Milgram Experiments*, Special Issue. *Journal of Social Issues* 51(3):1–20.

Miller, George A. 1992. "The Consitutive Problem of Social Psychology." Pp. 40–46. In *A Century of Psychology as Science.* Edited by S. Koch and D. E. Leary. Washington, DC: American Psychology Association.

Millett, Kate. 1970. *Sexual Politics.* New York: Doubleday.

Mixon, D. 1971. "Beyond Deception." *Journal for the Theory of Social Behaviour* 2(2):145–77.

Moffitt, Terrie E. 1993. "Adolescent-Limited and Life-Course Persistent Antisocial Behavior: A Developmental Taxonomy." *Psychological Review* 100:674–701.

Money, John and Anke A. Ehrhardt. 1972. *Man and Woman, Boy and Girl: The Differentiation and Dimorphism of Gender Identity from Conception to Maturity.* Baltimore, MD: Johns Hopkins University Press.

Moscovici, Serge. 1972. "Society and Theory in Social Psychology." Pp. 17–96 in *The Context of Social Psychology: A Critical Assessment*, edited by J. Israel and H. Tajfel. New York: Academic Press.

Mulvey, E. P. and J. L. Haugaard. 1986. *Pornography and Public Health.* Washington, DC: U.S. Department of Health and Human Services.

Murchison, Carl, A. 1935. *A Handbook of Social Psychology.* New York: Russell & Russell.

Murphy, G., L. B. Murphy, and T. M. Newcomb. 1937. *Experimental Social Psychology: An Interpretation of Research upon the Socialization of the Individual* (rev. ed.). New York: Harper.

National Council for Research on Women. 1998. "The Girl's Report: What We Know and Need to Know about Growing Up Female," Washington, DC: NCRW.

National Institute of Mental Health. 1982. *Television and Behaviour: Ten Years of Scientific Progress and Implications for the Eighties*. Washington, DC: NIMH.

Nesselroade, John R. and Raymond B. Cattell. 1988. "Psychological Theory and Scientific Method." *Handbook of Multivariate Experimental Social Psychology*. Chicago: Rand McNally.

Newcomb, Theodore M. and E. L. Hartley (Eds.). 1947. *Readings in Social Psychology*. New York: Holt.

Nova Films. 2001. *Sex Unknown*. Boston PBS.

Olweus, Dan. 1979. "'Stability of Aggressive Reaction Patterns in Males': A Review." *Psychological Bulletin* 86:852–75.

Orne, M. T. 1959. "The Nature of Hypnosis: Artifact and Essence." *Journal of Abnormal Social Psychology* 58:277–99.

Orne, M. T. 1961. "The Potential Uses of Hypnosis in Interrogation." Pp. 169–215 in *The Manipulation of Human Behavior*, edited by A. D. Biderman and H. Zimmer. New York: Wiley.

Orne, M. T. 1962. "On the Social Psychology of the Psychological Experiment with Particular Reference to Demand Characteristics and their Implications." *American Psychologist* 17:777–83.

Orne, M. T. 1979. "The Use and Misuse of Hypnosis in Court." *International journal of Clinical and Experimental Hypnosis* 27:311–41.

Orne, M. T. and C. H. Holland. 1968. "On the Ecological Validity of Laboratory Deceptions." *International Journal of Psychiatry* 6:282–93.

Orne, M. T. and K. E. Scheibe. 1964. "The Contribution of Non-Deprivation Factors in the Production of Sensory Deprivation Effects: The Psychology of the 'Panic Button.'" *Journal of Abnormal and Social Psychology* 68:3–13.

Orne, M. T., P. W. Sheehan, and F. J. Evans. 1968. "Occurrences of Posthypnotic Behavior Outside the Experimental Setting. *Journal of Personality and Social Psychology* 9:189–96.

Owens, Anne Marie. 2002. "Feminist Shifts Focus to Boys." *Toronto Globe and Mail*, June 27.

Parsons, H. M. 1974. "What Happened at Hawthorne?" *Science* 183:922–32.

Patten, S. 1977a. "The Case That Milgram Makes." *Philosophical Review* 86(3):350–64.

Patten, S. 1977b. "Milgram's Shocking Experiments." *Philosophy* 52(4):425–40.

Penner, Louis. [1978] 1987. *Social Psychology: A Contemporary Approach*. New York: Oxford University Press.

Pepitone, Albert. 1999. "Historical Sketches and Critical Commentary About Social Psychology in the Golden Age." Pp. 170–99 in *Reflections on 100 Years of Experimental Social Psychology*, edited by A. Rodrigues and R. Levine. New York: Basic Books.

Perry, William James. 1935. *The Primordial Ocean: An Introductory Contribution to Social Psychology*. London: Methuen.

Pfungst, O. [1911] 1965. *Clever Hans (The Horse of Mr. Von Osten): A Contribution to Experimental, Animal, and Human Psychology*. Translated by C. L. Rahn. New York: Holt, Rinehart and Winston.

Popper, Karl R. 1959. *The Logic of Scientific Discovery*. New York: Harper Torchbacks.

Popper, Karl R. [1961] 1976. "The Logic of the Social Sciences." Pp. 87–104 in *The Positivist Dispute in German Sociology*. Theodor W. Adorno, Hans Albert, Ralf Dahrendorf, Jurgen Habermas, Harold Pilot, and Karl. L Popper. Translated by Glyn Adey and David Frisby. London: Heinemann.

Posner, Richard A. 1988. *Law and Literature: A Misunderstood Relation*. Cambridge, MA: Harvard University Press.

Proshansky, Harold and Bernard Seidenberg (eds.) 1965. *Basic Studies in Social Psychology*. New York: Holt, Rinehart and Winston.

Rainville, Pierre, Robert K. Hofbauer, M. Catherine Bushnell, Gary H. Duncan, and Donald D. Price. 2002. "Hypnosis Modulates Activity in Brain Structures Involved in the Regulation of Consciousness." *Journal of Cognitive Neuroscience* 14:887–901.

Rainville, Pierre, Robert K. Hofbauer, Tomas Paus, Gary H. Duncan, M. Catherine Bushnell, and Donald D. Price. 1999. "Cerebral Mechanisms of Hypnotic Induction and Suggestion." *Journal of Cognitive Neuroscience* 11:110–25.

Raudenbush, S. W. 1984. "Magnitude of Teacher Expectancy Effects on Pupil IQ as a Function of the Credibility of Expectancy Induction: A Synthesis of Findings from 18 Experiments." *Journal of Educational Psychology* 76:85–97.

Raven, Bertram. 1999. "Reflections on Interpersonal Influence and Social Power in Experimental Social Psychology." Pp. 114–34 in *Reflections on 100 Years of Experimental Social Psychology*, edited by A. Rodrigues and R. Levine. New York: Basic Books.

Raz, Amir and Theodore Shapiro. 2002. "Hypnosis and Neuroscience: A Cross Talk Between Clinical and Cognitive Research." *Archives of General Psychiatry* 59:85–90.

Ridley, Matt. 2003. *Nature via Nurture: Genes, Experience and What Makes Us Human*. Toronto: Harper Collins.

Ring, Kenneth. 1967. "Experimental Social Psychology: Some Sober Questions About Some Frivolous Values." *Journal of Experimental Social Psychology* 3:113–23.

Robinson, Virginia P. 1930. *A Changing Psychology in Social Case Work*. Chapel Hill: University of North Carolina Press.

Rodrigues, Aroldo and Robert V. Levine (Eds.). 1999. *Reflections on 100 Years of Experimental Social Psychology*. New York: Basic Books.

Roethlisberger, F. J. and William J. Dickson. 1939. *Management and the Worker*. Preface by Elton Mayo. Cambridge MA: Harvard University Press.

Rosenhan, David L. 1973. "Being Sane in Insane Places." *Science* 179:250–58.

Rosenthal, Robert. 1966. *Experimenter Effects in Behavioral Research*. New York: Meredith.

Rosenthal, Robert. 1969. "Empirical vs. Decreed Validation of Clocks and Tests." *American Educational Research Journal* 6:689–91.

Rosenthal, Robert. 1985. "From Unconscious Experimenter Bias to Teacher Expectancy Effects." Pp. 37–65 in *Teacher Expectancies*, edited by J. B. Dusek. Hillsdale, NJ: Lawrence Erlbaum Associates.

Rosenthal, Robert. 1987. *Judgment Studies: Design, Analysis, and Meta-Analysis*. New York: Cambridge University Press.

Rosenthal, R., S. S. Baratz, and C. M. Hall. 1974. "Teacher Behaviour, Teacher Expectations, and Gains in Pupils' Rated Creativity." *Journal of Genetic Psychology* 124:115–21.

Rosenthal, Robert and Lenore Jacobson. 1968. *Pygmalion in the Classroom: Teacher Expectations and Pupils' Intellectual Development.* New York: Holt, Rinehart and Winston.

Rosenthal, Robert and Lenore Jacobson. 1969. "Teacher Expectations for the Disadvantaged." *Scientific American* 218(4):19–23.

Rosenwald, George. 1986. "Why Operationism Doesn't Go Away: The Extrascientific Incentives of Social-psychological Research." *Philosophy of the Social Sciences* 16(3):303–30.

Ross, Edward A. 1908. *Social Psychology: An Outline and Source Book.* New York: Macmillan.

Russell, Diana. 1993. "The Experts Cop Out." Pp. 151–167 in *Making Violence Sexy,* edited by Diana Russell. Williston, VT: Teachers College Press.

Sabini, John. 1986. "Stanley Milgram (1933–1984)" (obituary). *American Psychologist* 41(12):1378–79.

Satcher, David. 1999. *Youth Violence: A Report of the Surgeon General.* Washington, DC: Public Health Service.

Schachter, Stanley. 1971. *Emotion, Obesity and Crime.* New York: Academic Press.

Schachter, Stanley. 1980. "Non-Psychological Explanations of Behavior." Pp. 131–57 in *Retrospections on Social Psychology,* edited by Leon Festinger. New York: Oxford.

Schachter, Stanley and J. E. Singer. 1962. "Cognitive, Social and Physiological Determinants of Emotional State." *Psychological Review* 69:379–99.

Scott, J. and L. A. Schwalm. 1988. "Rape Rates and the Circulation Rates of Adult Magazines." *Journal of Sex Research* 24:241–50.

Sherif, M. 1935. "A Study of Some Social Factors in Perception." *Archives of Psychology* 27(187):1–60.

Sherif, M. 1936. *The Psychology of Social Norms.* New York: Harper.

Sherif, M. [1936] 1965. *The Psychology of Social Norms.* Introduction by Gardner Murphy. New York: Octagon.

Sherif, M. 1937. "An Experimental Approach to the Study of Attitudes." *Sociometry* 1:90–98.

Silverman, Irwin. 1971. "Crisis in Social Psychology: The Relevance of Relevance." *American Psychologist* 26:583–604.

Silverman, Irwin. 1977. "Why Social Psychology Fails." *Canadian Psychological Review* 18(4):353–408.

Skinner, B. F. [1948] 1976 . *Walden Two.* New York: Macmillan.

Slocombe, Charles S. 1940. "Million Dollar Research," *Personnel Journal* 18:162–172.

Smith, M. Brewster. 1972. "Is Experimental Social Psychology Advancing?" *Journal of Experimental Social Psychology* 8:86–96.

Smith, M. Brewster. 1973. "Is Psychology Relevant to New Priorities?" *American Psychologist* 28:463–71.

Smith, M. L. 1980. "Teacher Expectations." *Evaluation in Education: An International Journal* 4:53–55.

Smoke, Kenneth. 1935. "The Present Status of Social Psychology in America." *Psychological Review* 42:537–53.

Sobol, M. G. 1959. "Panel Mortality and Panel Bias." *Journal of the American Statistical Association* 54(285).

Sokal, Alan. 1996a. "A Physicist Experiments with Cultural Studies." *Lingua Franca* 6(4):62–64.

Sokal, Alan. 1996b. "Transgressing the Boundaries: Towards a Transformative Hermeneutics of Quantum Gravity." *Social Text* 14(1, 2):217–52.

Sommers, C. H. 1994. *Who Stole Feminism? How Women Have Betrayed Women*. New York: Simon & Schuster.

Sommers, C.H. 2000a. The War Against Boys, New York: Simon and Schuster.

Sommers, C. H. 2000b. "The War Against Boys: How Misguided Feminism Is Harming Our Young Men." *Atlantic Monthly* 285(5):59–74.

Sorokin, P. 1954. *Fads and Foibles in Modern Sociology*. Chicago: Regnery.

Stam, H. J., H. L. Radtke, and I. Lubek. 1998. "Repopulating Social Psychology Texts." Pp. 153–86 in *Reconstructing the Psychological Subject*, edited by B. M. Bayer and J. Shotter. London: Sage.

Stam, H. J., H. L. Radtke, and I. Lubek. 2000. "Strains in Experimental Social Psychology: A Textual Analysis of the Development of Experimentation in Social Psychology." *Journal of the History of the Behavioral Sciences* 36(4):365–83.

Stricker, Lawrence. 1967. "The True Deceiver." *Psychological Bulletin* 68(1):13–20.

Surgeon General's Scientific Advisory Committee. 1972. *Television and Growing Up: The Impact of Televised Violence*. Washington, DC: USPGO.

Swaab, Dick F., Wilson C. J. Chung, Frank P. M. Kruijver, Michel A. Hofman, and Tatjana A. Ishunina. 2001. "Structural and Functional Sex Differences in the Human Hypothalamus." *Hormones and Behavior* 40:93–98.

Tannenbaum, Percy H. 1972. "Studies in Film- and Television-Mediated Arousal and Aggression: A Progress Report. Pp 309–50 in *Television and Social Behavior:* Vol. 5, *Television's Effects: Further Explorations*, edited by George A. Comstock, Eli A. Rubinstein, and John P. Murray. Washington, DC: USGPO.

Tavris, Carol. 2002. "The High Cost of Skepticism." *Skeptical Inquirer*, July–August (on-line).

Tedeschi, James T., Svenn Lindskold, and Paul Rosenfeld. 1985. *Introduction to Social Psychology* (4th ed.). New York: West.

Thoma, S. 1986. "Estimating Gender Differences in the Comprehension and Preferences of Moral Issues." *Developmental Review* 6:165–80.

Thorndike, Robert L. 1968. "Review of Pygmalion in the Classroom." *American Educational Research Journal* 5:708–11. Reprinted in Janet D. Elashoff and Richard E. Snow (eds.) *Pygmalion Reconsidered*, Worthington. Ohio: Charles Jones, 1971.

Tolkien, J. R. R. 1966. *The Lord of the Rings*. London: Grafton. pp 65–68.

Triplett, Norman. 1897. "The Dynamogenic Factors in Pace-Making and Competition." *American Journal of Psychology* 9:507–32.

Twain, Mark. 1885. *The Adventures of Huckleberry Finn*. New York: Random House.

U.S. Department of Education Statistics. 1999. Digest of Educational Statistics 1998. Washington, DC: U.S. Department of Education.

Vander Zandem, James. 1987. *Social Psychology* (4th ed.). New York: Random House.

Wadden, Thomas and Charles Anderton. 1982. "The Clinical Use of Hypnosis." *Psychological Bulletin* 91(2):215–43.

Walker, L. 1984. "Sex Differences in the Development of Moral Reasoning: A Critical Review." *Child Development* 55:677–91.

Webster's Seventh New Collegiate Dictionary. 1977. Toronto, ON: Thomas Allen and Sons Limited.

Wertham, Frederic. 1954. *Seduction of the Innocent.* New York: Rinehart.

Wheeler, Ladd. 1987. "Social Comparison, Behavioral Contagion, and the Naturalistic Study of Social Interaction." Pp. 46–65 in *A Distinctive Approach to Psychological Research: The Influence of Stanley Schachter.* Neil E. Grunberg, Richard E. Nisbett, Judith Rodin, and Jerome E. Singer. Hillsdale, NJ: Lawrence Erlbaum Associates.

Whitehead, T. North. 1938. *The Industrial Worker.* Cambridge, MA: Harvard University Press.

Wiegman, O., M. Kuttschreuter, and B. Baarda. 1992. "A Longitudinal Study of the Effects of Television Viewing on Aggression and Prosocial Behaviors." *British Journal of Social Psychology* 31:147–64.

Wilson, Edward O. 1975. *Sociobiology.* Cambridge, MA: Harvard University Press.

Wilson, James Q. and Richard J. Herrnstein. 1985. *Crime and Human Nature: The Definitive Study of the Causes of Crime.* New York: Simon and Schuster.

Wineburg, S. S. 1987. "The Self-Fulfillment of a Self-Fulfilling Prophecy." *Educational Researcher* 16(9):28–37.

Wineburg, S. S. 1987. "Does Research Count in the Lives of Behavioral Scientists?" *Educational Researcher* 16(9): 42–44.

Wittgenstein, Ludwig. 1922. *Tractatus Logico-Philosophicus.* London: Routledge and Kegan Paul.

Wittgenstein, Ludwig. 1951. *Philosophical Investigations.* Oxford: Macmillan.

Worchel, S., J. Cooper, G.R. Goethals and J.M. Olson. 2000. *Social Psychology*, Belmont, CA: Wadsworth.

Wuebben, P., B. Straits, and G. Schulman (Eds.). 1974. *The Experiment as a Social Occasion.* Berkeley, CA: Glendessary.

Wurtzel, Alan and Guy Lometti. 1984. "Smoking Out the Critics." *Society* (September/October):36–40.

Zajonc, Robert B. 1997. "One Hundred Years of Rationality Assumptions in Social Psychology." Pp. 200–14 in *Reflections on 100 Years of Experimental Social Psychology*, edited by Aroldo Rodrigues and Robert V. Levine. New York: Basic Books.

Zillmann, Dolf. 1984. *Connections between Sex and Aggression.* Hillsdale, NJ: Lawrence Erlbaum Associates.

Zillmann, Dolf. 1991. "Television Viewing and Physiological Arousal." Pp. 103–33 in *Responding to the Screen: Receptions and Reaction Processes*, edited by Jennings Bryant and Dolf Zillmann. Hillsdale, NJ: Lawrence Erlbaum Associates.

Zillmann, D. and W. J. Bryant. 1982. "Pornography, Sexual Callousness and the Trivialization of Rape." *Journal of Communication* 34:10–21.

Zillmann, D. and W. J. Bryant. 1984. "Effects of Massive Exposure to Pornography." Pp. 115–38 in *Pornography and Sexual Aggression,* edited by N. Malamuth and E. Donnerstein. Orlando, FL: Academic Press.

Zillmann, Dolf and Jennings Bryant. 1988. "Response," *Journal of Communication* 38(2): 185–92.

Zimbardo, P. 1972. "Comment: Pathology of Imprisonment." *Society* (April):4–8.

Zimbardo, P. 1999. "Experimental Social Psychology: Behaviorism with Minds and Matters." Pp. 135–57 in *Reflections on 100 Years of Experimental Social Psychology,* edited by A. Rodrigues and R. Levine. New York: Basic Books.

Znaniecki, F. 1925. *The Laws of Social Psychology.* New York: Russell & Russell.

Index

183